How to have your cake & eat it too!

How to have your cake & eat it too!

Diet Cooking for the Whole Family:
diabetic, hypoglycemic,
low-cholesterol/low-fat, low-salt
and low-Calorie diets

Norma M. MacRae, R.D.
Consulting Dietitian
Foreword by Robert H. Williams, M.D.

ALASKA NORTHWEST PUBLISHING COMPANY
Anchorage, Alaska

First printing: January 1976
Second printing: June 1976

Library of Congress Cataloging in Publication Data

MacRae, Norma M   1924-
    How to have your cake & eat it too!

    Bibliography: p.
    Includes index.
    1. Sugar-free diet.   2. Low-fat diet.   3. Salt-
free diet.   4. Low-calorie diet.   I. Title.
RM219.M23   641.5'63   75-41392
ISBN 0-88240-025-8

Design and illustrations by Cheri Vigna
Alaska Northwest Publishing Company

Printed in U.S.A.

For Robert Hardin Williams, M.D.

In grateful appreciation of his friendly support over the years and his faith in the capabilities of the skinny young redhead he hired.

Table of Contents

The public is very fortunate to have available this splendid book. It was written by a dietitian who had splendid training at the Johns Hopkins Hospital. She then had magnificent additional training and experience as the head dietitian on the research ward of Harvard Medical School, at the Thorndike Laboratory. Thereafter, she worked in my metabolic research laboratory for 3 years, thereby acquiring an excellent understanding of metabolic and nutritional problems and appropriate diets. Thereafter, while serving 20 years as a consultant dietitian she formulated an increasing variety of tasty and practical diets best suited to the patient problems. The fact that she developed such an excellent private practice in dietetics is testimony to the great faith and appreciation by physicians, patients and others.

As clinical research has progressed, it has become evident that we do not need to restrict carbohydrates as vigorously for diabetics as in the past. Thus, Miss MacRae's recipes allow the diabetic to enjoy almost the same good things as everyone else although they are lower in free sugar than the usual foods. The diet provides for food that is appetizing to the patient's family. Moreover, many diets are suitable to serve guests because they have relatively good taste appeal.

This is the first cookbook that provides for the needs of patients with cholesterol and triglyceride restriction, made necessary by various types of alteration in the blood fats. There are tasty recipes for pickles, soups, casseroles and all types of desserts, including low-cholesterol and low-sugar ice cream. There are also directions for canning and freezing fruits, suggestions for low-Calorie dips and nibbling foods. There are a number of tables and charts that help the patients when they eat at picnics, restaurants and elsewhere.

The chapter on replacements and substitutions has material that has not been presented in previous diet cookbooks. The recipes are original and were developed to fit the needs of individual patients.

Moreover, there are explanations of why the various diets are provided. The basic rules are presented simply and clearly. Each recipe gives the content of protein, fat, carbohydrate and Calories, along with the cholesterol level per serving, and the sodium content.

In conclusion, this book is a magnificent one dealing with diets for patients with diabetes, hypoglycemia, excess cholesterol and triglyceride, obesity, and salt and water retention.

Robert H. Williams, M.D.
Professor of Medicine
University of Washington, and
Head, Diabetes Research Center

The Author

The author Norma M. MacRae was the first full-time consulting dietitian in the United States. For more than 20 years she has had a busy practice in Seattle, with offices both downtown and in the Northgate medical complex.

During her years of practice the need for a cookbook such as this became apparent. As a result of requests from patients and physicians she has developed many special recipes; until now they have never been put together in book form. Thus this cookbook is the result of many years experience, and the recipes have been used and approved by her patients. She is constantly experimenting with new products to develop tastier foods for dieters.

The author is a native of Detroit, Michigan. She is a graduate of Alma College (St. Thomas, Ontario), Michigan State College, and the Johns Hopkins School of Dietetics in Baltimore. She is a Registered Dietitian.

At Johns Hopkins she did research in the laboratories of Dr. and Mrs. Elmer V. McCollum, the biochemists who discovered vitamins A and D. She was later employed by Harvard University Medical School as the dietitian for the Fourth Harvard Medical Service at Thorndike Memorial Laboratory. There, she was dietitian for Dr. Robert H. Williams, one of the world's

foremost endocrinologists, and accompanied him to the University of Washington in Seattle to work in metabolic research.

She has been president of both the Seattle and Washington State Dietetic Associations and has served as a committee chairman for the American Dietetic Association. She has been a panelist on medical forums and is in demand as a speaker.

Along with her love of cooking and good food, the author likes to fish, raises orchids and has Norwegian elkhounds. She loves the Northwest life and spends much of her free time at a cabin in the San Juan Islands, where most of the basic experimental work for this book was done.

1. Why Did I Write This Cookbook?

When a patient is told to limit sugar, cholesterol and Calories* the common reaction is, "What's left?" As you'll see in the recipe sections, there's plenty left.

When I'm seeing patients for dietary consultation, I like to be able to recommend one or more cookbooks for their use. But after telling several new patients that I knew of no recipe book for limiting sugar, cholesterol, fat *and* salt, I realized that a large number of patients had these combined dietary limits, and that a recipe book was needed. So I prepared this book for them. Diabetics, hypoglycemia patients, persons on the new hyperlipoproteinemia (Fredrickson) diets of types 3, 4 and 5 (low sugar, low cholestrol) and those with sodium or salt restrictions will find this book useful.

Variety is the key to being able to stay on a restricted diet for a long time. Now that recipes for tasty, appetizing foods are available, there is no excuse for not making diet meals attractive and palatable.

Hypoglycemia has become a popular subject for diet articles in the last few years (diabetes has been recognized for centuries). Physicians are diagnosing hypoglycemia in more patients, and the public is aware of the disease and of the dietary problems it involves. Although the problems of hypoglycemia and diabetes are quite different (insulin excess versus insulin shortage), the two conditions have some points of relationship, and the diet plans are similar.

Most recipes in this cookbook are designed for both diabetics and hypoglycemics. This of course presumes use in reasonable quantities. Too many dietetic cookies—too many anythings, dietetic or not—will cause problems. Used as directed, these recipes offer a safe diet that is anything but dull. The desserts fill the cravings to which people with these metabolic disorders are prone.

We recognize how frustrating it is for the good cook to find that one of the family must be on a restricted diet and cannot eat the usual meals. This cookbook should help the person doing the food preparation to plan attractive meals and to prevent monotony and lack of appeal for the dieter.

Unfortunately not all foods can be modified to fit into a low-sugar diet, or a low-cholesterol diet, or a low-saturated-fat diet. So some foods are missing from this cookbook.

---

*The food Calorie is the kilocalorie (1,000 x calorie). It is written with a capital "C" in this book.

The dessert recipes, however, are especially numerous. Most dieters will watch the rest of what they eat if they can have a nice dessert to end the meal. Some of the combinations of ingredients may seem odd to the person just learning how to adapt recipes, but the important thing is that the recipes do work. The food is tasty and attractive to the dieter.

For the person wanting to reduce his weight, these recipes are lower in Calories than the same items made with sugar, cream or added eggs. Just the same, too many servings means too many Calories just as any other food would. Let the dieter beware of eating too much of the pie or too many of the cookies. Although they are prepared dietetically, they are still not free of Calories!

We hope you will experiment with our recipes and come up with some of your own as well. A good cook will always be challenged by a change in meal plans; these suggestions should show the way.

Dieting needn't be dull—use your imagination and *enjoy* food.

2. General Information on Diets

Blood Fats: Cholesterol and Triglycerides

Most people do not realize that fats are perfectly normal parts of the blood in any human body. They are found largely in the serum, not in the blood cells, and they have specific functions in the chemistry of the body. It is only when the body manufactures too much of these fats, so that the blood becomes overloaded with them, that we have to worry about it.

The best-known blood fat is *cholesterol*. This substance is an important chemical source from which the body manufactures several hormones, vitamin D and other body chemicals. Cholesterol is normally found in the liver, in nerve tissue and in gallstones. The hormones produced by the adrenals and the various sex glands are also related to cholesterol.

Perhaps 75 percent of the cholesterol in the body has been manufactured from other materials. The average American eats about 40 percent of his daily Calories as fat. Almost half of this fat is saturated because the main sources are meat, eggs, cheese, cream, whole milk, butter and other dairy foods. These saturated fats tend to increase the level of cholesterol in the blood; the unsaturated fats (polyunsaturated and monounsaturated) tend to lower the level of cholesterol in the blood.

People have been told about "saturated" and "polyunsaturated" fats for several years. Few understand what they are. In general, the saturated fats are those which are solid at body temperature. One exception is coconut oil, a very saturated fat but liquid at 98 degrees. The unsaturated fats are mostly those that stay liquid at body temperature.

These adjectives describe the chemical structure of the fats. Because of their structure, saturated fats may attach themselves to the artery walls, in a sludgelike deposit, unless the blood flow is able to carry them along. Most are found in the high-cholesterol foods and in the so-called "non-dairy creamers," which are usually coconut oil. Avoiding excessive amounts of the saturated fats helps prevent fat deposits in the arteries and the narrowing of the channel. Instead of forming sludge deposits in the arteries, the unsaturated fats tend to carry the sludge along with them, thus helping prevent accumulation on the artery wall.

More simply—think of the saturated fats as lazy, sludge-forming materials and the unsaturated fats as scrubbing brushes: The monounsaturated fat has only 2 scrubbing surfaces while the polyunsaturated fat may have 14 or more. Obviously, the polyunsaturated fats do a better job of acting as detergents because they have a larger capacity. These polyunsaturated fats are found in fish (oils), walnuts, corn oil, soybean oil and safflower oil. The monounsaturated fats are found in poultry, olives, other nuts (except coconut) and cottonseed oil. Many foods contain small amounts of these substances, but only those listed have enough to be effective.

Polyunsaturated fats, eaten in reasonable amounts, apparently tend to lower the blood levels of cholesterol and triglycerides and may also help remove the fat already deposited, provided that fat has not been hardened by the addition of calcium by the body. The ratio of unsaturated to saturated fats found effective for controlling fatty deposits is at least 2:1.

Any human body will make cholesterol if given excess Calories. The Calories do not have to be from any specific food. Whenever a person is gaining weight, he is making extra cholesterol, and he is making other blood fats, too. Which of the blood fats will be increased the greatest amount depends on the metabolic balance and chemistry of the individual. Some persons make extra cholesterol only; others make that plus extra triglycerides and phospholipids. Either of the first two can cause artery and heart damage if there's too much for too long.

Altering the diet can control the level of blood cholesterol in many cases. The biggest factor in this control is getting the body to a normal weight, thus ridding it of fat in both blood and tissues. This is important. The defatting also desludges at the same time, leaving the body with a limited reservoir for fat formation.

One should cut down or stop eating foods high in cholesterol. These foods include egg yolk, liver and glandular meats, milk fat, meat fat and some shellfish, especially shrimp. Coconut oil turns into cholesterol very readily, so this should be avoided, too. The fats eaten should be primarily from the polyunsaturated groups. By switching the fat intake in this manner, the body is often

encouraged to reduce the cholesterol deposits and to no longer manufacture it at an increased rate.

Triglycerides are fats that are also found in the blood serum. The usual sources of triglycerides are sugars, excessive amounts of starch and alcohol. Many persons with diabetes mellitus or hypoglycemia have high triglyceride levels, since the metabolic upset caused by these diseases inclines the body to manufacture these fats. The excess fat can then become artery deposits—which can lead to heart attacks and strokes.

Many physicians place diabetics (and sometimes hypoglycemics) on fat-restricted diets in an attempt to prevent the development of this secondary artery problem. Diabetics develop early heart and artery problems at a rate many times higher than that for normal people. Control of diabetes helps prevent the development of the related vascular disease. When the blood sugar is in balance, the fuel is used for energy and heat with only the excess going to storage. If the metabolic balance is off, the body tends to produce excess cholesterol and triglycerides. These are made mostly in the liver and distributed throughout the body and blood.

The rules for prevention of high cholesterol and triglyceride levels are similar; combined, there are six rules—on which the recipes in this cookbook are based:

1. Lose weight until a normal level is reached. This is necessary for control of both cholesterol and triglycerides.

2. Avoid free sugar and limit natural sugars in order to reduce triglycerides.

3. Avoid or limit the intake of high-cholesterol foods. That means cut animal fats and red meats to three meals per week—no more—and eliminate milk fat and coconut fat entirely (including non-dairy creamers). Use fish, poultry, low-fat cheese and cottage cheese to supply much of the diet protein.

4. Include unsaturated fats in the diet (soybean oil, safflower oil or corn oil) to help desludge cholesterol and triglyceride deposits. The polyunsaturated fats do not produce excess fat in the blood unless consumed in large amounts.

5. Limit or avoid the use of alcohol. This will have to be decided by your doctor on the basis of your blood content of triglycerides. Be sure to discuss this frankly with your physician. Diet control in every aspect but this one may cause you to still have excess triglycerides and therefore develop vascular disease.

6. Limit food intake to give no excess over the body's needs. This is necessary for control of both cholesterol and triglycerides.

Diabetes versus Hypoglycemia

Diabetes mellitus is caused by a shortage of insulin, a hormone needed to regulate the use of sugar in the body. This disease has been recognized from ancient times. The Egyptians and Greeks were known to have suffered from it, and the symptoms we see are unchanged from the way their physicians described them.

Patients who cannot control diabetes by just watching what they eat must have medicine to supply the lacking insulin. No human can live without insulin. Either it must be made by the body in adequate amounts, or the drugs given must extend the insulin to cover needs, or injected insulin must be used. There is no alternative substance to fill this need.

Hypoglycemia is a newer recognized disease. In many cases it is a prediabetic condition. (The pancreas seems to overwork, and then slow down and quit—or partly quit.) Hypoglycemia is frequently found in families where there are diabetics. Since many of the symptoms are the same, it is often difficult to know which disease a person is suffering from. Extensive blood tests may be needed to establish a diagnosis. Some persons have a delayed production of insulin (diabetes) and then over-make it (hypoglycemia). This creates a medical condition that is difficult to control.

Hypoglycemia is the overproduction of insulin. This leads to the lowering of the blood sugar level and subsequent cell starvation. Headaches, forgetfulness, dizziness, nausea, anxiety, heart palpitations, excessive fatigue and shakiness may all be symptoms of this disease. Much of this is due to the lack of adequate sugar supply for the brain. (Most parts of the body are able to convert other foods into the energy they need, but the brain has difficulty doing this.) People who suffer from this disease frequently show personality changes which are quite violent. (Perhaps Dr. Jekyll/Mr. Hyde suffered from this disease.)

It seems logical that persons with hypoglycemia would need only to eat sugar often to control their low blood sugar. Not so. Sugar unfortunately stimulates the production of still more insulin and the result is even lower blood sugar. The only way we know to prevent the production of excess insulin in people with hypoglycemia is to eliminate from the diet those foods which directly stimulate the production of insulin.

Obesity makes hypoglycemia harder to control, and yet hypoglycemia may be the basis for the weight gain in the first place. The constant, unsatisfied hunger caused by hypoglycemia makes people crave food, eat, and gain weight. The weight gain places the insulin balance under greater stress, and the hypoglycemia becomes more severe as a result. This is a vicious circle for many people.

Whether the hypoglycemia is the prediabetic or the flat curve variety, control of body weight is a vital factor. Control of weight is as important as eating the correct foods.

Although diabetes and hypoglycemia are different in cause and effect, their treatment by diet is much the same. The main difference is that the hypoglycemic must eat small, frequent meals with protein at each, but the diabetic usually needs only three normal meals and a bedtime snack. Recipes which are suitable for one are usually suitable for the other, unless the carbohydrate level is too high for the hypoglycemic to handle at one time.

There are seven rules for control of diabetes and hypoglycemia by diet. The first five apply to both disorders:

1. Concentrated sugars (sugar, molasses, syrup, etc.) must be avoided.

2. Natural sugars and starches must be eaten sparingly, and the amounts must be spread throughout the day in order to moderate blood sugar level and insulin demand.

3. Weight must be normal for body size. Excess fat increases the need for insulin in diabetics and increases the strain on insulin production in hypoglycemics. In either case, it makes the disease harder to control.

4. Exercise should be taken so the body is firm and muscular, not soft and flabby. Exercise helps the body use food with less insulin needed.

5. Total Calories must not exceed the amount needed to maintain normal body weight and supply fuel for usual activities.

Two additional rules apply only to the control of hypoglycemia:

6. Alcohol must be drastically limited or avoided. For many people with hypoglycemia alcohol is similar to a sugar, and the reaction is as bad but slower to occur.

7. Protein foods (meat, fish, poultry, eggs, cheese) must be taken every few hours. The exact plan of the diet should depend on the results of the glucose tolerance tests; mealtimes must be planned to prevent low blood sugar levels.

Nobody should self-diagnose medical problems. If you think you may have either diabetes or hypoglycemia, be sure to have a doctor test you. In the case of diabetes, a simple blood test may be enough, or the doctor may want to do a glucose tolerance test to determine the degree of the disease. In the case of hypoglycemia, a longer glucose tolerance test (at least 5 hours) preceded by a diet high in sugar and starch for 3 days is the only accurate test. These tests indicate the level of insulin function and so show the existence of any disorders.

There is some medical controversy about the diagnosis of hypoglycemia. It is a popular disease at the moment, and people may believe they have it when they really do not. The only accurate way to find out is to have the blood test. Psychological problems may give similar symptoms—but hypoglycemia may cause emotional upsets and instability. Find out!

Salt and Sodium

There is a lot of difference between the food which is low-salt and that which is low-sodium. Everyone involved in the care of patients who require diets low in salt should clearly understand the differences between the two and know what changes they make in the food allowed the dieter.

Table salt is sodium chloride. It is the *sodium* part of the formula that is the troublemaker. Sodium is also found in baking soda (sodium bicarbonate), in monosodium glutamate and in baking powder (mostly disodium phosphate).

Sodium eaten in food stimulates the body to hold water in its tissues. This extra water gives additional work for the heart and kidneys. It can cause high blood pressure, heart failure and even strokes. So you can understand that when the doctor decides that a patient must limit salt intake, it is a serious matter. The strictness of the limitation depends upon how badly that person is holding water in his body. If he has only a slight problem, perhaps a low-salt diet is enough cutting down; if he has a major problem, a low-sodium diet may be needed.

The difference between these two diets is a matter of how strict you must be in avoiding foods with salt. The first level (low-salt) omits free salt (added salt) and any foods prepared with large amounts of salt, such as bacon, ham, pickles and olives. The second level (low-sodium) omits all of these, *plus* limiting foods which are naturally high in salt, such as celery, dark green leafy vegetables, beets, carrots and shellfish. On both levels salt, soda, monosodium glutamate and baking powder are forbidden. You may use a salt substitute for flavoring, but sparingly; too much causes an unpleasant taste.

The usual American diet contains 8 to 10 grams of salt a day. Forty percent of the salt molecule is sodium. If you multiply the salt figures by 0.4 you will get the sodium value.

The low-salt diet contains 3 to 4 grams of salt: 1-1/4 to 1-1/2 grams of sodium. The low-sodium diet contains 1 to 2 grams of salt: 1/2 gram or less of sodium. This last comes from naturally occurring sodium in foods, not from anything added by man. If all of your food is prepared without salt, including salt-free bread and margarine, and you limit milk (or milk products) to a cup a day or less, you will be following a low-sodium diet.

If your doctor wants you to follow a very strict low-sodium diet, you will not be able to use some of the recipes in this book. If the recipe is labeled "This cannot be made low in salt," don't try to use the food. The other recipes give the amount of sodium when made with the low-salt directions. A reasonable rule is that you should not use anything with more than 25 to 30 milligrams of sodium in a serving if you are on a low-sodium diet.

If such a rigid diet is required, you should purchase a low-sodium cookbook. There are several good ones in print. If you can't find one, ask your local heart association which ones they recommend. Recipes in these will not be low in sugar, and if you have diabetes or hypoglycemia along with the salt problem you will have to be careful what you make from such a cookbook. The recipe may be low enough in salt but too high in sugar and starch for your diet.

If you don't understand or can't remember your diet prescription, recheck with your doctor. If possible, have a registered dietitian explain the diet limits and help you plan your meal pattern. Write down what the doctor and dietitian tell you. It is confusing when two diets sound so much alike and are so different in foods allowed.

The following may help you to distinguish between these diets:

The *low-salt diet* is 1,250 to 1,500 milligrams of sodium a day. Omit all free salt; omit all salt in cooking; avoid excessively salty foods such as bacon, ham, lunch meat, pickles, olives, salted nuts or salted crackers.

The *low-sodium diet* is 400 to 800 milligrams of sodium a day. Omit all the items omitted for the low-salt diet and observe the following additional restrictions: Limit milk and milk products to 1 cup a day or less. Avoid all canned or processed food unless it is diet-packed without salt. Omit beets and beet greens, carrots, spinach, kale, chard, celery and turnips.

If your doctor orders this strict a diet, you must have a diet plan for your meals and a low-sodium cookbook for recipes.

Salt free is a rather vague term, and not a definite diet level. It usually means a low-sodium diet, but with no limit on the amounts of foods eaten (such as milk) as long as the items are prepared without added salt.

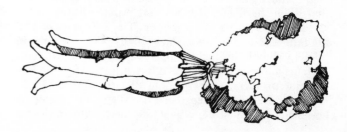

Do's and Don'ts for Dieting

Do's

Do be home for as many meals as possible. It is better not to struggle with meals out when they can be avoided.

Do take a snack with you when you know you may be delayed. This is the easiest way to say no to temptation.

Do expect to be able to follow your diet most places. The chapter on eating out has tips that make it less complicated than you might think.

Do remember that if you have one bad day with dieting, the next day you have a new chance. Because you blew it once doesn't give you a corner on doing it again. If you do, it is because you want to go off your diet.

Don'ts

Don't go shopping when you are hungry. You will buy all sorts of goodies and then they will be there to tempt you. A good rule is not to shop more than 1-1/2 hours after a meal.

Don't go to a party so hungry that you eat (and drink) everything you see. Have something to eat before you go—perhaps your usual nighttime snack if you are having a late dinner.

Don't have several drinks and then expect your will power to work when the food comes. Alcohol not only adds Calories, it relaxes your will to control what you eat. It's double dynamite.

Don't stock up on goodies for visitors. The only person who will end up enjoying them is you.

Don't think, "I'll have just one bite." It won't work. You will end up eating what you know you shouldn't. The food-aholic has to learn what the alcoholic does, namely that the first bite (drink) is the fatal one.

Don't make everyone miserable by talking about your diet all the time. Show people results and they will do the talking, and the compliments will be music to your ears. Save your energy for working at your diet instead of wearing out your tongue (and your friends' ears).

Don't set yourself up for temptation. If you deliberately put yourself in a situation where you can't follow your diet, then take the consequences without complaining.

Remember

People find time and opportunity for things they really want to accomplish. If they want to find excuses to fail, that is easy enough. The really hard job is to stick with it and prove that your brain is boss, not your stomach.

Notes

3. A Little Home Chemistry

How To Read a Label and Understand What It Says

Most people can't interpret a label—whether they're on a diet or not. Our new labeling laws will make this simpler, but it still can require a mathematics degree to figure out the values in some cases. Try following the tips given here and see how easy it is once you know how to do it.

What Does a Label Tell You?

Many people don't know that the federal rules regarding the labeling of products apply only to products which cross state lines. Products made and sold within a state are subject only to the laws of that state. It is the products made in one state and sold in another that come under federal law.

Some products, such as mayonnaise, peanut butter and many others, are not required to have ingredients listed on the label as long as they meet federal standards. You can purchase from the government a booklet that will tell you what ingredients are allowed to be in these foods, but still not know whether those ingredients are there. The product might have all the allowed items, some of them or none of them; you have no way of knowing for sure. You must assume that all the allowed ingredients are

there. If sugar is one of the allowed items, you will have to skip that product or buy one which states "no sugar added" or "dietetic—no sugar." Dietetic products must show the nutritional breakdown (protein, fat and carbohydrate) and other information on the label. Our new laws on labeling dietetic foods make it much easier for a person to read and interpret data.

The following rules will make it easier for you to read a label and know what you are reading:

1. Look to see whether it is a local product. Local products will be covered by state laws which probably do not require that the contents be labeled. If there are no food values given, do not use it. Buy a brand that is labeled, so you know what you are getting.

2. Ingredients are listed in the order of amount in a product. If wheat is the largest ingredient, it is listed first; the other ingredients are listed in descending order. Many of the ingredients at the bottom of the list represent a very tiny amount and don't matter.

3. If the ingredient you want to avoid (for example, sugar) is one of the first three ingredients on a label, DO NOT USE IT. If it is the fourth listed, consider how sweet the product is. If it is a sweet product (or salty, or

whatever you want to avoid) then still don't use it. After the fourth-listed ingredient, however, there is not enough to matter, and you may use the food. The one exception to this is the person on a low-sodium diet.

4. These words mean sugar: dextrose, sucrose, glucose, maltose, lactose, malt, corn syrup, corn solids, sugar, honey, invert sugars, molasses.

These sweeteners may give trouble, too: Sorbitol and mannitol are both alcohols which have a sweet taste. Most people who must limit sugar must limit these, too. They are apt to cause a reaction like excess sugar in persons with hypoglycemia, but it will take longer. If this is your problem, avoid these alcohols.

5. If you are really concerned about a product that you would like to use, write to the manufacturer and ask for information. Give specific data from the label so that the reply can be specific in answering your questions. They will be prompt in answering; most large manufacturers are prepared for consumers to consult them about their products. They employ home economists for just this purpose.

6. If you want information and don't know where to write, call a library and ask them to look up the company's business address. Address your letters to the company's Customer Relations Department.

If you want to look up the ingredients of standard products in the government's Standard of Identity booklet you can obtain a copy for $1.75 from the Superintendent of Documents, Government Printing Office, Washington, D.C. 20402. Ask for the *Code of Federal Regulations Number 21, Food & Drugs,* Parts 1 to 119, January 1, 1972.

Now That You Have Read the Label, What Does It Mean?

Perhaps you wonder what the percent figures on the label mean in food amounts. The following will give you some means to judge whether the food is worth what it has to replace.

Percents—The percent figures given on the label (% protein, % fat, % carbohydrates) also express the number of grams of protein, or whatever, found in 100 grams of the product. 100 grams is slightly less than a half cup, or 20 teaspoons. In other words, the percentage on the label divided by 20 equals the number of grams in 1 teaspoon.

Teaspoons—Percent (%) given on label ÷ 20 = grams in 1 teaspoon of the product. For example, diet jelly may contain carbohydrate 20%, protein 1%, fat 1%. Carbohydrate 20% = 20 grams of carbohydrate per 100 grams of product. Carbohydrate 20 grams ÷ 20 teaspoons = 1 gram per teaspoon. No replacement is needed for 1 to 2 grams per meal extra. The protein and fat contents are low enough to ignore.

Portions—Percent (%) given on label x package weight ÷ 100 = grams per package. Amount in 1 serving = grams per package ÷ number of servings. For example, diet gelatin may contain carbohydrate 2%, protein 68%, fat 0.1%. Let's say the package weighs 5/8 ounce. 1 ounce = 30 grams. 5/8 ounce x 30 grams = 19 grams per package. Protein, then, is 68 x 19 ÷ 100 = 13.8 grams per package. Protein replacement is 13.8 grams per package ÷ 4 servings per package = 3.5 grams per serving. 3.5 grams protein = 1/2-ounce low-fat meat. Find a food equal in value and use it as a replacement (see Tables, pages 203-222). The carbohydrate and fat content are low enough to ignore.

Calories—When Calories only are given, assume that they are whatever you are avoiding, whether sugar or starch. A gram of carbohydrate contains 4 Calories. Calories ÷ 4 = grams carbohydrate; up to 2 grams may be used at a meal without replacement. For example, dietetic pop may contain 2 Calories per 8 ounces. Carbohydrate per bottle is 2 Calories ÷ 4 Calories per gram = 1/2 gram, so you could consume 3 bottles in a day without replacement.

All dietetic foods will fit into one of three families—calculated by teaspoons, by portions, or by Calories. As labels improve, you will have less trouble figuring them out. We suggest that you keep a card file (like a recipe file) of information about replacements for the dietetic foods you use. Then when you buy a new supply you will only have to check to be sure the label is the same; you won't have to refigure the product. You might cut out the original label and stick it on the back of the card. Write on the card the substitute for one serving and your meal planning will be easy.

Substitutions and Equivalents

Balancing the flavorings and seasonings in dietetic recipes makes them appeal to everyone. Don't be afraid to experiment with new combinations; use your imagination to give new touches to common dishes.

The Sugar Substitutes

No other food substitutes draw so much attention as the sugar substitutes. It's easy to see why. And isn't it lucky that substitution is so easy? The substitutes available for 1 cup of sugar allow room for choice: either 1/2 cup of granular substitute, 6 teaspoons of a liquid substitute or 48 quarter-grain saccharine tablets.

Here's how to use the three types:

Granules—Use half as much volume of granular substitute as sugar called for in the recipe. Taste and add more if desired. Used to excess this is apt to give a bitter taste and an unpleasantly sweet aftertaste.

Liquids—Read label to determine how much is used to replace 1 teaspoon of sugar; multiply by 3 to get amount needed to replace 1 tablespoon of sugar. Use less than the recipe calls for by about one-fifth. (If it calls for 1 teaspoon liquid sweetener to replace the sugar in recipe, use 4/5 teaspoon instead.) Sometimes the sweetening power is greater than the label shows so be sure to check out each new product you use. If you find a particular sweetener is less strong, you can easily add more.

Tablets—Dissolve a tablet in a little warm water before adding to the recipe. Most tablets are equivalent to 1 teaspoon of sugar; 3 tablets would equal 1 tablespoon of sugar.

Both the liquid and granular sweetening agents are capable of making foods taste sweet, but they vary in their capacity to make a product with satisfactory texture and appearance.

The most common basis of substitute sweeteners is saccharine. Saccharine is a derivative of coal; it is a totally noncaloric substance. Several other sweetening materials are expected to be marketed soon, but until these are available and proven satisfactory, the use of the saccharine-based sweeteners is expected.

Saccharine may change taste when subjected to high temperatures for any length of time. It should be added at the end of the cooking, so that it does not change taste due to prolonged heating. Of course, this cannot be done with baked goods or foods which are cooked in a sealed container (jam, canned fruits). Always add saccharine as late in a recipe as you can—after removing from the heat is the best time. The concentrated soluble saccharine powder used in commercial canning has virtually no aftertaste; about 1 teaspoon equals 5 pounds of sugar. This concentrated form is not usually available to the householder; saccharine for domestic use is cut with an inert substance.

Dissolve saccharine tablets in warm water before using in a recipe. Liquid saccharine need not be diluted or changed in any way before using.

Each package label tells how much sweetening is in a measured portion of the contents. Usually it tells how many drops (or what volume) is required to replace a teaspoon of sugar. There are 48 level teaspoons in 1 cup. If you change brands, be sure you check the strength of the new product as there may be a large difference. (Some of the cheaper products are not good bargains because they contain less sweetening.)

When you start using sugar substitutes, you will notice that it is hard to get enough sweetening without having a bitter or strong aftertaste. The trick is to undersweeten and use other things to enhance the sweetness. Try using less sugar substitute than you think you want. Soon your taste for sugar will decrease, the less-sweet items will taste good to you, and there will be no aftertaste.

Use natural fruit sugars to provide some of the sweetening, especially for tart fruits such as rhubarb or cranberry. Many recipes in this book call for apple or applesauce. The natural sugar of the apple lessens the need for a sugar substitute. Lemon juice will also bring out the natural sweetening in fruit, sometimes enough that no other sweetening is needed. Lemon rind will serve this purpose, too, although too much of it will give a strong taste and overpower the food's proper flavor. The Calories in lemon juice and lemon rind are negligible and they do not add appreciably to the total value of the food.

The Calories in this book have been calculated for granular substitutes. Use of a totally noncaloric sweetener will drop the food value 3 Calories or less per serving, and probably less than 1 Calorie. If you are watching Calories closely enough for that difference to matter, use the liquid sweeteners. Foods prepared with liquid sweeteners will have fewer Calories, but their texture and appearance will be not as close to the real thing as those made with the granular products.

Among the new sweeteners under development is one taken before eating that changes the taste buds' sensitivity to sugar. Foods are prepared with no added sweetening; sweetness appears only in the mouth of the person using the substance. Other persons would probably find the foods unsatisfactory.

Most of the granular substitutes are combinations of saccharine and a natural sugar (not sucrose) or starch. They have some Calories, but so few compared with comparable amounts of sugar that there is a large reduction in food value. The granular substitutes require one-third to one-half the volume required in sugar for the same sweetening. One product uses glycine as a sweetening agent. Glycine is a protein compound (amino acetic acid) that can be used in cooking without giving an aftertaste. However it does not give quite the same baked product as the granular sugar substitutes which are combinations of saccharine and a carbohydrate.

If you remove the sugar from a recipe and do not use anything to replace the carbohydrate, the appearance of the food will be different. It may fail to brown satisfactorily, and if sugar was a major ingredient in the recipe, the food made without it will be heavier in texture.

Sodium-Free Baking Powder

You may buy sodium-free baking powder or have your druggist make this mix, recommended by the American Heart Association:

Potassium bicarbonate	39.8 grams
Cornstarch	28.0 grams
Tartaric acid	7.5 grams
Potassium bitartrate	56.1 grams

This makes about 4 ounces. Store it in a tight container. Use 1-1/2 teaspoons of this in place of 1 teaspoon of regular baking powder. Avoid overbeating mixtures containing this powder.

Milk

Whole milk—Use equal volume skim milk plus 2 teaspoons oil per cup. Add oil with other liquid ingredients. One to two drops of butter flavoring added to the oil will give the flavor which skim milk lacks.

Evaporated milk—Use equal volume evaporated skim milk plus 4 teaspoons oil per cup. Add to other liquids in recipe.

Half-and-half—Use 1 cup skim milk plus 3 table-spoons oil. Put this in the blender and blend at top speed for about 1 minute until the oil is homogenized into the milk. This will be approximately 18 percent fat, equal to the fat content of half-and-half. It will stay homogenized for several hours.

Dry milk—Use 1/3 cup dry skim milk per cup of whole milk in recipe. Then add 1 cup (less 1 tablespoon) of water to the other liquid ingredients. This is the same as using liquid skim milk.

Cream

The so-called non-dairy creamers are usually mixtures of coconut oil and corn solids (syrup); unless the label specifically says otherwise, don't use them. The first item contributes to the forming of cholesterol and the second (sugar) may add to the blood triglycerides. These cream substitutes are not only empty Calories which give only fuel, but they also do harm by contributing to the formation of blood fats. It is better to use dry skim milk, evaporated skim milk or even small amounts of whole milk; these would at least provide some vitamins and minerals along with the protein.

Eggs

For 1 egg use 2 egg whites plus 1-1/4 teaspoons oil and 6 drops of yellow food coloring. Add oil with coloring to other liquid ingredients. Add the egg whites as directed for whole eggs.

Egg substitutes—Read the package directions for the amount to use. Most liquid egg substitutes call for 1-1/2 ounces per medium egg. Use the substitute as you would fresh eggs. If the recipe calls for separating the egg yolk and white, use 1 fresh egg white, 2/3 ounce of egg substitute and 1/4 teaspoon oil or melted margarine. Add the oil to the egg substitute. Use the white separately as the recipe directs.

Watch for the sodium content of egg substitutes: 1 whole egg contains approximately 41 milligrams of sodium.

Flour

Instant flour—You may use all-purpose flour in recipes that call for instant flour, but the product will be heavier and tougher. Use 1 tablespoon per cup less of all-purpose flour.

Oat flour—Do not substitute any other flour for oat flour. The result will be unsatisfactory. Oat flour may be made by putting old-fashioned oats in a blender and running it for a minute at top speed. Put the result into a sieve; the fine matter that goes through the mesh is oat flour. Or put the oats through a food mill; whatever part goes through the mill is usable as oat flour.

Fats

Margarine—Never use soft margarine unless a recipe calls for that type. Use the stick variety (one that is high in unsaturated fat).

To use margarine in a recipe that calls for butter, be sure to add a little extra flour (1 teaspoon per cup) or the dough will be too soft.

Oil—Use oil only if the recipe calls for it.

Don't use oil to replace butter or margarine in a recipe in which you are also using a sugar substitute. The use of oil requires extra sugar for satisfactory texture. There is no way to correct this in a dietetic recipe.

You may use either oil or melted margarine in the egg substitution described previously.

Flavorings

As a general rule, food sweetened artificially needs a little more of whatever other flavoring is called for in the recipe. (If vanilla is the other flavoring, for instance, it might need to be increased from 1/2 teaspoon to 3/4 teaspoon.)

Use combinations of flavorings to get interesting results. Try less vanilla and more almond, black walnut, maple, rum and even anise extract. Use sparingly any flavoring that you have not tried before, because some have a stronger flavor than vanilla. To start, for the quantity of vanilla called for, substitute half vanilla and half (or slightly less) another flavoring. Adjust to taste with each change of flavoring.

Citrus Rind and Juice

You may substitute the following for 1 teaspoon of grated lemon rind:

  1 teaspoon grated orange rind
  2/3 teaspoon grated grapefruit rind
  1/2 teaspoon dried lemon rind
  2 tablespoons lemon juice

Since lemon and other fresh citrus fruits give out their oils gradually, the flavor will become stronger as the product stands. If you make something ahead of time, use a little less rind or it may prove too strong-tasting when you serve it.

Fruit Natural Sweetenings

Combinations of tart fruits and naturally sweet ones give an end product which requires less artificial sugar substitute. Adding lemon juice also brings out the natural sweet flavor in fruit. Try using 1 teaspoon of lemon juice per cup of fruit and taste before adding any sweetener.

Two fruits which are difficult to sweeten alone are rhubarb and lemon. Both can be sweetened by combining with sweeter fruits such as apples or berries. Try a proportion of half each, and then add more of the tarter fruit until you find out what proportion is best.

Dried fruits such as raisins or dates may furnish all the sweetening needed in some combinations.

Don't be afraid to use your imagination when trying fruit mixtures. Very few fruits fail to blend well with others, however unlikely some combinations may seem.

Food Values

No dietetic cookbook would be complete without some form of chart showing approximate food values and replacements. These are given in the least complicated form possible. So many factors are involved in the growing and processing of foods that there are great variations in the value. For this reason, it is ridiculous to try to measure food to the fraction of the gram. The type of measurement that is used in this book is fully as accurate as the foods themselves. The current trend is away from dwelling on detailed weighing, emphasizing instead the planning of meals that approximate each other in food content and volume. This makes it much easier to live comfortably with one's family.

The tables of equivalent values begin on page 203.

Notes

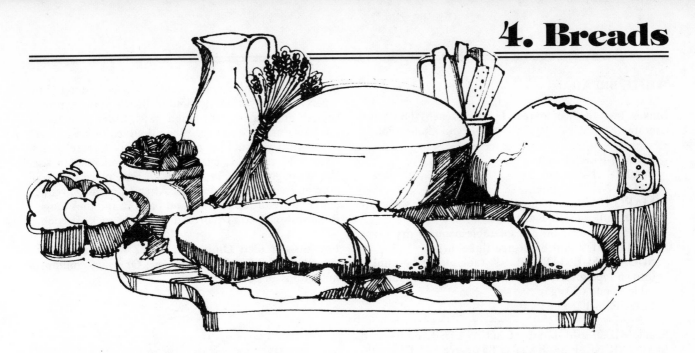

Most breads contain a small amount of sugar to give food for rapid yeast growth. This sugar is converted into gas (carbon dioxide) and is part of what causes the bread to rise. Breads made with no free sugar will take longer to rise and are likely to be heavier and less attractive than those made with sugar.

None of the bread and biscuit recipes in this section are sweet-tasting except the sweet rolls. If you wish a sweeter taste, use additional sugar substitute. Excess sugar substitute causes most people to notice a bitter taste. Be conservative in your use of substitutes, and the results will be excellent.

WHITE BREAD

Makes two 18-slice loaves, 1 pound each. One slice contains 81 Calories (P3, F1, C15),* no cholesterol.

SKIM MILK, 1 cup
WATER, 1 cup hot
SALT, 2-1/2 teaspoons
MARGARINE, 3 tablespoons. Use corn-oil, soybean-oil or safflower-oil margarine.
YEAST, 1 cake; or 1 scant tablespoon of dry yeast
WATER, 1/2 cup 85-degree (lukewarm)
SUGAR SUBSTITUTE, 3 tablespoons granular (brown type gives best taste); or substitute equal to 6 tablespoons of sugar
FLOUR, 6-1/2 cups sifted

Scald MILK; add 1 cup of hot WATER, SALT and MARGARINE. Put YEAST in 85-degree WATER; add 1 teaspoon of SUGAR SUBSTITUTE. Stir to dissolve. Let stand 10 minutes. Add yeast mixture to milk mixture; stir well; add sugar substitute. Add FLOUR

*These figures express grams of protein, fat and carbohydrate per serving; they are given with each recipe.

gradually, beating after each addition. Divide dough into 2 parts. Knead on lightly floured board until texture is smooth and elastic. Oil dough balls; cover with towel; put in warm place to rise. When doubled in size, knead again until all bubbles are out; shape. Grease dough again with vegetable oil and put in bread pans to rise. When dough has again doubled in size, place in a cool oven and set it at 400 degrees. After 15 minutes, reduce temperature to 350 degrees and bake 25 minutes longer. Remove bread from pan and place on rack to cool.

For low-salt diet: Omit salt; use 2 teaspoons of salt substitute. Use salt-free margarine. One slice contains 4 milligrams of sodium.

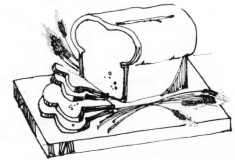

LIGHT WHEAT BREAD

Makes two 18-slice loaves. One slice equals 1 slice of bread with 1/2 teaspoon of fat; contains 94 Calories (P3, F2, C16), 7 milligrams of cholesterol if made with egg, no cholesterol if made with egg substitute.

YEAST, 2 cakes; or 2 scant tablespoons of dry yeast
WATER, 1/2 cup at 85 degrees (lukewarm)
SUGAR SUBSTITUTE, 2 tablespoons granular; or substitute equal to 1/4 cup of sugar
SKIM MILK, 2 cups
MARGARINE, 1/3 cup soft-type. Use corn-oil, soybean-oil or safflower-oil margarine.
EGG, 1; or 1-1/2 ounces of liquid egg substitute
SALT, 1-1/2 teaspoons
ALL-PURPOSE FLOUR, about 5-1/2 cups
WHOLE WHEAT FLOUR, 1 cup
WHEAT GERM, 3 tablespoons unsweetened

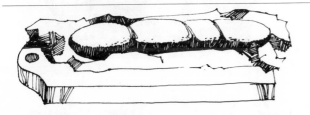

Add YEAST to 85-degree WATER, add 1 teaspoon of SUGAR SUBSTITUTE, stir to dissolve and let stand 10 to 15 minutes. Scald MILK, add MARGARINE and set aside to cool to 85 degrees. Add milk mixture to yeast, then add EGG, SALT and remainder of SUGAR SUBSTITUTE. Save 1/2 cup ALL-PURPOSE FLOUR for the board. Combine WHEAT GERM with FLOUR and add gradually. Knead on lightly floured board until texture is even. Form 2 loaves. Grease sides and tops of loaves with vegetable oil. Put in warm place to rise. Cover with towel.

When loaves have doubled in size, knead again on lightly floured board until all bubbles are gone and dough has an even, elastic texture. Grease bread pans with vegetable oil. Put shaped dough into pans; oil sides and top, as before. Allow to double in size. Put pans in a cool oven and set it for 400 degrees. After 15 minutes, lower temperature setting to 350 degrees. Bake 25 to 30 minutes more, until well browned. Remove loaves; grease tops sparingly with margarine. Place loaves on rack to cool.

For low-salt diet: Omit salt; use 1 teaspoon of salt substitute. Use salt-free margarine. One slice contains 10 milligrams of sodium.

BAKING POWDER BISCUITS - Plain and Herbed.

Makes 12 biscuits. One biscuit equals 1 slice of bread with 1/2 teaspoon of fat; contains 117 Calories (P3, F5, C15), no cholesterol.

FLOUR, 2 cups
BAKING POWDER, 3 teaspoons double-acting
SALT, 1/2 teaspoon
MARGARINE, 1/3 cup soft-type. Use corn-oil, soybean-oil or safflower-oil margarine.
SKIM MILK, 3/4 cup
Optional:
CHIVES, 1 tablespoon finely diced
OREGANO, 1/2 teaspoon dried
THYME, 1/4 teaspoon dried
PARSLEY, 1 teaspoon fresh or dried, chopped fine

Sift DRY INGREDIENTS together. Cut in MARGA-RINE with pastry blender. Add MILK to make a soft dough. Sprinkle HERBS over the dough, spreading evenly through the mixture. Roll out dough 1/2-inch thick on lightly floured board. Cut into 12 parts (may use 2-inch round cutter). Place biscuits on oiled pan. Bake at 450 degrees for 12 to 15 minutes until brown.

For low-salt diet: Omit salt; use 1/2 teaspoon of salt substitute. Use 4 teaspoons of sodium-free baking powder. Use salt-free margarine. All pure dried herbs are low in salt, so you may use them. One biscuit contains 10 milligrams of sodium.

BLUEBERRY MUFFINS

Makes 14 muffins. One muffin equals 1 slice of bread with 1 teaspoon of fat; contains 107 Calories (P2, F5, C13). Contains 17.5 milligrams of cholesterol if made with egg, 1 milligram if made with egg substitute.

SUGAR SUBSTITUTE, 1/3 cup granular (brown type is best); or substitute equal to 2/3 cup of sugar
MARGARINE, 1/3 cup. Use corn-oil, soybean-oil or safflower-oil margarine.
EGG, 1 beaten; or 1-1/2 ounces of liquid egg substitute
INSTANT FLOUR, 1-1/2 cups
BAKING POWDER, 1-1/2 teaspoons double-acting
SALT, 1/2 teaspoon
CINNAMON, 1/8 teaspoon
NUTMEG, 1/16 teaspoon
YOGURT, 3/4 cup plain low-fat
SKIM MILK, 4 tablespoons
LEMON RIND, 1/2 teaspoon
BLUEBERRIES, 1 cup. If using frozen, partially thaw before adding.

Cream SUGAR SUBSTITUTE with MARGARINE and beaten EGG. Combine FLOUR, BAKING POWDER, SALT and SPICES in separate bowl. (You may use a sifter to mix them thoroughly.) Add YOGURT to creamed mixture. Blend until smooth. Add about 1/3 of flour mixture to creamed mixture; beat until smooth; add SKIM MILK and LEMON RIND, mix again. Gradually add remaining flour and beat until mixture is smooth and creamy. Add BLUEBERRIES, mixing with spoon to spread evenly through batter. Using paper liners in standard-size muffin tins, spoon into 14 evenly portioned muffins. Bake at 375 degrees for 45 minutes. Remove muffins from pan and place on a rack to cool.

Suggestions: Muffins will keep fresh and moist in airtight plastic container. Other berries (boysenberries or raspberries, for example) may be used, but the best is blueberry. You may alter the taste by using different spices and flavorings. Lemon rind in the blueberry batter is best, but you may want to use orange rind with other berries.

For low-salt diet: Use salt-free margarine. Use 2-1/4 teaspoons of sodium-free baking powder. Omit salt; use 1/2 teaspoon of salt substitute. One muffin contains 20 milligrams of sodium.

SWEET ROLLS WITH RAISINS

Makes 36 rolls. One roll equals 1 slice of bread, 1/2 teaspoon of fat and 1/4 cup of fruit; contains 102 Calories (P3, F2, C18), no cholesterol.

WHITE BREAD (see recipe)
MARGARINE, 4 tablespoons. Use corn-oil, soybean-oil or safflower-oil margarine.
SUGAR SUBSTITUTE, 1 cup granular (brown type gives best taste); or substitute equal to 2 cups of sugar
CINNAMON, 1/2 teaspoon
RAISINS, 1/2 cup, soaked in hot water

Follow the recipe for WHITE BREAD to the point of dividing dough into 2 parts. With a rolling pin, roll out dough about 1/2-inch thick. Try to make it rectangular, so it can be made into an even roll. Spread dough with softened MARGARINE, leaving edges ungreased. Mix SUGAR SUBSTITUTE and CINNAMON; sprinkle over margarine. Scatter drained RAISINS over sugared area. Roll from one of the long sides to make a long, narrow roll. Dampen edges with warm water and seal. Cut roll into 3/4-inch slices. Place slices on greased cookie sheet and let rise until doubled in size. Bake in preheated oven at 425 degrees until brown, 15 to 18 minutes. Remove rolls from sheet and put on rack to cool.

For low-salt diet: Make white bread, using low-salt directions. Use salt-free margarine for filling. One roll contains 5 milligrams of sodium.

SCOTCH SCONES WITH RAISINS

Makes 12 scones. One scone equals 1 slice of bread with 1 teaspoon of fat; contains 112 Calories (P3, F4, C16), no cholesterol.

FLOUR, 2 cups
BAKING POWDER, 3 teaspoons
SALT, 1/2 teaspoon
MARGARINE, 1/4 cup (1/2 cube). Use corn-oil, soybean-oil or safflower-oil margarine.
SKIM MILK, 2/3 cup
SUGAR SUBSTITUTE, 1-1/2 teaspoons granular; or substitute equal to 1 tablespoon of sugar
RAISINS, 2 tablespoons, soaked in hot water

Sift DRY INGREDIENTS together. Cut in MARGA-
RINE as if for pie crust, using pastry blender or fork.
Add SKIM MILK and SUGAR SUBSTITUTE and mix
well. Drain RAISINS, add to dough and mix again.
Knead lightly on floured board. Divide into 2 equal
parts. Roll each half into a circle about 1/2-inch thick.
Cut into 6 wedges, as if cutting a pie. Place on Teflon
baking sheet or sheet sprayed with nonstick coating.
Bake at 425 degrees for 15 to 18 minutes, until browned.

For low-salt diet: Omit salt; use 1/2 teaspoon of salt
substitute. Use 4 teaspoons of sodium-free baking
powder. Use salt-free margarine. One scone contains 9
milligrams of sodium.

OLD-FASHIONED DUMPLINGS

Makes 8 dumplings. One dumpling equals 1 slice of
bread with 1/2 teaspoon of fat; contains 98 Calories (P3,
F2, C17), no cholesterol.

FLOUR, 2 cups
BAKING POWDER, 4 teaspoons double-acting
SALT, 1/2 teaspoon

MARGARINE, 1-1/2 tablespoons. Use corn-oil,
soybean-oil or safflower-oil margarine.
SKIM MILK, 1/2 cup
WATER, 1/4 cup

Sift DRY INGREDIENTS together. Cut in MARGA-
RINE with pastry blender, as for pie crust. Combine
LIQUIDS; add slowly to flour mixture; mix gently. Put
onto lightly floured board. Roll or pat into about
1/2-inch thickness. Cut with 2-inch biscuit cutter.
Should make 8 portions. Drop onto boiling stew or soup.
Cover and cook 12 to 15 minutes, until cooked through.

Alternative methods: Drop dough, 1/3 cup at a time, into
boiling stew or soup, and cook as directed. If you wish
smaller dumplings, divide the dough into 12 parts (about
3 tablespoons per serving), then cook as directed. This
latter method makes 12 dumplings. One small dumpling
equals 2/3 slice of bread with 1/4 teaspoon of fat;
contains 67 Calories (P2, F1, C11).

For low-salt diet: Omit salt; use 1/2 teaspoon of salt
substitute. Use 5 teaspoons of sodium-free baking
powder. Use salt-free margarine. One dumpling contains
7 milligrams of sodium.

PANCAKE AND WAFFLE BASIC MIX

Makes 5 cups. One cup contains 495 Calories (P13, F19, C68), no cholesterol.

DRY MILK POWDER, 1 cup instant
FLOUR, 3-1/2 cups unsifted
BAKING POWDER, 1-1/2 tablespoons double-acting
SALT, 3/4 teaspoon
SUGAR SUBSTITUTE, 1 tablespoon granular; or substitute equal to 2 tablespoons of sugar
MARGARINE, 1/2 cup (1 cube). Use corn-oil, soybean-oil or safflower-oil margarine.

Mix DRY INGREDIENTS thoroughly. With pastry blender, cut in MARGARINE until mixture is like fine corn meal. Put in tight container and store in cool place.

For low-salt diet: Omit salt. Use 3/4 teaspoon of salt substitute. Use 2-1/4 teaspoons of sodium-free baking powder. Use salt-free margarine. One cup contains 69 milligrams of sodium.

PANCAKES

Makes 8 pancakes, 5-1/2-inch size. One pancake equals 1 slice of bread with 1/2 teaspoon of fat; contains 101 Calories (P4, F3, C17), 32 milligrams of cholesterol if made with egg, no cholesterol if made with egg substitute.

BASIC MIX, 2 cups (see recipe)
WATER, 1-1/2 cups
EGG, 1; or 1-1/2 ounces of liquid egg substitute

Combine INGREDIENTS; stir until moistened well and free of lumps. Do not beat. Bake on griddle sprayed with nonstick coating or lightly brushed with vegetable oil. Have griddle hot, but not smoking. Cook until bubbles form on top. Turn and brown other side. Serve with dietetic jam or sauce (see recipes).

For low-salt diet: Make basic mix with salt-free ingredients (see recipe). One pancake contains 36 milligrams of sodium.

WAFFLES

Makes 4 waffles. One square equals 1 slice of bread, 1/2 teaspoon of fat and 1/2 ounces of meat; contains 142 Calories (P5, F6, C17), 32 milligrams of cholesterol if made with egg, no cholesterol if made with egg substitute.

WATER, 1-1/2 cups
EGG, 1; or 1-1/2 ounces of liquid egg substitute
VEGETABLE OIL, 1 teaspoon
BASIC MIX, 2 cups (see recipe)
EGG WHITES, 2

Place BASIC MIX in a medium-size bowl. Combine WATER, beaten EGG and OIL. Do not add whites. Gradually add wet mixture to BASIC MIX, stirring to remove lumps. Beat EGG WHITES until fluffy and dry. Fold egg whites gently into batter, being careful not to over-mix. Bake in hot waffle iron, oiled or sprayed with nonstick coating, on medium setting until brown. Serve with dietetic sauce or jam (see recipes).

Suggestions: Waffles are good when they contain fresh fruit for variety. You may add 1/2 cup of blueberries just before you fold in the egg whites. Follow the other directions and bake as usual. Omit 1/2 tablespoon of fruit per waffle square from your meal.

For low-salt diet: Make basic mix according to low-salt instructions. Use 2-1/4 ounces of egg substitute and only 1 egg white in recipe. One square contains 36 milligrams of sodium.

Notes

Soups are a good way to use leftovers economically. They are nutritious and appealing when well prepared and seasoned. When you have a dab of leftover vegetable, don't throw it away—make soup! For example, almost any vegetable can be substituted for the cauliflower in the Cream of Cauliflower Soup.

The recipes in this chapter are planned for quick preparation, but they still have the good flavor and appeal of the old-style, long-cooked soup pot.

Experiment with seasonings and herbs to suit your taste. Learn to use herbs freely. They help to bring out flavors and enhance the appetizing aroma of hot soup.

Note that a few of these recipes cannot be made to suit a low-salt diet: Cream of Tomato Soup, Northwest Fish Soup and Oyster Chowder à la Maryland.

BASIC CHICKEN BROTH

Makes about 5 cups. One cup equals 1/3 ounce of meat; contains 17 Calories (P2, F1, C0) and about 5 milligrams of cholesterol.

CHICKEN backs and necks, about 3 pounds
ONION, 1 large slice, chopped
CELERY, 1 large stalk with leaves, chopped
GARLIC, 1/2 small clove, minced
BAY LEAF, 1
BOILING WATER, 7 cups
SALT, 1/2 teaspoon
PEPPER, 1/8 teaspoon

Bake CHICKEN in roasting pan in 450-degree oven for 45 to 60 minutes. Remove to large soup kettle; discard fat. Add VEGETABLES, BAY LEAF and WATER. Simmer, covered, 3-1/2 to 4 hours, until meat falls from bones. Strain; add SEASONINGS to liquid; taste and adjust to suit. Line sieve with a white disposable tissue; strain liquid. (Tissue works as well as a filter and is cheaper and easier to get.) Pour strained liquid into jars and allow to stand at room temperature until completely cool. Refrigerate until liquid is jelled. Discard any fat from top. Use jellied liquid in any recipe that requires chicken broth or as a clear soup. Pick all the lean meat from sieved solids; use in any recipe calling for cooked chicken or add to broth to make a heartier soup. (Allow for at least 1 ounce of meat serving per cup if you add the shredded meat.)

For low-salt diet: Omit salt; use 1/2 to 3/4 teaspoon of salt substitute. One cup contains about 35 milligrams of sodium.

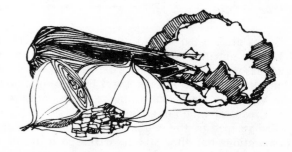

JO'S BROWN BEEF BROTH

Makes about 8 cups. One cup of broth equals 1/2 ounce of meat; contains 36 Calories (P5, F1, C2), about 5 milligrams of cholesterol.

BEEF BONES, about 4 pounds, cut into pieces
YELLOW ONION, 1 large, including skin, chopped
CELERY, 2 large stalks with leaves, chopped
PARSLEY, 1 small bunch chopped; or about 1 teaspoon of dried parsley
CARROT, 1 medium, sliced
POTATO, 1 small, cut into small cubes
GARLIC, 1/2 clove, chopped fine
BOILING WATER, 10 cups
SALT, 2/3 teaspoon
PEPPER, 1/8 teaspoon

Place BONES and ONION in roasting pan; bake 45 to 60 minutes in 450-degree oven, until bones are brown. Drain off fat. Place bones and onions in a very deep soup pot; add REMAINING INGREDIENTS. Cover and cook about 4 hours. About every half hour, skim off the gray scum that forms on the surface. Keep covered between skimmings. Remove from heat; pour through a colander to separate solids from liquids. Strain liquid through a sieve, using a white disposable tissue for a filter. (A tissue works well and is cheaper and easier to get than filter paper.) Pour strained liquid into jars; cool completely; place in refrigerator. Do not refrigerate while still warm. After broth is chilled, remove any fat congealed on the surface. Use in any recipe that calls for beef broth.

Suggestions: This is a pleasant, mild-flavored broth that will blend well with any recipe. You can make it a stronger-flavored soup by adding herbs or more garlic or onion.

For low-salt diet: Omit salt; if desired, add 2/3 teaspoon of salt substitute near the end of the cooking process. One cup contains 40 milligrams or less sodium.

TOMATO MADRILENE (Bouillon)

Makes 4 servings, about 3/4 cup each. One serving equals 1/3 slice of bread; contains 24 Calories (P2, F0, C4), 2 milligrams of cholesterol.

BEEF BROTH, 10-1/2-ounce can fat-free; or use 10-1/2 ounces of brown beef broth (see recipe)
TOMATO JUICE, 10-1/2 ounces
BAY LEAF, 1. Use 2 if you like it spicy.
LEMON JUICE, 1 tablespoon
PARSLEY SPRIG, 1, finely chopped
TABASCO, 4 to 6 drops
SALT and PEPPER, to taste
CLOVES, 4
LEMON, 4 thin slices

Combine BROTH, TOMATO JUICE and BAY LEAF; simmer these about 1 hour: Then add ENOUGH WATER to replace evaporation loss until you have 21 ounces total liquid. Add LEMON JUICE, PARSLEY and TABASCO; simmer for 1/2 hour. Taste and add SALT and PEPPER. Remove bay leaf; insert CLOVE at angle in each LEMON SLICE; serve soup with lemon slice on top.

Suggestions: If you want this to really warm the throat as it goes down, cook for 2 hours with the bay leaf, then add twice the Tabasco. This is an excellent soup to start a heavy dinner, because it is light and refreshing and does not take away the appetite for other food.

For low-salt diet: Omit salt; use salt substitute. Use 10-1/2 ounces of salt-free tomato juice. Use homemade chicken or beef broth, made without salt and skimmed of all fat (see recipe). One serving (1/4 recipe) contains 14 milligrams of sodium.

QUICK CHICKEN SOUP

Makes 6 servings. One serving equals 2 ounces of meat and 2/3 slice of bread; contains 162 Calories (P16, F6, C11), 49 milligrams of cholesterol.

CHICKEN BROTH, 10-1/2-ounce can fat-free. Chill before opening.
CHICKEN or TURKEY, 6 ounces cooked, trimmed of fat and skin
WATER, 2/3 can
ONION or CHIVES, 1/2 teaspoon diced
CELERY, 1/4 cup diced
CARROT, 1 small, peeled and diced
BAY LEAF, 1 large or 2 small
SKIM MILK POWDER, 1/2 cup
FLOUR, 2 tablespoons
SALT, 1/2 teaspoon
PEPPER, 1/4 teaspoon
ONION POWDER, to taste (optional)
WATER, to make 1-1/2 quarts final volume

Remove any fat from chilled CHICKEN BROTH. Blend CHICKEN, broth and WATER on "puree" setting for 1 minute. Cook diced VEGETABLES and BAY LEAF in water to cover, until soft but not mushy. Combine with chicken puree. Add MILK POWDER; stir to dissolve completely. Make a thin paste with FLOUR and a little cold WATER (or use instant flour, which will dissolve by itself). Add flour paste to chicken-vegetable mixture; stir well. Cook until slightly thickened. Add SALT and PEPPER; mix well. Taste and add more seasonings if desired; add ONION POWDER if you want the onion flavor stronger; remove bay leaf. Add WATER to bring total volume to 1-1/2 quarts. Heat and serve.

Suggestions: This is a good way to serve some of the leftover holiday fowl. You can make it a vegetable-chicken soup by doubling the vegetable amounts given. The additions won't increase the food value enough to change what must be given up for a serving of soup.

For low-salt diet: Omit salt; use salt substitute to taste. Omit canned chicken broth; use 3 cups of chicken broth made without salt (see recipe). Be sure the chicken or turkey has been cooked without salt; do not use canned or smoked poultry. One serving (1/6 recipe) contains 48 milligrams of sodium.

VEGETARIAN VEGETABLE SOUP

Makes 5 servings, about 7 ounces each. One serving equals 1 slice of bread; contains 68 Calories (P4, F0, C13), no cholesterol.

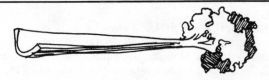

CELERY, 1/4 cup chopped
GREEN PEPPER, 1/4 cup chopped
CARROT, 1/2 cup diced
POTATO, 1/2 cup diced; or 1/8 cup of macaroni
ONION, 1 medium, diced
TURNIP, 1/2 cup diced (optional)
PARSLEY, 1 teaspoon chopped
PEELED TOMATOES, 2 cups canned
CONSOMME, 10-1/2-ounce can; or 2 beef bouillon cubes and 10-1/2 ounces of water
SALT, 1 teaspoon. Cut to 1/2 teaspoon if bouillon cubes are used.
PEPPER, 1/4 teaspoon
TABASCO, 3 to 6 drops
GARLIC, 1 clove (optional)
WATER to make 5 cups total

Combine prepared VEGETABLES, except tomatoes; cover with water; simmer until tender. Chop TOMATOES and add. Add CONSOMME and SEASONINGS to taste. Heat to blend flavors; add hot WATER to adjust volume. Serve with toast cubes or oyster crackers, if you have an additional bread serving.

Suggestions: This soup can be varied endlessly. You may add any leftover vegetables. You can keep a pot of soup in the refrigerator, add leftovers, and adjust the seasonings when soup is heated for serving. Add consomme or bouillon cubes and water to increase the liquid, if needed.

For low-salt diet: Omit salt; use 1 teaspoon of salt substitute. Use fresh or diet-pack tomatoes. If using fresh tomatoes, drop into boiling water for about 30 seconds to loosen skin, then peel, chop and measure. Omit consomme; use about 2 cups of unsalted, fat-free beef broth (see recipe). One serving (1/5 recipe) contains 33 milligrams of sodium.

CHINESE CHICKEN VEGETABLE SOUP

Makes 4 servings. One serving equals 1 serving of semistarchy vegetable; contains 28 Calories (P2, F0, C5), 5 milligrams of cholesterol. With chicken added, 1/4 recipe equals 2 ounces of meat and 1 serving of semistarchy vegetable; contains 151 Calories (P15, F7, C7), 41 milligrams of cholesterol.

CHICKEN BROTH, 10-1/2-ounce can, chilled before opening
WATER, 10-1/2-ounce can
BAY LEAF, 1
FINE NOODLES, 2 tablespoons, broken into small pieces
CELERY, 1 large stalk, sliced thin diagonally
BOK CHOY or NAPA CABBAGE, 1 large stalk, sliced thin diagonally
FROZEN PEAS, 1/4 cup
MUSHROOMS, 1/4 cup, sliced thin
GREEN ONIONS, 2, including tops, chopped into small pieces
MONOSODIUM GLUTAMATE, 1/4 teaspoon
SWEET BASIL, 1/8 teaspoon dried
WHITE PEPPER, 1/8 teaspoon

Optional:
CHICKEN, 8 ounces (bone and skin removed), sliced diagonally

Combine BROTH and WATER; add BAY LEAF and NOODLES; cover and simmer for 5 minutes. Add sliced CELERY and BOK CHOY; cook, covered, another 3 minutes. For milder flavor, remove bay leaf now. Add REMAINING INGREDIENTS, including sliced CHICKEN (if used); cook until peas are tender. Serve immediately.

For low-salt diet: Omit monosodium glutamate; use 1/2 teaspoon of salt substitute. Use homemade chicken broth (see recipe) made according to low-salt directions. Use fresh mushrooms only. If adding chicken or turkey, be sure it was cooked without salt. One serving (1/4 recipe) contains 81 milligrams of sodium when made with chicken, 45 milligrams without chicken.

MOCK PEA SOUP

Makes 6 servings, about 7 ounces each. One serving equals 1/2 slice of bread or 1 serving of semistarchy vegetable; contains 28 Calories (P1, F0, C6), no cholesterol.

ZUCCHINI, 1 medium, sliced thin (2-1/2 cups)
CARROT, 1 medium, sliced thin
CELERY, 1 large stalk, diced
ONION, 1 small, diced
BAY LEAF, 1
WATER, 1 quart
SAGE, 1/4 teaspoon. Use 1/8 teaspoon if you prefer less sage flavor.
GARLIC SALT, 1/2 teaspoon
SWEET BASIL, pinch
PEPPER, 1/8 teaspoon
CHICKEN BROTH, 1-1/2 cups (see recipe)

Place VEGETABLES and BAY LEAF in saucepan; add WATER; simmer until very tender. Remove bay leaf; put vegetables in blender with enough liquid to make blending easy; blend at top speed for about 1 minute, until no pieces of vegetable are visible. Return mixture to pan; add other SEASONINGS and CHICKEN BROTH; add enough vegetable liquid to make consistency of pea soup. Add extra water if needed for desired consistency. Heat thoroughly; taste; add more seasonings if desired.

Suggestions: You may add small pieces of lean ham or lean ground beef that has been browned and drained well to remove fat. Use 6 ounces of meat in all and allow 1 ounce of meat per serving of soup in addition to equivalent in bread or vegetable.

For low-salt diet: Substitute garlic powder for garlic salt. Use chicken broth made without salt and with all fat removed. Do not add ham or ground beef. Add 1/2 teaspoon of salt substitute. One serving contains 14 milligrams of sodium.

CONNORS' ONION AND CARROT PUREE
Hot or Chilled

Makes 5 cups soup. One 6-ounce serving equals 1/2 slice of bread or 1 serving of semistarchy vegetable; contains 53 Calories (P3, F1, C9), no cholesterol.

ONION, 1-1/2 cups chopped
CARROTS, 3/4 cup peeled and chopped
GARLIC, 1 small clove, minced
HOT WATER, 1 cup
CHICKEN BROTH, 3 cups
CREAM OF WHEAT or FARINA, 1 tablespoon (not instant)
SALT, 1/2 teaspoon, more if unsalted broth is used
PEPPER, 1/8 teaspoon
SWEET BASIL, 2 large pinches dried
TABASCO, 4 to 6 drops
YOGURT, 1/4 cup plain low-fat

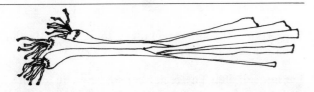

Place chopped VEGETABLES in deep kettle; add the WATER; cover and cook over low heat about 20 minutes. Add CHICKEN BROTH; cover and simmer 40 minutes more, until vegetables are very soft. Add CREAM OF WHEAT; stir to mix; cook uncovered about 15 minutes, until slightly thickened. Remove from heat; add SEASONINGS; taste and adjust to suit. Dilute with HOT WATER to total volume of 4-3/4 cups. Whip in the YOGURT; blend thoroughly. Serve hot immediately, or chill and serve as cold soup. Garnish with shredded fresh or dried parsley.

Suggestions: For those who don't care much for onion, this will be a pleasant surprise. The onion flavor is subtle, despite the amount used. If you wish an even milder onion flavor, use 3/4 cup of onion and 1-1/2 cups of carrot.

For low-salt diet: Omit salt; use 3/4 teaspoon of salt substitute. Use salt-free chicken broth (see recipe) or use 3 salt-free bouillon cubes and 3 cups of hot water. Use regular cream of wheat, not quick-cooking, which is higher in sodium because of the processing it goes through to make it instant. Eight ounces contain 36 milligrams of sodium.

CREAM OF TOMATO SOUP

Makes 5 servings. One serving equals 1/2 ounce of meat and 1 slice of bread; contains 123 Calories (P7, F3, C17), 3 milligrams of cholesterol.

WATER, 1 cup
ONION, 1 tablespoon grated
SALT, 2/3 teaspoon
SUGAR SUBSTITUTE, 2/3 teaspoon granular; or substitute equal to 1-1/2 teaspoons of sugar
BAY LEAF, 1/2
CLOVES, 2
PEPPERCORNS, 2; or 1/8 teaspoon of pepper
INSTANT FLOUR, 2-1/2 tablespoons
MARGARINE, 1 tablespoon. Use corn-oil, soybean-oil or safflower-oil margarine.
BUTTER FLAVORING, 6 drops
SODA, 1/16 teaspoon
TOMATO PUREE, 2 cups
SKIM MILK POWDER, 2/3 cup
SKIM MILK, 1 cup

Add ONION, SALT, SUGAR SUBSTITUTE, BAY LEAF, CLOVES and PEPPER to the cup of WATER; simmer slowly for 5 to 10 minutes but no longer. Remove bay leaf, cloves and peppercorns. Add FLOUR, stirring to prevent lumps. Cook over slow heat until mixture thickens slightly. Add MARGARINE and BUTTER FLAVORING; cook a minute or two longer, stirring often. Add SODA to TOMATO PUREE; stir to dissolve. Add to thickened vegetable and spice mixture; stir to mix well. Dissolve DRY MILK in LIQUID MILK; beat to be sure all is in solution; warm slightly but do not heat to boiling point. Add warm milk mixture to previous combination, stirring to avoid curdling; taste and add more seasonings if you wish. Heat to serving temperature; serve at once.

Suggestions: If you want a bulkier soup, use half canned tomato and half puree.

For low-salt diet: This recipe cannot be made low in salt.

CREAM OF POTATO SOUP

Makes 3 servings. One serving (about 7 ounces) equals 2 servings of semistarchy vegetable, or 1 slice of bread and 2 teaspoons of fat; contains 179 Calories (P5, F11, C15), 2 milligrams of cholesterol.

ONION, 2 tablespoons diced; or 1 tablespoon of diced onion and 1 tablespoon of diced chives
CELERY, 2 tablespoons diced
CELERY LEAVES, 1 teaspoon diced
PARSLEY (preferably fresh), 1 teaspoon diced
MARGARINE, 2 tablespoons. Use corn-oil, soybean-oil or safflower-oil margarine.
INSTANT FLOUR, 1-1/2 tablespoons
SKIM MILK, 1 cup
MASHED POTATOES, 3/4 cup
SALT, 1/4 teaspoon. Use 1/2 teaspoon if potato was not salted in cooking.
PEPPER, 1/8 teaspoon

Cover raw VEGETABLES with just enough water to simmer them in, about 1/2 cup; cover and cook until tender. Make a roux by melting the MARGARINE and stirring in the FLOUR. Add MILK gradually, stirring to avoid lumps. Cook over low heat until slightly thickened. Add POTATOES and cooked VEGETABLES with liquid. Add SALT and PEPPER; mix well; add enough hot water to make 2-1/2 cups. Heat, stirring constantly, about 1 minute to blend seasonings. Serve immediately.

Suggestions: This is an excellent use for the dab of leftover mashed potatoes that isn't enough for anything else. You may extend leftovers with instant dry potato flakes. Just make up the needed amount according to the recipe on the package, then use like fresh potato.

For low-salt diet: Omit salt; use 1/2 teaspoon of salt substitute. Be sure potato is cooked in unsalted water; do not use instant potato. Use salt-free margarine. Omit diced celery; use only celery leaves. Increase the parsley to 1-1/2 teaspoons for additional flavor. One serving (1/3 recipe) contains 56 milligrams of sodium.

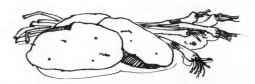

CREAM OF ASPARAGUS SOUP

Makes 3 servings. One serving equals 1 slice of bread, 1/2 ounce of meat and 1/2 teaspoon of fat; contains 113 Calories (P5, F5, C12), 2 milligrams of cholesterol.

MARGARINE, 1 tablespoon. Use corn-oil, soybean-oil or safflower-oil margarine.
INSTANT FLOUR, 3 tablespoons
SKIM MILK, 1 cup
SALT, 1/3 teaspoon
PEPPER, 1/16 teaspoon
CHIVES, 2 teaspoons chopped; or 1 teaspoon of diced onion
LIQUID, 1 cup combined asparagus liquid and water
CUT ASPARAGUS, 8-ounce can; or 1 cup asparagus ends cooked with 1/4 teaspoon of salt.

Melt MARGARINE; stir in FLOUR to make roux. Add MILK gradually, stirring to keep mixture smooth. Add SALT, PEPPER and CHIVES. Cook over low heat in double boiler, stirring often, until thickened. Using part of LIQUID, puree ASPARAGUS in blender for about 30 seconds. Add pureed asparagus and remaining liquid to milk mixture. Cook 3 to 5 minutes to blend flavors and bring to serving temperature. Taste; adjust seasonings to suit.

Suggestions: When asparagus is in season, cook the tips to serve as a vegetable and save the coarser stems for soup. Chop stems, cover with water and cook until tender. Blend in blender until smooth, then strain to remove any tough fibers. This gives you asparagus for two meals at the price of one.

For low-salt diet: Omit salt; use 1/3 teaspoon of salt substitute. Use fresh asparagus cooked without salt, or diet-pack asparagus. Use salt-free margarine. One serving (1/3 recipe) contains 45 milligrams of sodium.

CREAM OF CAULIFLOWER SOUP -
(Basic Creamed Vegetable Soup)

Makes 3 servings. One serving equals 1/2 slice of bread; contains 52 Calories (P4, F0, C9), 2 milligrams of cholesterol.

SKIM MILK, 1 cup
HOT WATER, 1 cup
MINCED ONION, 1/4 teaspoon dried; or 3/4 teaspoon fresh, chopped fine
SALT, 1/2 teaspoon
PEPPER, 1/4 teaspoon
PARSLEY FLAKES, 1/4 teaspoon
CELERY SALT, sprinkle
BAY LEAF, 1/2 small
TABASCO, 2 drops (optional)
BUTTER FLAVORING, 4 to 6 drops
INSTANT FLOUR, 1-1/4 tablespoons
CAULIFLOWER or other vegetable, 1 cup mashed or pureed

Combine MILK and WATER; add SEASONINGS and simmer about 3 minutes. Remove BAY LEAF; add BUTTER FLAVORING and FLOUR; stir until smooth. Return to heat and cook until slightly thick. Add mashed or pureed VEGETABLE. Heat 1 minute to combine seasonings. Taste and add salt if needed.

Suggestions: For celery soup, dice 1 cup of celery, cover with water and cook until tender. Save liquid and use as part of liquid in soup. For cabbage or broccoli soup, use 1/4 teaspoon of dry mustard in place of celery salt and bay leaf. If using fresh vegetables (not leftovers), chop, cover with water and cook until tender. This basic vegetable soup recipe can be used for almost any vegetable normally eaten. If you wish to use mixed vegetables, cook them and add them whole in place of the mashed vegetable.

For low-salt diet: Omit salt and celery salt; use 1/2 teaspoon of salt substitute. Be sure to use fresh vegetables cooked in unsalted water, or diet-pack canned vegetables. Do not use frozen mixed vegetables, as they are salted in preparation. Do not use celery. One serving (1/3 recipe) contains 49 milligrams of sodium.

NORTHWEST FISH SOUP

Makes 5 cups, 6 servings. One 7-ounce serving equals 1 ounce of meat; contains 60 Calories (P8, F2, C2), 34 milligrams of cholesterol.

CARROTS, 2 cups peeled and sliced
ONION, 1 tablespoon chopped
GARLIC, 1 small clove, diced
MARGARINE, 1 tablespoon. Use corn-oil, soybean-oil or safflower-oil margarine.
BOILING WATER, 1-1/2 cups
SKIM MILK, 1 cup
PARSLEY, 1/4 teaspoon dried
SWEET BASIL, 1/16 teaspoon dried
TARRAGON or OREGANO, 1/16 teaspoon dried
CUMIN, 1/16 teaspoon (optional)
TABASCO, 2 to 3 drops
SALT, 3/4 teaspoon
PEPPER, 1/8 teaspoon
HALIBUT, 1 cup cooked, shredded fine
WATER, to bring volume to 5 cups

In soup kettle, combine CARROTS, ONION, GARLIC, MARGARINE and BOILING WATER. Cover and cook over low heat about 1 hour or until tender. Place in blender; blend until quite smooth. Return to kettle; add MILK and SEASONINGS. Heat gently to blend flavors. Taste and add more seasonings if desired. (Remember, there's fish to add, so you don't want it weakly seasoned at this stage.) Add shredded FISH; heat over low temperature about 5 minutes; dilute to 5 cups in all. Taste; add more seasonings if necessary. Serve immediately.

Suggestions: You may use sole, snapper, cod or any of the white fish for this recipe, or use combinations of them. Cook until tender in a minimum amount of liquid. Cool and shred. You could use leftovers—or use crab for the protein if you don't have to watch your cholesterol and saturated fat.

For low-salt diet: Omit salt; use 3/4 to 1 teaspoon of salt substitute instead. Cook fish in unsalted water. Substitute 1 cup of diet-pack stewed tomatoes for 1 cup of carrots. Do not use on low-sodium diet. One serving (1/6 recipe) contains 96 milligrams of sodium.

SALMON BISQUE (Cream of Salmon Soup)

Makes 8 servings, about 3/4 cup each. One serving equals 3 ounces of meat and 1/2 slice of bread; contains 149 Calories (P20, F5, C6), 30 milligrams of cholesterol.

SALMON, 1-1/2 pounds cooked (1-1/2 cans)
CELERY, 1/4 cup diced
ONION, 1/4 cup diced
PARSLEY, 2 teaspoons chopped
WATER, 1 cup
SWEET BASIL, ROSEMARY, THYME, 2 pinches each
SALT, 1 teaspoon. Use less with canned salmon.
PEPPER, 1/4 teaspoon
TABASCO, 2 to 4 drops
SKIM MILK, 4 cups
FLOUR, 3 tablespoons
WATER, 1 to 1-1/2 quarts

Drain SALMON and pick over to remove skin and bones. Flake fish fine with fork. Simmer VEGETABLES in 1 cup of WATER until tender; remove from heat; add SEASONINGS; place in blender to smooth if you wish. Add SKIM MILK and FLOUR to vegetable mixture; cook over low heat until thickened slightly, stirring frequently to avoid lumping or sticking. Add fish; mix well. Thin with WATER to desired consistency. One quart of water will make it a thick soup (3/4 cup equals 1 serving); 1-1/2 quarts of water will make it thin (1-1/4 cups equal 1 serving). Taste; add more seasonings if desired. If you have used fresh fish, you may want more salt. You may want to increase the pepper or Tabasco, or add some onion powder. Heat to serving temperature and serve.

Suggestions: For a filling and welcome change, serve this as a luncheon dish on a cold day. You may add a small potato and cut the flour down to 1-1/2 tablespoons. If you do this, mince the potato and add with the other vegetables. The food value will not change. You may substitute plain white fish for the salmon.

For low-salt diet: Use fresh fish that has been cooked without added salt. Decrease skim milk to 2 cups; add 2 more cups of water. Omit salt; use 2/3 to 1 teaspoon of salt substitute. One serving (1/8 recipe) contains 65 milligrams of sodium.

HALIBUT CHOWDER

Makes 6 servings of approximately 1-1/2 cups each (large soup bowl). One serving equals 3 ounces of meat and 1/2 slice of bread; contains 172 Calories (P25, F4, C9), 34 milligrams of cholesterol.

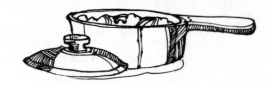

HALIBUT or other white fish, 1-1/2 pounds fresh
HOT WATER, 2 cups
BAY LEAF, 1
ONION, 2-1/2 tablespoons minced
PARSLEY, 1 teaspoon diced
POTATO, 1 cup cubed
CELERY, 1/4 cup diced
WATER, 1-1/2 quarts
FLOUR, 2 tablespoons
MARGARINE, 1 tablespoon. Use corn-oil, soybean-oil or safflower-oil margarine.
SALT, 2 teaspoons
PEPPER, to taste. Use at least 1/4 teaspoon.

Simmer FISH in HOT WATER with BAY LEAF until fish flakes easily. Drain (save liquid) and cool. Cook VEGETABLES in 1 quart of WATER until barely tender. Flake fish; discard skin and bones. Combine remaining 2 cups of water with fish liquid. Add the FLOUR, stirring to prevent lumping. Cook until thickened. Combine thickened liquid with vegetables in their liquid; add flaked fish. Add MARGARINE, SALT and PEPPER; heat thoroughly for about 1 minute; taste; add more salt and pepper if desired. Serve immediately.

Suggestions: If you prefer more bay and less fish taste, cook a bay leaf with the vegetables as well as with the fish. Discard the leaves when you combine the ingredients for final heating.

For low-salt diet: Omit salt; use 2 teaspoons of salt substitute. Use salt-free margarine. Be sure the fish you use has never been frozen. Some frozen fish is packed in brine, and that would greatly increase the sodium in the fish. One serving (1/6 recipe) contains 86 milligrams of sodium.

OYSTER CHOWDER À LA MARYLAND

Makes 4 servings. One serving equals 2 ounces of meat and 1/2 slice of bread; contains 128 Calories (P13, F4, C10), 60 milligrams of cholesterol.

FRESH OYSTERS, 1 pint
CARROTS, 1/4 cup julienne
CELERY, 1/4 cup julienne
GREEN PEPPER, 1/8 cup julienne
ONION, 1 teaspoon diced
PARSLEY, 1/4 teaspoon chopped
SALT, 1/2 teaspoon
PEPPER, 1/4 teaspoon
MARGARINE, 1 teaspoon; or 4 to 6 drops of butter flavoring. Use corn-oil, soybean-oil or safflower-oil margarine.

Cover OYSTERS with water; bring to boil and cook until edges curl; set aside. Cut VEGETABLES in julienne strips; combine with SEASONINGS, except margarine or butter flavoring; cook in 1 cup water until barely tender. Combine vegetables and MARGARINE or butter flavoring with oysters and add water to make 1 quart.

Taste; add seasonings to suit. Heat to serving temperature, about 2 minutes. Serve at once.

Suggestions: If you prefer a slightly thicker soup, drain cooked oysters and vegetables and thicken the liquid with 2 tablespoons of flour. Cook until clear and slightly thick, then add oysters and vegetables and proceed from adding margarine. (One serving of thickened soup equals 2 ounces of meat and 1 slice of bread.)

This type of chowder could be made with clams, shrimp or even white fish. The slowest part of the preparation is slicing the vegetables. The rest takes only a few minutes.

For low-salt diet: Because of the natural salt in oysters and carrots, this recipe cannot be made low in salt.

EASY CORN CHOWDER

Makes 4 servings, about 7 ounces each. One serving equals 1-1/2 slices of bread and 1 teaspoon of fat; contains 156 Calories (P4, F4, C26), 1 milligram of cholesterol. This is no recipe for a low-Calorie diet!

WHOLE-KERNEL CORN, #303 can
WATER, 1 can
SALT, 1/2 teaspoon
PEPPER, 1/8 teaspoon
TABASCO, 3 to 4 drops
ONION, 1 tablespoon diced. Double if you like onion flavor.
PARSLEY, 1 teaspoon chopped
FLOUR, 1 tablespoon
SKIM MILK, 1/2 cup
MARGARINE, 1 tablespoon. Use corn-oil, soybean-oil or safflower-oil margarine.

Put half the CORN and all the corn LIQUID and WATER in blender set on "chop" and blend for 1 to 2 minutes. Pour into saucepan; add SEASONINGS, ONION, PARSLEY and remaining CORN. Simmer, uncovered, about 15 minutes, stirring often. When onion seems quite soft, remove from heat; add FLOUR; stir to prevent lumping. Return to heat and cook slowly about 5 minutes. Add MILK and MARGARINE; heat thoroughly, about 1 minute; taste; adjust seasonings. Serve immediately.

Suggestions: For a more colorful soup, add 1-1/2 tablespoons of chopped green pepper and 1 tablespoon of chopped pimento when you add the corn.

For low-salt diet: Use fresh or diet-pack canned corn. If using fresh, use 1-1/2 cups of kernels and cook in unsalted water until tender. Omit salt; use 1/2 teaspoon of salt substitute. Use salt-free margarine. One serving (1/4 recipe) contains 12 milligrams of sodium.

6. Salads

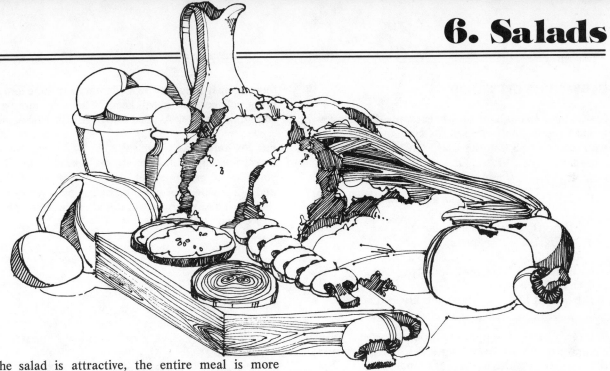

If the salad is attractive, the entire meal is more appealing. These recipes are unusual combinations that will add greatly to mealtime pleasure.

Try the dressings on your favorite green salads—even lettuce becomes more appealing. You may find you like a change.

For a really spicy, nippy taste, try the Vinaigrette Dressing. Your palate will certainly stand up and take notice!

CABBAGE FRUIT SALAD

Makes lots—enough for the whole family. You may want to cut recipe in half. Two-thirds cup equals 1/2 cup of fruit; contains 48 Calories (P2, F1, C10), no cholesterol.

CABBAGE, 1 head, about 2 pounds
CARROT, 1 small, peeled and grated fine
CELERY, 1/2 cup diced
PIMENTO, 2 tablespoons, cut fine
YOGURT, 1/4 cup plain
VINEGAR, 1 tablespoon white
CELERY SEED, 1 teaspoon (optional)
SALT, 1/2 teaspoon
PINEAPPLE, 1 can diet-pack crushed

Put CABBAGE through old-fashioned meat grinder, using coarse blade. Grate or grind CARROT. Combine cabbage, carrot, diced CELERY and PIMENTO; mix well. Combine YOGURT, VINEGAR, CELERY SEED and SALT; mix well. Add dressing to vegetables; mix thoroughly. Add PINEAPPLE; mix again; if too dry, add a small amount of juice from the pineapple. Taste; add more salt if needed.

Suggestions: This may be made ahead of time and stored in the refrigerator. It will keep 24 hours or more without changing texture. A good salad to take on a picnic.

For low-salt diet: Omit salt; use 1/2 teaspoon of salt substitute. Omit celery, celery seed and pimento. Use 1/4 cup of diced green pepper to restore volume, if you wish, and 1/2 teaspoon of unsalted poppy or caraway seed for texture. These changes will not alter the food value. One cup contains 48 milligrams of sodium.

COLESLAW

Makes about 3 cups. One cup equals 1 serving of semistarchy vegetable or 1/2 slice of bread; contains 45 Calories (P3, F1, C6), 1 milligram of cholesterol.

CABBAGE, 2 cups finely shredded
PARSLEY, 1 tablespoon chopped
ONION, 2 teaspoons chopped
GREEN PEPPER, 1 tablespoon finely chopped (optional)

Dressing:
  YOGURT, 1/2 cup plain; or use buttermilk
  DRY MUSTARD, 1/8 teaspoon, or 1/16 teaspoon
  of mustard seed
  SALT, 1/2 teaspoon
  PEPPER, 1/8 teaspoon coarse
  CIDER VINEGAR, 1 tablespoon
  SUGAR SUBSTITUTE, 1-1/2 teaspoons granular, or
  substitute equal to 1 tablespoon of sugar

Combine CABBAGE, PARSLEY, ONION and GREEN PEPPER; mix. Combine DRESSING ingredients; taste; add more vinegar if you want it more tart, more sugar substitute if you want it sweeter. Combine vegetables and dressing; mix well; let stand at least 1/2 hour so vegetables will absorb dressing flavor.

For low-salt diet: Omit salt; use 1/2 teaspoon of salt substitute. Omit yogurt or buttermilk; use 1/2 cup of evaporated skim milk plus 1 tablespoon more vinegar. Add vinegar to milk and allow to stand about 5 minutes to thicken slightly. One cup (1/3 recipe) contains 52 milligrams of sodium.

Warning: Do not make this far ahead of serving time, or it may separate because it has nothing to bind the dressing to the vegetables.

THREE-BEAN SALAD

Makes about 7 cups. One-half cup equals 1 serving of semistarchy vegetable and 1 teaspoon of fat, or 1/2 slice of bread and 1 teaspoon of fat; contains 81 Calories (P2, F6, C7), no cholesterol.

OIL, 1/3 cup
WHITE VINEGAR, 1/2 cup
SUGAR SUBSTITUTE, 1/3 cup granular; or substitute equal to 2/3 cup of sugar
BEAN SPROUTS, #303 can (about 2 cups)
GREEN BEANS, #303 can julienne (about 2 cups)
YELLOW WAX BEANS, #303 can (about 2 cups)
CELERY, 1/2 cup diced
ONION, 1/4 cup diced
GREEN PEPPER, 1/4 cup diced
PIMENTO or TOMATO, 1/8 cup finely chopped

Prepare MARINADE from first three ingredients. Drain CANNED VEGETABLES; save juices for soup. Combine BEANS and chopped VEGETABLES; mix well. Pour marinade over vegetables; stir so all will be well covered with liquid. Let stand at least 2 hours, stirring occasionally. Chill; serve on lettuce leaf.

Suggestions: This salad improves with age, so make a large batch and use it over a week or more. You may double recipe using larger, more economical cans. ical

For low-salt diet: Use diet-pack vegetables, or fresh vegetables cooked without salt. Cook until barely done, as a crisp texture is more appealing. Omit celery; increase green pepper and onion to 1/2 cup each. Omit pimento; use tomato for color. One serving (1/7 recipe) contains 6 milligrams of sodium.

VEGETABLE POTPOURRI

Makes 6 cups of vegetables. One 1-cup serving of vegetables equals 1 serving of semistarchy vegetables or 2/3 slice of bread and 1 teaspoon of fat; contains 48 Calories (P2, F0, C10), no cholesterol.

Makes 5-1/2 tablespoons of dressing. One-sixth of the dressing contains 36 Calories (P0, F4, C0).

Vegetables:
　BEAN SPROUTS, 1 cup canned
　CARROTS, 1 cup canned
　GREEN PEAS, 1 cup canned
　GREEN BEANS, 1 cup canned regular-cut
　SLICED BEETS, 1 cup canned
　ASPARAGUS SPEARS, #1 can

Dressing:
　MAYONNAISE, 2 tablespoons
　SKIM MILK, 1-1/2 tablespoons
　WHITE VINEGAR, 1-1/2 teaspoons
　SUGAR SUBSTITUTE, 1/2 teaspoon granular;
　or substitute equal to 1 teaspoon of sugar
　PIMENTO or SWEET RED PEPPER, 1 teaspoon
　finely diced

Chill VEGETABLES well before opening cans. Arrange drained vegetables on large platter, interspersing colors; refrigerate until serving time. Combine DRESSING ingredients; taste; add more sugar substitute if you like a sweet dressing on vegetable salad. Serve with dressing separate—perhaps in a small bowl in middle of platter.

Suggestions: This is an attractive platter for a buffet luncheon. Other vegetables, like Mexican-style corn or packaged mixed vegetables, may be used, but if so, the food value would be increased by at least half so portions must be adjusted accordingly.

For low-salt diet: Use diet-pack vegetables or fresh vegetables cooked without salt. Do not overcook; they are better crisp. Omit sliced beets; substitute raw cherry tomatoes, cut in half. Use salt-free mayonnaise in dressing (buy or see recipe). Omit pimento. One serving of vegetables contains 28 milligrams of sodium; of dressing, 4 milligrams of sodium.

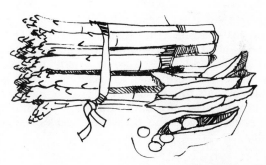

CRANBERRY SALAD

Makes 6 servings, about 2/3 cup each. One serving equals 1/2 cup of fruit; contains 52 Calories (P2, F0, C11), no cholesterol.

FRESH CRANBERRIES, 2 cups
ORANGE, 1 large
SUGAR SUBSTITUTE, 1-1/2 teaspoons granular; or substitute equal to 1 tablespoon of sugar
DIET GELATIN, 1 package orange or raspberry
BOILING WATER, 1 cup
ORANGE JUICE, 1/2 cup fresh or frozen
LEMON JUICE, 1 teaspoon
SALT, sprinkle

Put CRANBERRIES and ORANGE through grinder, using coarse blade. Add SUGAR SUBSTITUTE; mix well. Dissolve GELATIN in WATER; stir well. Add cold JUICES and SALT. Refrigerate gelatin mixture until almost set. Remove from refrigerator; fold in ground fruit; pour into fruit mold or ring, large or individual (6). Return to refrigerator until firm. Unmold onto lettuce; serve with mayonnaise or cooked salad dressing (see recipes).

Suggestions: This is a good holiday salad which will take the place of cranberry sauce for dieting diners. If made in individual molds, it can be dressed and served individually, thus giving complete control of each portion.

For low-salt diet: Omit salt; use sprinkle of salt substitute. Use unsalted diet gelatin; check label to be sure. One serving (1/6 recipe) contains 3 milligrams of sodium.

JELLIED CITRUS SALAD

Makes 7 servings. One serving equals 1/2 cup of fruit; contains 52 Calories (P2, F0, C11), no cholesterol.

UNFLAVORED GELATIN, 1 envelope
COLD WATER, 1/4 cup
FROZEN JUICE, 1-3/4 cups orange or grapefruit, diluted
YELLOW FOOD COLORING, 2 to 4 drops if grapefruit juice is used (optional)
LEMON JUICE, 1-1/2 tablespoons
SALT, sprinkle
SUGAR SUBSTITUTE, 1-1/2 tablespoons granular; or substitute equal to 3 tablespoons of sugar
GRAPEFRUIT SECTIONS, 3/4 cup, diet-pack or fresh
ORANGE SECTIONS, 3/4 cup, diet-pack or fresh

Dissolve GELATIN in WATER; let stand 5 minutes. Heat slightly if necessary to dissolve gelatin completely. Add ORANGE JUICE, or GRAPEFRUIT JUICE with FOOD COLORING. Add LEMON JUICE, SALT and SUGAR SUBSTITUTE; stir to blend. Chill until slightly thicker than unbeaten egg white. Add well-drained CITRUS FRUITS. If using individual molds, arrange fruits on bottom of mold to form a design. Return to refrigerator and chill until very firm. Serve individually, on lettuce leaf with 1 teaspoon of mayonnaise on top. Allow 1 fat serving for topping (see recipe).

Suggestions: You may add dietetic maraschino cherries, cut in half, to enhance design in bottom of mold. Add 3-1/2, and they need not be counted as added food value.

For low-salt diet: Omit salt; use salt substitute. One serving (1/7 recipe) contains 3 milligrams of sodium.

MOLDED BEET SALAD

Makes 4 servings. One serving equals 1 serving of semistarchy vegetable or 1/2 slice of bread; contains 45 Calories (P3, F1, C6), no cholesterol.

DIETETIC GELATIN, 1 package lemon-flavored
COLD WATER, 1-1/4 cups
BEET LIQUID, 3/4 cup
SALT, 1/4 teaspoon
WHITE VINEGAR, 1-1/2 tablespoons
TABASCO, 4 drops
HORSERADISH, 1 teaspoon (optional)
WORCESTERSHIRE SAUCE, 1 teaspoon
BEETS, 1-1/2 cups diced
CELERY, 1/2 cup diced
ONION, 1 teaspoon grated or finely chopped

Dissolve GELATIN in WATER; heat slowly to complete dissolving. Add BEET LIQUID and SEASONINGS; mix well. Combine BEETS, CELERY and ONION with gelatin mix; stir well. Refrigerate until almost set; stir to distribute vegetables evenly; return to refrigerator and allow to set until firm. Cut into squares and serve on lettuce leaf; or, if made in individual molds, unmold onto lettuce leaf. Top with 1 teaspoon of cooked salad dressing or mayonnaise (see recipes).

Suggestions: This salad gives a cheerful color to a meal. If you like salad vinegary, use an extra 1/2 tablespoon of white vinegar. It will almost bite back!

For low-salt diet: This recipe cannot be made low in salt because of the beets and celery.

NEW ORLEANS VEGETABLE ASPIC

Makes 6 servings, 1/2 cup each. One serving equals 1 serving of semistarchy vegetable; contains 20 Calories (P2, F0, C3), no cholesterol.

UNFLAVORED GELATIN, 1 envelope
COLD WATER, 1-3/4 cups
WHITE VINEGAR, 3 tablespoons
SUGAR SUBSTITUTE, 2 tablespoons granular; or substitute equal to 1/4 cup of sugar
TABASCO, 1/8 teaspoon
SALT, 1/4 teaspoon. Use 2/3 teaspoon if all vegetables are fresh
FOOD COLORING, 4 drops yellow or green
CELERY, 1/2 cup finely diced
CARROT, 1/4 cup grated
CANNED OKRA, 1/2 cup, diced; or 1/2 cup French-cut green beans
PIMENTO or SWEET RED PEPPER, 1/4 cup chopped

Dissolve GELATIN in WATER; stir well; heat slightly if necessary to complete dissolving. Add VINEGAR, SEASONINGS and FOOD COLORING; stir thoroughly. Mix VEGETABLES together. (Be sure to drain any canned vegetables well before adding them.) Pour gelatin mixture over vegetables; mix well. Pour into 6 individual molds and let set in refrigerator until firm; or pour into a large mold and divide when serving. Serve on lettuce leaf with cooked salad dressing (see recipe) for topping.

Suggestions: You may substitute tomato juice for 1 cup of water and omit the food coloring. This will not increase the food value enough to change the replacement required.

For low-salt diet: Omit celery; use 1/2 cup of finely chopped cabbage. Omit salt; use 1/2 teaspoon of salt substitute. Use diet-pack green beans and omit okra. Omit pimento; use a small tomato, diced very fine and drained of liquid and seeds. One serving (1/6 recipe) contains 10 milligrams of sodium.

SUBMARINE SALAD

Makes 4 servings. One serving equals 1 ounce of meat and 1/2 cup of fruit; contains 65 Calories (P6, F1, C8), 3 milligrams of cholesterol.

DIETETIC LIME GELATIN, 1 package
BOILING WATER, 1-1/2 cups
PEAR JUICE, 1/2 cup
SALT, 1/4 teaspoon
WHITE VINEGAR, 2/3 teaspoon
GROUND GINGER, 1/8 teaspoon
DIETETIC PEARS, 1 cup sliced
COTTAGE CHEESE, 4 ounces low-fat, well washed and drained

Mix GELATIN with WATER; stir well to dissolve. Add PEAR JUICE, SALT, VINEGAR and GINGER. Put 1/3 of this mixture into mold and chill until firm. Place sliced PEARS on top of firm gelatin in mold. When it is almost set, beat 1/2 of remaining gelatin to consistency of egg whites; pour over sliced pears; refrigerate until firm. Add COTTAGE CHEESE to remaining gelatin; beat until smooth; pour on top of two previously set layers; allow to set until very firm. Serve on lettuce with mayonnaise topping (see recipe); white layer (with cottage cheese) should be on the bottom, so it will look as if pears are on the bottom of the ocean. (Now you know why it is called Submarine Salad!)

Suggestions: This is a sweet salad, so serve it with tart or spicy vegetable and meat dishes.

For low-salt diet: Omit salt; use 1/4 teaspoon of salt substitute. Wash cottage cheese thoroughly by placing it in a colander and running cold water over it until the water comes off clear. Stir as you wash it to eliminate all the salt you can. One serving (1/4 recipe) contains 78 milligrams of sodium. Because of the sodium in the cottage cheese, which comes from the milk, this salad should not be used in a 1-gram salt diet, even though you wash the cottage cheese well. Washing removes only the salt added in preparation, not the natural salt.

VINAIGRETTE MOLDED SALAD

Makes 6 servings. One serving equals 1 serving of semistarchy vegetable, or 1/2 slice of bread and 1/2 ounce of meat; contains 52 Calories (P6, F0, C7), no cholesterol.

UNFLAVORED GELATIN, 2 envelopes
LEMON JUICE, 2 tablespoons
CIDER VINEGAR, 2-1/2 tablespoons
SALT, 1/2 teaspoon
SUGAR SUBSTITUTE, 2 tablespoons granular; or substitute equal to 1/4 cup of sugar
SALT, 1/2 teaspoon
CARROTS, 1 cup shredded
CELERY, 3/4 cup diced
GREEN PEAS, 3/4 cup cooked, well drained
PIMENTO or SWEET RED PEPPER, 2 tablespoons chopped
GREEN PEPPER, 1 small, chopped
DIETETIC GINGER ALE or FRESCA, 2 cups well chilled

Soak GELATIN in 1/4 cup of cold water for 5 minutes; dissolve in 1/3 cup of boiling water; if necessary, heat mixture to dissolve gelatin completely. Add LEMON JUICE, VINEGAR, SALT and SUGAR SUBSTITUTE, mix to blend. Chill until almost set; chill VEGETABLES also. Add GINGER ALE or FRESCA and vegetables. Pour into ring mold or 6 individual molds; chill until very firm. Serve on bed of lettuce or (if individual) a lettuce leaf.

Suggestions: For a more colorful salad, you may add yellow food coloring, but the interesting color combination of the vegetables shows off well if no color is added.

For low-salt diet: This recipe cannot be made low in salt because of the sodium in the celery, the pimento and the diet drink.

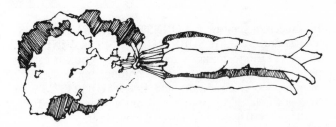

COOKED SALAD DRESSING

Makes 1-1/2 cups. One tablespoon contains 4 Calories (P0, F0, C1), no cholesterol. Three tablespoons equal 1/4 slice of bread; contain 12 Calories.

CORNSTARCH, 2 tablespoons
SALT, 1 teaspoon
DRY MUSTARD, 1/2 teaspoon
SUGAR SUBSTITUTE, 2 teaspoons granular; or substitute equal to 1-1/2 tablespoons of sugar
CIDER VINEGAR, 3/4 cup
WATER, 1/3 cup
LIQUID EGG SUBSTITUTE, 3 ounces. Use 2 whole eggs for regular diet.

In saucepan, combine CORNSTARCH, SALT, MUSTARD and SUGAR SUBSTITUTE. Stir in VINEGAR and WATER to make a smooth paste. Cook over low heat, stirring frequently, until boiling; cook about 3 minutes more. Gradually add EGG SUBSTITUTE or beaten whole eggs, stirring constantly to avoid curdling. Cool and refrigerate in covered container.

Suggestions: You may substitute white vinegar for cider vinegar for a milder flavor.

For low-salt diet: Omit salt; use 1 teaspoon of salt substitute. One tablespoon contains 6 milligrams of sodium.

EGGLESS SALAD DRESSING

Makes 1-1/2 pints. One tablespoon equals 2 teaspoons of fat; contains 89 Calories (P1, F9, C1), no cholesterol.

NONFAT MILK POWDER, 1/3 cup
SALT, 1-1/2 teaspoons
DRY MUSTARD, 1-1/2 teaspoons
SUGAR SUBSTITUTE, 1 tablespoon granular; or substitute equal to 2 tablespoons of sugar
WATER, 1/3 cup
OIL, 2 cups. Use corn, safflower or soybean oil.
CIDER VINEGAR, 1/2 cup

With rotary beater or wire whip, beat together DRY MILK, SALT, MUSTARD, SUGAR SUBSTITUTE and

WATER. Add half the OIL, 1/4 cup at a time, beating smooth after each addition; add VINEGAR; beat until smooth and thick; add remainder of oil gradually. Store, covered, in refrigerator.

Suggestions: If you like a spicy salad dressing, add herbs to liven it up. A small amount of sweet basil or oregano is compatible with the other ingredients.

For low-salt diet: Omit salt; use 1-1/2 teaspoons of salt substitute. One tablespoon contains 2 milligrams of sodium.

EASY FRENCH DRESSING

Makes about 2-1/2 cups. One tablespoon equals 1 teaspoon of fat; contains 54 Calories (P0, F6, C0), no cholesterol.

OIL, 1 cup
CIDER VINEGAR, 1/2 cup
TOMATO PUREE, 1/2 cup
SUGAR SUBSTITUTE, 1/2 teaspoon granular; or substitute equal to 1 teaspoon of sugar
PAPRIKA, 1/2 teaspoon
DRY MUSTARD, 1/2 teaspoon
GARLIC, 1/4 clove, mashed
EGG WHITE, 1
SALT, 1/2 teaspoon or more
UNFLAVORED GELATIN, 1/2 envelope
WATER, 1/2 cup

Combine ALL INGREDIENTS except gelatin and water in blender jar. Blend until smooth. Combine GELATIN and WATER; heat slowly to dissolve; cool slightly. Add gelatin to blended ingredients and blend for 1 minute. Store in refrigerator, covered, until needed; then allow to stand at room temperature until oil loses its cloudiness. Shake well before using.

Suggestions: This is not a thick dressing but the consistency is good on green salads. Dressing will not separate when poured on vegetables. It can be used for marinating chicken or fish before cooking.

For low-salt diet: Omit salt; use 1/2 teaspoon of salt substitute. Use salt-free tomato puree (be sure it says salt-free on the label). One tablespoon contains 2 milligrams of sodium.

ITALIAN DRESSING

Makes 1 cup. One tablespoon equals 1 teaspoon of fat; contains 45 Calories (P0, F5, C0), no cholesterol.

SALT, 1/2 teaspoon
PEPPER, 1/4 teaspoon
GARLIC POWDER, 1/8 teaspoon
ONION POWDER, 1/8 teaspoon
PAPRIKA, 1/8 teaspoon
RED WINE VINEGAR, 1/3 cup
WATER, 1/3 cup
OIL, 1/3 cup

Mix DRY INGREDIENTS. In glass jar with tight lid, add WATER to VINEGAR; add dry ingredients. Add OIL; cover and shake well. Keep refrigerated. Before using, allow to stand at room temperature until oil loses cloudiness; shake well.

Suggestions: In place of garlic powder you may add a piece of garlic clove, and in place of onion powder, a section of fresh onion. Dressing will absorb the flavors during storage. Don't do this unless you really love garlic!

For low-salt diet: Omit salt; use 1/2 teaspoon of salt substitute. No sodium.

OIL-FREE ITALIAN DRESSING

Makes 5-1/2 ounces. No replacement needed; contains no Calories (P0, F0, C0), no cholesterol.

RED WINE VINEGAR, 1/3 cup
WATER, 1/3 cup
GARLIC POWDER, 1/16 teaspoon
ONION POWDER, 1/8 teaspoon
PEPPER, 1/16 teaspoon coarse-ground
PAPRIKA, 1/16 teaspoon

Combine INGREDIENTS and mix well.

Suggestions: In place of garlic powder you may add a piece of garlic clove, and in place of onion powder, a section of fresh onion. Dressing will absorb the flavors during storage. An excellent marinade for chicken or fish.

For low-salt diet: Recipe is salt-free.

SALT-FREE, OIL-FREE ITALIAN DRESSING

Makes 12 ounces. No replacement needed. Two tablespoons contain 2 Calories (P0, F0, C1/2), no cholesterol.

TOMATO JUICE, 1 cup salt-free
RED WINE VINEGAR, 1/2 cup
GARLIC POWDER, 1/8 teaspoon
ONION POWDER, 1/8 teaspoon
PEPPER, 1/8 teaspoon
PAPRIKA, 1/8 teaspoon
SUGAR SUBSTITUTE, 1/2 teaspoon
granular; or substitute equal to 1 teaspoon
of sugar

Combine INGREDIENTS and mix well.

Suggestions: In place of garlic powder you may add a piece of garlic clove, and in place of onion powder, a section of fresh onion. Dressing will absorb the flavors during storage. An excellent marinade for chicken or fish.

For low-salt diet: Recipe is salt-free.

VINAIGRETTE DRESSING

Makes about 3-3/4 cups. One and one-half tablespoons equal 1 teaspoon of fat; contain 36 Calories (P0, F4, C0), no cholesterol.

> WATER, 1-1/2 cups
> CIDER VINEGAR, 5/8 cup
> RED WINE VINEGAR, 5/8 cup
> OIL, 3/4 cup
> GREEN PEPPER, 1/4
> PIMENTO, 2 teaspoons
> GARLIC, 2 teaspoons
> PARSLEY, 1-1/2 tablespoons
> SALT, 1 tablespoon
> PEPPER, 1/4 teaspoon
> CAYENNE PEPPER, 1/8 teaspoon (optional)
> SUGAR SUBSTITUTE, 2 teaspoons granular; or substitute equal to 4 teaspoons of sugar

Combine LIQUIDS. Grind, or blend on coarse-chop setting, GREEN PEPPER, PIMENTO, GARLIC and PARSLEY. Combine with liquids, SEASONINGS and SUGAR SUBSTITUTE; mix well. Refrigerate, tightly covered; before using, let stand at room temperature until oil loses cloudiness; shake well.

Suggestions: This is a very tangy dressing, excellent on dandelion greens, beet greens and spinach.

For low-salt diet: Omit salt; use 1 tablespoon of salt substitute. Omit pimento; use 1/4 teaspoon of paprika for color. No sodium.

LOW-CHOLESTEROL MAYONNAISE

Makes 2-1/2 cups. One tablespoon equals 1 teaspoon of fat, or 1-1/2 teaspoons of fat if made with egg substitute; contains 58 Calories (P0, F6, C1), no cholesterol.

> FLOUR, 1/3 cup
> SALT, 1 teaspoon
> DRY MUSTARD, 1/3 teaspoon
> SUGAR SUBSTITUTE, 1/2 teaspoon granular; or substitute equal to 1 teaspoon of sugar
> WATER, 3/4 cup
> CIDER VINEGAR, 1/3 cup
> EGG WHITES, 3; or 2-1/4 ounces of liquid egg substitute
> OIL, 1 cup. Use corn, safflower or soybean oil.
> YELLOW FOOD COLORING, 2 to 6 drops

Make paste with FLOUR, SALT, MUSTARD, SUGAR SUBSTITUTE, WATER and VINEGAR; stir constantly as you add liquids. Cook in double boiler, stirring constantly until thick, boiling at least 1 minute. Remove from heat and cool slightly. Beat EGG WHITES with rotary beater, wire whip or mixer; add to cooked mixture, beating as you add. (Be sure cooked material is cool enough that egg whites do not curdle.) Add OIL gradually, beating after each addition to be sure all oil is absorbed. Add enough FOOD COLORING to give the creamy yellow color of mayonnaise. Cover and store in refrigerator until needed.

Suggestions: Add more sweetenings or seasonings if you wish, though proportions given are those for real mayonnaise—normally a rather bland mixture.

For low-salt diet: Omit salt; use 1 teaspoon of salt substitute. One tablespoon contains 4 milligrams of sodium.

HOW TO STRETCH MAYONNAISE

Makes 1/2 cup. One tablespoon equals 1-1/2 teaspoons of fat; contains 66 Calories, 63 milligrams of cholesterol.

One teaspoon equals 1/2 teaspoon of fat; contains 22 Calories, 21 milligrams of cholesterol.

PURE MAYONNAISE, 4 tablespoons
EVAPORATED SKIM MILK, 3 tablespoons
CIDER VINEGAR, 1 tablespoon
LIQUID SWEETENER, 3 drops; or substitute equal to 1/2 teaspoon of sugar
SALT, PEPPER and ONION POWDER, to taste
PAPRIKA, sprinkle (optional)

Put MAYONNAISE, MILK and VINEGAR into mixing bowl; stir well; let stand for 15 minutes. Add SWEETENER; add SEASONINGS to taste; mix. Refrigerate.

Suggestions: If your diet allows very little mayonnaise, try stretching it with this. It is fine for sandwiches and salads. You may use 7 tablespoons of low-fat yogurt for the milk and mayonnaise. It will be a thinner dressing, but not significantly different in food value.

For low-salt diet: Use salt-free mayonnaise. Omit salt; use sprinkle of salt substitute. One teaspoon contains 9 milligrams of sodium.

Notes

Meats—To keep lean meats from becoming dry and unappetizing, without adding fat, requires effort. Spiced marinades and slow, low-temperature cooking help tenderize these dishes.

Casseroles—Never hurry a mixed dish as you will lose much of the expected taste and texture. Using very dry wine in recipes improves taste and tenderness. The alcohol evaporates during cooking so the Calories do not have to be counted.

Vegetables are your most useful foods for making meals both filling and eye-catching. A little variety in taste and appearance does wonders for preventing boredom in a diet. When you have tried the vegetable combinations given here, experiment to see what other dishes you can come up with.

Sauces—Most conventional main course sauces contain either cream or fat. Sauce recipes in this cookbook are low in saturated fats (butter and eggs). Use them to make meals more appetizing, to give a change of appearance when you have leftovers or to lend elegance to your meal. Pamper your palate and dieting will be much easier.

Beef

BEEF STEW WITH VEGETABLES

Makes 5 servings. One serving equals 3 ounces of meat, 1 serving of bulky vegetable and 1 slice of bread; contains 219 Calories (P22, F7, C17), 64 milligrams of cholesterol.

LEAN BEEF, 1 pound cubed. Buy a little extra and trim off fat.

OIL, 1 tablespoon corn or soybean

POTATOES, 3 small, peeled and cut into 5 pieces each

CARROTS, 3 medium, peeled and cut into pieces. Try to have 10 or 15 pieces for easy division.

ONION, 1 medium, peeled and cut into 5 pieces

GREEN PEPPER, 1/4, cut into small pieces (optional)

CELERY, 2 large stalks, cut into 2-inch pieces

SALT, 1/2 teaspoon

PEPPER, 1/8 teaspoon

GARLIC, 1/4 clove (optional)

INSTANT FLOUR, 1 tablespoon

TABASCO, 3 to 4 drops (optional)

Trim all fat from BEEF; weigh to make sure you have 1 pound. Brown beef cubes in OIL in pressure cooker; turn to brown all surfaces and prevent sticking; be sure heat is low enough that oil does not smoke. Arrange VEGETABLES on top of browned beef cubes; pour 1-1/2 cups of water over vegetables; add SEASONINGS; close pressure cooker. Cook at 10 pounds of pressure for 20 minutes from time pressure indicator starts to jiggle. Remove cooker from heat; hold under cold water to reduce pressure quickly. Remove lid; drain liquid into a bowl; retain solids in colander. Return liquid to cooker; add 1/2 cup hot water; thicken with FLOUR; cook until slightly thick. Add more salt and pepper and 3 or 4 drops TABASCO if you wish. Add drained vegetables and meat to gravy and reheat quickly. Serve immediately, dividing into 5 equal portions.

For low-salt diet: Omit salt; use 1/2 teaspoon of salt substitute. One serving (1/5 recipe) contains 94 milligrams of sodium.

BURGER CHOP SUEY

Makes 3 servings, about 1 cup each. One serving equals 3 ounces of meat and 1/2 slice of bread; contains 154 Calories (P19, F6, C6), 53 milligrams of cholesterol.

GROUND BEEF, 1/2 pound very lean
ONION, 3 tablespoons
OIL, 1 teaspoon corn or soybean
BEEF BOUILLON, 1 cube
BOILING WATER, 1 cup
SUGAR SUBSTITUTE, 1/2 teaspoon granular; or substitute equal to 1 teaspoon of sugar
SOY SAUCE, 1 teaspoon
TABASCO, 2 drops
BEAN SPROUTS, 1 cup. If fresh, blanch with boiling water.
CELERY, 1/2 cup diced
MUSHROOMS, 1/2 cup fresh, sliced (optional)
WATER CHESTNUTS, 1/2 cup sliced (optional)
INSTANT FLOUR, 1 tablespoon

Saute BEEF and ONION in OIL until brown. Dissolve BOUILLON CUBE in BOILING WATER; add to beef and onions; add SUGAR SUBSTITUTE, SOY SAUCE and TABASCO; mix well. Add VEGETABLES; cover and cook slowly until vegetables are just tender; add more water if needed. Drain liquid into separate pan; add water to make about 2/3 cup; stir in FLOUR and cook until thick. Add sauce to vegetables in original pan; heat thoroughly; serve immediately over rice or noodles. (Allow 1 slice of bread for each 1/2 cup of cooked rice or noodles.)

For low-salt diet: Omit soy sauce; use 1/2 teaspoon of salt substitute. If salt-free soy sauce is available, you may use 1 teaspoon. Omit beef bouillon cube; use homemade salt-free broth (see recipe) in place of bouillon cube and water. Or, if salt-free bouillon cubes are available, you may use 1, with the water. Omit water chestnuts; use 1 cup of fresh mushrooms. Omit celery; increase bean sprouts to 1-1/2 cups. Be sure to use fresh bean sprouts, as the canned are high in salt. One serving (1/3 recipe) contains 47 milligrams of sodium.

MEAT LOAF

Makes good hamburgers, too! Makes 5 servings. One serving equals 3 ounces of meat; contains 141 Calories (P21, F5, C3), 63 milligrams of cholesterol.

EGG WHITE, 1
BEEF, 1 pound extra-lean, coarsely ground
SAUERKRAUT, 1/2 cup, washed and chopped
ONION, 2 tablespoons diced
GREEN PEPPER, 2 tablespoons diced
SAGE or POULTRY SEASONING, 1/2 teaspoon
SALT, 1/2 teaspoon
PEPPER, 1/4 teaspoon
OATMEAL, 1/4 cup quick-cooking

Beat EGG WHITE slightly. Add BEEF, SAUER-KRAUT, ONION and GREEN PEPPER; mix well. Sprinkle SEASONINGS evenly over mixture; add OATMEAL and mix well. Form into a loaf; use a few drops of warm water if it feels dry. Place loaf in open roasting pan, on a rack so drippings will collect in pan and not be reabsorbed by the loaf. Bake at 325 degrees until outside crust is well browned, about 1 hour.

Suggestions: To change the taste completely, add 2 tablespoons of horseradish to meat loaf and omit sauerkraut and sage or poultry seasoning. Use leftover meat loaf cold for sandwich filling, or make it for use in sandwiches. For variety, form raw mixture into meatballs. For hamburgers, make 5 equal patties from raw mixture; brown on Teflon pan.

For low-salt diet: Omit salt; use 1/2 teaspoon of salt substitute. Replace sauerkraut with an extra 1/2 teaspoon of sage and 1/8 teaspoon of dry mustard, mixed into the meat before other ingredients are added. One serving (1/5 recipe) contains 101 milligrams of sodium.

POOR MAN'S STROGANOFF

Makes 5 servings. One serving equals 3 ounces of meat and 1/2 slice of bread; contains 174 Calories (P23, F6, C7), 78 milligrams of cholesterol.

GROUND BEEF, 1 pound extra-lean
ONION, 1 small, diced
GARLIC, 1/4 clove
CELERY and CELERY LEAVES, 1/4 cup diced
OIL, 1 teaspoon corn or soybean
BOUILLON CUBES, 2 beef or chicken
HOT WATER, 1 cup
DRY WHITE WINE, 1 cup
MOCK SOUR CREAM, 1/2 cup (see recipe); or 1/2 cup plain low-fat yogurt
INSTANT FLOUR, 2 tablespoons
PEPPER, 1/4 teaspoon
TABASCO, 6 to 8 drops (optional)

Saute BEEF, ONION, GARLIC and CELERY in OIL until vegetables are tender. Dissolve BOUILLON CUBES in HOT WATER; pour over meat mixture; cook slowly until all liquid is evaporated. Pour WINE over meat mixture; simmer, covered, until half of wine is evaporated. Add SOUR CREAM, FLOUR and SEASONINGS; mix; cook until mixture is thick and smooth, about 5 minutes; add a little hot water if it gets too thick to pour readily. Pour over cooked noodles and serve. (Allow 1 slice of bread for each 1/2 cup of noodles.)

Suggestions: You may add sliced mushrooms to this recipe without adding to the food value replacements. Use about 1/2 cup, sliced; add last and cook only enough to heat them through.

For low-salt diet: Omit salt; use fresh homemade unsalted chicken broth (see recipe); use 1/2 teaspoon of salt substitute. Do not use canned mushrooms; if using fresh mushrooms, cook in unsalted liquid or use uncooked and add before mixture is simmered. Omit Tabasco; use 1/8 teaspoon of black pepper or 1/16 teaspoon of cayenne. One serving contains 65 milligrams of sodium.

STUFFED STEAK

Makes 5 servings. One serving equals 3 ounces of meat and 1/2 slice of bread; contains 196 Calories (P22, F8, C9), 63 milligrams of cholesterol.

TOP-ROUND STEAK, 1 pound, thin-sliced; or use 1 pound of flank steak. Trim off fat before weighing.
POULTRY STUFFING 1/2 recipe (see recipe)

Pound STEAK with mallet to tenderize and flatten evenly. Prepare POULTRY STUFFING. Place flattened steak on board; spread on dressing, leaving edges bare. Roll; tie with string at ends and 1 or 2 places midway. Place on rack in roasting pan; cover with foil or lid. Bake at 300 degrees for about 1-1/2 hours; uncover for last 15 to 20 minutes to brown.

Suggestions: For a different flavor, add sliced mushrooms to stuffing. If you wish, make a thin gravy from the fat-free drippings. It will taste like gravy from a stuffed turkey or chicken.

For low-salt diet: Follow low-salt directions given for stuffing recipe. Do not use canned mushrooms; use fresh mushrooms, if any; slice and steam in a covered pan before adding them to the stuffing. One serving (1/5 recipe) contains 73 milligrams of sodium.

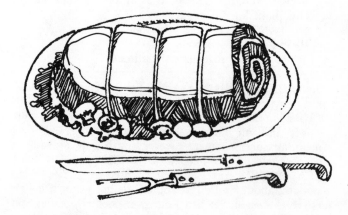

Poultry

CHICKEN ITALIENNE

Makes 4 to 6 servings. One 4-1/2 ounce serving equals 3 ounces of meat; contains 182 Calories (P21, F10, C2), 90 milligrams of cholesterol.

LEMON JUICE, 1/2 to 2/3 cup
ITALIAN DRESSING, 1 to 1-1/2 cups low-Calorie (see recipe)
CHICKEN FRYER, 1-1/2 to 2 pounds, cut up
PAPRIKA

Combine LEMON JUICE and ITALIAN DRESSING; marinate CHICKEN in this for at least 2 hours, turning frequently to keep meat covered. Broil chicken in oven or table-top broiler; use marinade to baste chicken as it cooks, basting with pastry brush to be sure you cover it well. Sprinkle both sides of chicken with PAPRIKA the first time you turn it. Serve portion as permitted on your diet; allow at least 4-1/2 ounces, including skin and bone, for each 3 ounces of meat permitted.

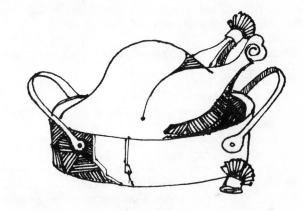

Suggestions: Cook more than you need for one meal. It's a wonderful leftover for a cold lunch and a good picnic dish.

For low-salt diet: Use salt-free, oil-free Italian dressing; purchase or see recipe. One serving (1/6 recipe) contains 68 milligrams of sodium.

CRUNCHY CHICKEN LOAF

Makes 8 servings. One serving equals 3 ounces of meat and 1 serving of bulky vegetable; contains 129 Calories (P15, F7, C2), 59 milligrams of cholesterol.

CHICKEN FRYER, 2-pound; or Cornish game hen
BAY LEAF, 1
GARLIC, 1/4 clove
CELERY, 1 large stalk, coarsely chopped
WATER, 1-1/2 quarts, or enough to come 2/3 up on chicken
PARSLEY, 1 tablespoon chopped
CELERY, 1/4 cup diced
ONION, 1-1/2 tablespoons diced
GREEN PEPPER, 1 tablespoon diced
PIMENTO, 3 tablespoons diced; or sweet red pepper or tomato with seeds removed
BEAN SPROUTS, 1 cup coarsely chopped
OLIVES, 5 green or black, diced (optional)
PLAIN GELATIN, 1 to 2 envelopes (optional)
SALT, 1 teaspoon
PEPPER, 1/8 teaspoon
TABASCO, 4 drops

Put POULTRY in Dutch oven or stew kettle; add BAY LEAF, GARLIC, coarsely chopped CELERY and WATER; cook until meat falls off the bone, 3 to 3-1/2 hours; add liquid as needed to keep poultry at least half covered during cooking; turn about midway in cooking, if you wish, to get uniform doneness. Remove from heat; drain liquid and store in jars. (Do not refrigerate while liquid is still warm, or it will make a cloudy gelatin.) Pick meat from bones and skin, shredding so no piece is larger than 1/2 inch; discard skin, bones, fat and any connective tissue; set aside to cool completely. When liquid is cold, remove fat from top and discard; place 2 cups of the liquid in saucepan. Add VEGETABLES, including BEAN SPROUTS, if fresh, to chicken liquid and simmer until slightly soft, about 5 minutes; if using canned bean sprouts, add them now; add OLIVES. If liquid did not make a firm gel, add packaged GELATIN; add SEASONINGS; taste; add more seasonings if needed. Combine gelatin mixture and minced poultry. Spray loaf pan with nonstick coating; pour in mixture; chill until firm.

For low-salt diet: Omit salt; use 1 teaspoon of salt substitute. Use fresh bean sprouts. Omit olives. One serving (1/8 recipe) contains 53 milligrams of sodium.

TURKEY/CHICKEN NEWBURG

Makes 5 servings. One serving equals 3 ounces of meat and 1/2 slice of bread; contains 213 Calories (P24, F9, C9), 125 milligrams of cholesterol.

MARGARINE, 4 teaspoons. Use corn-oil, soybean-oil or safflower-oil margarine.
FLOUR, 3 tablespoons
SKIM MILK, 1 cup
ONION or CHIVES, 1 tablespoon finely diced
BUTTER FLAVORING, 4 drops
YELLOW FOOD COLORING, 3 drops
SALT, 1/2 teaspoon
PEPPER, 1/8 teaspoon
DRY WHITE WINE, 1/4 cup; or 1/2 teaspoon of sherry flavoring and 1/4 cup of water
CHICKEN or TURKEY, 2-1/2 cups diced
MUSHROOMS, 1 cup sliced, cooked

Melt MARGARINE; stir in FLOUR to make smooth paste; gradually add MILK, stirring to keep smooth. Add ONION or CHIVES, BUTTER FLAVORING and FOOD COLORING. Cook slowly, stirring constantly, about 5 minutes until thickened. Add SEASONINGS, CHICKEN or TURKEY, and MUSHROOMS. Heat, stirring to prevent sticking, but do not cook. Serve over rice, biscuits or toast. Allow 1 slice of bread serving for whatever you use, in addition to food value given.

Suggestions: Add 2 tablespoons of chopped pimento or sweet red pepper for additional color. Mix diced ham (trimmed of all fat) with turkey (equal parts) for variation and better use of leftovers.

For low-salt diet: Cook turkey or chicken without salt for use in recipe. Omit salt; use 1/2 teaspoon of salt substitute. Use salt-free margarine. Use fresh mushrooms (not canned) and cook without salt. One serving (1/5 recipe) contains 105 milligrams of sodium.

CHICKEN BAVARIAN

Makes 4 servings. One serving equals 3 ounces of meat and 1 serving of bulky vegetable; contains 177 Calories (P21, F9, C3), 90 milligrams of cholesterol.

TOMATO PUREE, 6 ounces
ITALIAN DRESSING, low-calorie. Purchase or see recipe.
SAUERKRAUT, 1/2 cup
CHICKEN BREASTS, 2 medium-size, cut in half

Combine TOMATO PUREE, ITALIAN DRESSING and SAUERKRAUT for marinade. Wash CHICKEN; drain dry; place in bowl and cover with marinade; let stand at least 2 hours. Remove chicken from marinade; arrange in Teflon baking dish or dish sprayed with nonstick coating. With slotted spoon, take sauerkraut from marinade and spread evenly over chicken parts; spoon liquid over garnished chicken. Bake at 325 degrees, uncovered, until chicken looks brown and dry, 1-1/4 to 1-1/2 hours. Discard liquid when serving, or spoon 1 to 2 tablespoons over each piece of chicken to moisten.

For low-salt diet: This recipe cannot be made low in salt because of the dressing and sauerkraut.

POULTRY STUFFING

Makes about 4 cups of stuffing, enough for a 3- to 4-pound chicken. One serving (1/2 cup) equals 1 slice of bread and 1/2 teaspoon of fat; contains 82 Calories (P3, F2, C13), no cholesterol.

BREAD CRUMBS, 4 cups firmly packed
CELERY, 1/4 cup diced
CELERY LEAVES, 2 tablespoons diced
ONION, 1/4 cup chopped
MARGARINE, 4 teaspoons melted. Use corn-oil, soybean-oil or safflower-oil margarine.
SALT, 1 teaspoon
PEPPER, 1/4 teaspoon
POULTRY SEASONING or SAGE, 1-1/2 teaspoons. Use 2 teaspoons if you like strong seasonings.
HOT WATER, 3 to 5 tablespoons
BACON BITS, 1 tablespoon imitation (optional)

Break BREAD into fine pieces, or crumble. Saute diced VEGETABLES in MARGARINE; cover after browning lightly, and allow to steam. Mix SEASONINGS together; sprinkle over crumbs in large bowl; mix well. Add margarine-vegetable mixture to bread-spice mixture; blend well. Add enough HOT WATER to make mix stick together, but not be heavy; add BACON BITS, if desired. Clean out body cavity of chicken; wipe it dry; stuff; skewer opening closed. In roasting pan, bake chicken as directed for any roast fowl, until skin is crisp and well browned—20 to 25 minutes per pound at 325 degrees. Remove any leftover stuffing from cavity and reheat before serving. NEVER leave leftover dressing in carcass to eat later.

Suggestions: This stuffing is a sure-fire favorite. Use under chicken breasts, in stuffed flank steak or as a side dish with other entrees.

For low-salt diet: Make stuffing with salt-free bread crumbs. Omit salt; use 1 teaspoon of salt substitute. Use salt-free margarine. Use pure sage, not poultry seasoning, which may contain salt. Do not use bacon bits. One serving (1/2 cup) contains 23 milligrams of sodium.

Fish/Seafood

BAKED SOLE VICHY

Makes 3 servings. One serving equals 3 ounces of meat and 1/4 slice of bread; contains 162 Calories (P23, F6, C4), 80 milligrams of cholesterol.

FILLET OF SOLE, 1 pound
MARGARINE, 4 teaspoons. Use corn-oil, soybean-oil or safflower-oil margarine.
LEMON JUICE, 1/3 cup
DRY WHITE WINE, 1/3 cup. Use Chablis, Rhine, mountain white or similar wine
CELERY LEAVES, 1-1/2 tablespoons chopped
PARSLEY, 1 tablespoon fresh chopped
THYME, 2 pinches
ROSEMARY, 1 pinch
LEMON-PEPPER MIX, 1/4 teaspoon
SALT, 1/2 teaspoon
LEMON, 3 paper-thin slices

Wash and dry SOLE; cut into 3 equal pieces. Melt MARGARINE in LEMON JUICE; add WINE, HERBS and SEASONINGS. Simmer about 5 minutes over low heat; bruise herbs with bowl of spoon to release their flavor. Pour over fish pieces, covering well; let stand to marinate. Spray baking dish, 8 to 9 inches square, with nonstick compound, or oil lightly with vegetable oil. Place fish in pan; pour on marinade slowly, so herbs are on fish rather than dish; place a LEMON SLICE on top of each piece of fish. Bake, uncovered, at 375 to 400 degrees for about 20 minutes. If you want the fish browner, baste with the marinade after 15 minutes. Turn on broiler; place dish close enough to heat element to brown fish slowly. Serve with lemon slice on top; spoon on enough marinade to moisten.

For low-salt diet: Use fresh fish. Frozen fish is sometimes brined. Use salt-free margarine. Omit salt; use salt substitute. Use only 1 tablespoon of celery leaves and fork them aside when eating fish. Omit lemon-pepper mix; use 1/8 teaspoon of black pepper. One serving contains 92 milligrams of sodium.

BARBECUED SALMON

Makes 8 servings or more. One 3-1/2 ounce serving equals 3 ounces of meat and 2 teaspoons of fat; contains 382 Calories, 109 per ounce (P7, F9, C0), 21 milligrams of cholesterol.

LEMON JUICE, 1/4 cup
PAPRIKA, 1/2 teaspoon
SALT, 1 teaspoon
PEPPER, 1/4 teaspoon
SALMON, 2-1/2 pounds fresh
GARLIC POWDER, 1/8 teaspoon
KETCHUP, 1/2 cup (see recipe)
VEGETABLE OIL, 1/2 cup

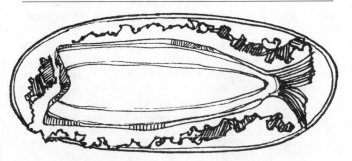

Make a marinade of LEMON JUICE, PAPRIKA, SALT and PEPPER; brush on SALMON, covering thoroughly; let stand for 2 hours, brushing often with marinade. Combine GARLIC POWDER, KETCHUP and OIL with remainder of marinade; coat fish well with this sauce. Preheat oven to 325 degrees; bake fish on rack, uncovered, about 1 hour, basting frequently with barbecue sauce.

Suggestions: This marinade/barbecue sauce and style of cooking are good with large fresh-water fish, such as lake trout, or you may use halibut. Cooking could be done outdoors on a large barbecue. Put grill far enough above the coals to avoid burning fish. Use the recipe for Diet Ketchup or combine the following: 1/2 cup of tomato puree; 1 tablespoon of diced onion; 1/2 clove of garlic, minced; and 1/2 tablespoon of vinegar.

For low-salt diet: Omit salt; use 1 teaspoon of salt substitute. Use the ingredients above for ketchup replacement; be sure puree is salt-free. One 3-1/2-ounce serving contains 54 milligrams of sodium.

FINNAN HADDIE SUPREME

Makes 3 servings. One serving equals 3 ounces of meat and 1/3 slice of bread; contains 165 Calories (P25, F5, C5), 60 milligrams of cholesterol.

FINNAN HADDIE, 1/2 pound
SKIM MILK, 1/2 cup
MARGARINE, 1 teaspoon. Use corn-oil, soybean-oil or safflower-oil margarine.
INSTANT FLOUR, 1 tablespoon
BUTTER FLAVORING, 4 drops
YELLOW FOOD COLORING, 3 drops. Omit if butter flavoring is colored.
CELERY, 1 teaspoon chopped
PARSLEY, 1/2 teaspoon fresh, finely chopped
ONION, 1/2 to 1 tablespoon chopped
SALT, 1/3 teaspoon
PEPPER, 2 sprinkles
PREPARED MUSTARD, 1/8 teaspoon
EGG WHITE, 1
COTTAGE CHEESE, 1/2 cup low-fat

Cover FISH with cold water; bring to slow boil. Discard this water; cover fish with boiling water and cook until very tender. Drain and cool fish; flake into fine pieces. To make cream sauce, melt MARGARINE in MILK and stir in FLOUR rapidly. Cook until slightly thickened. Remove from heat; add BUTTER FLAVORING, COLORING, SEASONINGS and lightly beaten EGG WHITE. Combine COTTAGE CHEESE and flaked fish; mix well; pour on sauce and mix again. Spray baking dish with nonstick coating, or oil lightly with vegetable oil. Put mixture in baking dish; bake at 350 degrees until nicely browned on top, 40 to 45 minutes.

Suggestions: For a more spicy and interesting casserole, try adding a pinch of sweet basil or dill weed, or a tiny pinch of cumin. Sliced mushrooms will vary the texture and give more volume without altering the food value.

For low-salt diet: This recipe cannot be made low in salt because it uses cured fish, which is processed in brine.

OVEN-POACHED HALIBUT

Makes 5 servings. One serving equals 3 ounces of meat; contains 128 Calories (P21, F4, C2), 58 milligrams of cholesterol.

HALIBUT FILLET or other white fish, 1 pound, cut into 5 equal pieces
SKIM MILK, 2/3 cup
HOT WATER, 2/3 cup
ONION, 5 large slices
MARGARINE, 5 teaspoons. Use corn-oil, soybean-oil or safflower-oil margarine.
CELERY LEAVES, 1 tablespoon chopped
CHIVES or PARSLEY, 1 tablespoon chopped
SALT, 1/2 teaspoon
PEPPER, 1/4 teaspoon

Wash and dry HALIBUT pieces; place in deep baking dish, 8 or 9 inches square, sprayed with nonstick coating or lightly greased with vegetable oil. Add MILK and WATER, mixed. This should come about even with the top of the fish but not cover it. Place slice of ONION on each piece; put 1 teaspoon of MARGARINE on each onion slice; sprinkle on chopped CELERY and CHIVES or PARSLEY. Season with SALT and PEPPER. Bake, uncovered, at 375 degrees for about 25 minutes. Spoon some of the liquid over the top of fish; place under broiler; allow to brown about 5 minutes. Discard cooking liquid. About half the margarine will be thrown away, too, so you don't have to count it.

Suggestions: This method of cooking can be used for any mild fish. If the pieces are thick, use additional skim milk and water to come to the top of fish, but not to cover it. If fish is more than 1 inch thick, allow more baking time.

For low-salt diet: Omit salt; use 1/2 teaspoon of salt substitute. Use salt-free stick margarine. Be sure to use fresh fish. Some frozen fish is brined in the freezing process. One serving (1/5 recipe) contains 68 milligrams of sodium.

WHITE FISH WITH HERB SAUCE

Makes 3 servings. One serving equals 3 ounces of meat and 1 serving of bulky vegetable; contains 139 Calories (P24, F3, C4), 113 milligrams of cholesterol.

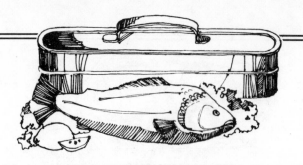

WHITE FISH, 1 pound. Use cod, halibut, halibut cheeks, sole or snapper.
LEMON JUICE, 1/3 cup
WATER, 1 cup
SKIM MILK, 1/4 cup
FLOUR, 1 tablespoon
OIL, 1 teaspoon
TARRAGON, 1 tablespoon fresh minced; or 2/3 teaspoons of dried
CHIVES, 1 tablespoon fresh minced; or 1-1/2 teaspoon of minced onion
SWEET BASIL, 1 sprig; or generous pinch of dry
ROSEMARY, 1 pinch
SALT, 1/4 teaspoon
PEPPER, 1/16 teaspoon
TABASCO, 3 drops
YELLOW FOOD COLORING, 2 drops

Marinate FISH in LEMON JUICE at least 30 minutes, turning often so it is well covered at all times. Put fish in steamer; add WATER; cook about 15 minutes, until done. Drain liquid and save 3/4 cup; put fish, covered, in warm place to stay hot until sauce is done. Add MILK to saved liquid; add FLOUR; stir to smooth; add OIL. Cook sauce over low heat until slightly thickened, stirring often. Add HERBS; cook 5 minutes longer; remove from heat. Add SEASONINGS and FOOD COLORING; stir well. Pour sauce over fish portions; serve immediately.

Suggestions: If there is any of this left, put in a covered casserole and save. It is excellent reheated.

For low-salt diet: Omit salt; use 1/4 teaspoon of salt substitute. Be sure fish is fresh, not salted or frozen in brine, which would increase the sodium content greatly. One serving contains 100 milligrams of sodium.

TUNA NOODLE MUSHROOM HOT DISH

Makes 4 servings. One serving equals 3 ounces of meat and 1 slice of bread; contains 214 Calories (P23, F6, C17), 30 milligrams of cholesterol.

NOODLES, 3/4 cup dry, broken into small pieces
SKIM MILK, 1 cup
FLOUR, 1-1/2 tablespoons
BUTTER FLAVORING, 6 drops
YELLOW FOOD COLORING, 3 drops. Omit if butter flavoring is colored.
TUNA, 6-ounce can, water-pack
COTTAGE CHEESE, 1/2 cup low-fat
ONION, 1 tablespoon dried
MUSHROOMS, 1/2 cup sliced
SWEET BASIL, 1/4 teaspoon dried
PARSLEY, 1/2 teaspoon dried
PIMENTO or SWEET RED PEPPER, 1 tablespoon chopped
SALT, 1/4 teaspoon
PEPPER, 1/16 teaspoon

Cook NOODLES in salted water until tender; drain well. Meanwhile, prepare sauce. Make paste with part of MILK and FLOUR; thin with remaining milk. Add BUTTER FLAVORING and COLORING; cook in double boiler until thickened; stir often to prevent lumping. Drain TUNA well; flake fine; combine with COTTAGE CHEESE, MUSHROOMS, ONION and HERBS. Combine all ingredients except sauce; mix well; add sauce; mix again. Spray loaf pan with nonstick coating, or oil lightly with vegetable oil. Fill loaf pan with mixture; sprinkle top lightly with paprika for color. Bake at 325 degrees until top is browned, about 40 minutes.

For low-salt diet: Cook noodles in unsalted water. Use water-pack tuna with no salt added; check label. Run cold water over cottage cheese, in colander, until water comes off clear, at least 2 minutes. Stir to wash thoroughly. Use fresh mushrooms instead of canned. Omit salt; use 1/2 teaspoon of salt substitute. One serving (1/4 recipe) contains 120 milligrams of sodium.

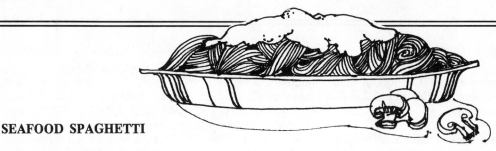

SEAFOOD SPAGHETTI

Makes 3 servings. One serving equals 3 ounces of meat and 1 slice of bread; contains 246 Calories (P23, F10, C16), 38 milligrams of cholesterol.

SPAGHETTI, 3/4 cup raw (1-1/2 cups cooked)
ONION, 1/4 cup diced
OIL, 3 teaspoons
TOMATO PUREE, 1 cup
GREEN PEPPER, 2 tablespoons diced
MUSHROOMS, 1/2 cup sliced
GARLIC, 1/4 clove, minced
OREGANO, 1/16 teaspoon or more (optional)
CIDER VINEGAR, 2 teaspoons
TABASCO, 2 to 4 drops
SALT, 1/3 teaspoon
PEPPER, 1/8 teaspoon
TUNA, 6 ounces water-pack

Cover SPAGHETTI with boiling water; cook until tender; drain. Saute ONION in OIL; add TOMATO PUREE, GREEN PEPPER, MUSHROOMS, SEASONINGS and 1/2 cup of WATER. Simmer, covered, about 10 minutes, until green pepper is tender. Flake TUNA fairly fine; add to sauce; mix well; heat to serving temperature. Divide cooked spaghetti into 3 half-cup portions; cover each with 1/3 of sauce.

Suggestions: If there is no cholesterol problem, shrimp can be used as a delicious substitution for tuna. Recipe would be higher in both cholesterol and salt and would contain 176 Calories.

For low-salt diet: Use water-pack tuna with no salt added; check label. Omit salt; use 1/3 teaspoon of salt substitute. Cook the spaghetti in unsalted water. One serving (1/3 recipe) contains 39 milligrams of sodium.

SALMON LOAF

Makes 5 servings. One serving equals 3 ounces of meat and 1/4 slice of bread; contains 128 Calories (P20, F4, C3), 46 milligrams of cholesterol.

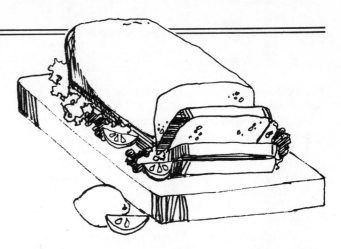

PINK SALMON, 16-ounce can; or 2 cups of cooked white fish
SALT, 1/2 teaspoon. Omit if you like food less salty.
PEPPER, 1/4 teaspoon
PARSLEY, 1 teaspoon dried
SWEET BASIL, 1/4 teaspoon dried
THYME, pinch of dried
ONION, 2 tablespoons finely chopped
EGG WHITES, 2, slightly beaten
TOASTED CRUMBS, 1/2 cup; or 1/2 cup of crumbled saltines

Break SALMON into small pieces, removing skin and bones. Add SEASONINGS, ONION and slightly beaten EGG WHITES; mix well. Stir in CRUMBS. If mixture seems dry, add about 2 tablespoons of hot water. Spray loaf pan with nonstick coating or oil lightly with vegetable oil. Form fish mixture into loaf; place in pan. Bake at 325 degrees for 1 hour.

Suggestions: This may be served with Spanish Barbecue Sauce (see recipe). Heat the sauce and pour it over the slices of salmon loaf.

For low-salt diet: Use fresh-cooked salmon, or leftovers from barbecued salmon if it was made by a low-salt recipe. Omit salt; use 1/2 teaspoon of salt substitute. (If using barbecued fish, omit salt substitute.) Use salt-free bread crumbs, or 1/4 cup of rolled oats, chopped fine in blender. One serving (1/5 recipe) contains 62 milligrams of sodium.

PATRICK'S SHRIMP DISH

Makes 3 servings. One serving equals 2 ounces of meat and 1 slice of bread; contains 172 Calories (P19, F4, C15), 104 milligrams of cholesterol.

FRESH MUSHROOMS, 1/2 cup, cut in pieces
MARGARINE, 2 teaspoons. Use corn-oil, soybean-oil or safflower-oil margarine.
FLOUR, 1-1/2 tablespoons
WATER, about 1/2 cup
FROZEN STRING BEANS, 10 ounce package French-cut
SHRIMP, 8 ounces cooked and deveined
SALT and PEPPER, to taste

Saute MUSHROOMS in MARGARINE until brown, stirring often. Stir FLOUR into margarine, mixing well; thin with WATER until runny. Steam STRING BEANS until tender; drain well. Put aside 1/4 of the beans for use in some other dish. Add 3/4 of the string beans to SHRIMP; pour on mushroom sauce; mix. Season with SALT and PEPPER. Heat and serve.

Suggestions: For added flavor, use a little of your favorite herb. A small pinch of rosemary or sweet basil blends well here.

For low-salt diet: This recipe cannot be made low in salt because of the natural salt in shrimp. One serving contains 119 milligrams of sodium.

Vegetable Protein

HOW TO USE VEGETABLE PROTEIN PRODUCTS

Soy protein is available in two general forms: soy granules and spun soy products that imitate various meat forms. Both are called textured vegetable protein (TVP). They are available dehydrated in grocery stores. Freeze-dried and frozen TVP products are now available on the commercial market and may soon be on the retail market.

These imitation meat products are made by a complicated process. First the soybean is separated into soy flour and soybean oil. The flour is then spun (extruded) into protein fibers or woven into a meatlike product. This is then fortified with natural nutrients similar to the product it is imitating, and finally it is given a meatlike flavor—beef, chicken, ham or tuna. Many of these textured vegetable protein products are used in the prepared foods you buy in the grocery store. Imitation bacon pieces are an example: The soy protein has been treated to look, taste and even smell like bacon.

The soy granules may be added to any mixed dish, such as meat loaf, fish loaf, meat or fish patties and meat sauces. They are used to stretch the meat or fish with which they are used. Soy protein may be substituted for up to half of the protein and it will be an acceptable product if you use seasonings and flavorings in the right amounts. It is not suitable for low-sodium diets.

The imitation protein products (spun protein derivatives) can be used alone to completely replace the meat, fish or poultry they copy. Use 1/3 cup (reconstituted) for each 1 ounce of meat in the recipe.

How To Reconstitute Protein Granules

For 1-1/2 ounces of granules (3 ounces dry in measuring cup), add 5 ounces of boiling water, mix well and allow to stand for at least 20 minutes. You may want to add a few drops of red coloring to match the color of the meat to which you plan to add the granules. Allow to cool. Mix with 1/2 pound of meat for a final volume of 3/4 pound. Form into loaf or patties, or add to sauce as recipe requires.

How To Reconstitute Spun Protein Products

Place 1-1/2 ounces (3 ounces dry in measuring cup) in large pan. Add 1 quart of water and 1/2 teaspoon of salt or salt substitute. Bring to a boil and cook for 7 to 8 minutes, until tender. Drain and cool. This amount will make 1 cup of meat substitute.

IMPORTANT: Treat these products just like fresh meat once they are cooked. Refrigerate if you are not going to use them immediately.

Be sure you season these products adequately. Onion, green pepper, spices and herbs will help disguise the substitution. The spun soy derivatives need less additions to make them tasty than the plain granules.

Substitutions

One-third cup reconstituted soy protein (either type) contains 7 grams of protein, 0 grams of fat, 4-1/2 grams of carbohydrate, no cholesterol and approximately 50 Calories. One-third cup plus 1 teaspoon of fat is equal to 1 ounce of meat and 1/3 slice of bread.

One cup of commercial Hamburger Helper (made with meat by package directions) equals 2 ounces of meat and 2 slices of bread, and contains 238 Calories, 16 grams of protein, 6 grams of fat and 30 grams of cholesterol.

IMITATION GOULASH

Makes 2 servings. One serving equals 2 ounces of meat and 2 slices of bread; contains 226 Calories (P19, F2, C33), 8 milligrams of cholesterol.

TEXTURED VEGETABLE PROTEIN, 1-1/2 ounces, beef flavor
MACARONI, 1/3 cup
SALT, 1 teaspoon
WATER, 1 quart
ONION, 1/4 cup diced
GREEN PEPPER, 1-1/2 tablespoons diced
TOMATOES, 1-1/2 cups canned, chopped
PEPPER, 1/16 teaspoon
SWEET BASIL or OREGANO, 1/8 to 1/4 teaspoon dried
CHEESE, 1 ounce low-fat (5% butterfat or less)

Place SOY TVP, MACARONI, half of SALT and the WATER in large pot; bring to boil and cook 7 minutes; drain. Combine ONION and GREEN PEPPER with TOMATOES; add SEASONINGS. Mix drained beef substitute, vegetables and seasonings. Place in casserole or baking dish that has been sprayed with a nonstick coating or lightly oiled. Chop or grate CHEESE; sprinkle over top of mixture. Bake at 350 degrees for 50 minutes; serve immediately.

For low-salt diet: Because of the sodium added in processing these items for the market, they should not be used on a sodium-restricted diet.

SOY HAMBURGERS

Makes 6 patties. One patty equals 2 ounces of meat and 1/3 slice of bread (P14, F5, C4.5); contains 95 Calories, 15 milligrams of cholesterol.

SOY GRANULES, 1-1/2 ounces dry (3 ounces measured in cup)
BOILING WATER, 5 ounces
RED FOOD COLORING, few drops
ONION, 1 to 2 tablespoons diced
GROUND BEEF, 1/2 pound lean
SALT and PEPPER, to taste. Use at least 1/2 teaspoon of salt.

Place SOY GRANULES in mixing bowl; mix BOILING WATER and FOOD COLORING; add to soy and allow to stand at least 20 minutes. Mix granules well so the coloring is even throughout. Add ONION to GROUND BEEF; add cooled granules and SEASONINGS to beef/onion mixture; work with hands until evenly blended (you should not be able to detect the granules). Mold into 6 patties; place on wax paper and refrigerate or freeze until ready to cook. Cook as you normally do meat patties, turning to be sure both sides are equally done; serve immediately. For meatballs or meat loaf: Use same directions, making 2 balls per patty. Add usual other ingredients to meat loaf. Bake or cook as you would all meat items.

For low-salt diet: Because of the sodium added in processing these items for the market, they should not be used on a sodium-restricted diet.

IMITATION HAM OMELETTE

Makes 1 serving. One serving equals 3 ounces of meat and 1/3 slice of bread; contains 228 Calories (P21, F14, C4.5);, no cholesterol.

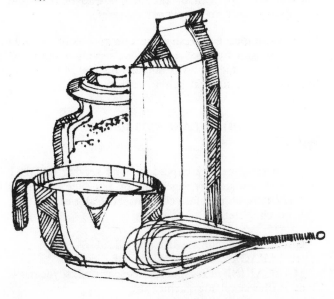

SKIM MILK, 1 tablespoon
LIQUID EGG SUBSTITUTE, 3 ounces
ONION, 1 teaspoon diced
GREEN PEPPER, 1 teaspoon diced
TEXTURED VEGETABLE PROTEIN, 1/3 cup ham flavor, reconstituted
SALT, 1/4 teaspoon
PEPPER, sprinkle
OIL, 1 teaspoon corn or soybean

Add SKIM MILK to EGG SUBSTITUTE; mix well. Add VEGETABLES with HAM SUBSTITUTE to egg mixture. Season with SALT and PEPPER as you would for normal omelette (use more if you wish). Place oil in heavy iron skillet or Teflon pan; use a brush or your fingers to spread it around the pan; heat pan until the oil is hot but not smoking. (Never cook at a heat level that causes fat to smoke.) Add egg mixture and cook, turning edges to form omelette and cooking all sides. Serve immediately.

For low-salt diet: Because of the sodium added in processing these items for the market, they should not be used on a sodium-restricted diet.

Vegetable Dishes

CARROTS VIENNESE

Makes 3 servings. One serving equals 1 serving of semistarchy vegetable (or 1/2 slice of bread) and 1/2 teaspoon of fat; contains 59 Calories (P1, F3, C7), no cholesterol.

CARROTS, 1-1/3 cups peeled and sliced about 1/4 inch thick
MARGARINE, 2 teaspoons. Use corn-oil, soybean-oil or safflower-oil margarine.
LEMON JUICE, 1 tablespoon
SUGAR SUBSTITUTE, 1-1/2 teaspoons granular; or substitute equal to 1 tablespoon of sugar
PARSLEY, 1/4 teaspoon chopped

Cook CARROTS in lightly salted water until tender. Drain off all but about 2 tablespoons of liquid (save for soup). Add MARGARINE, LEMON JUICE, SUGAR SUBSTITUTE and PARSLEY. Heat on low, stirring gently to mix ingredients well. Do not overcook.

Suggestions: This can be prepared ahead of time and reheated in oven in a covered casserole.

For low-salt diet: Use fresh carrots only; cook in unsalted water. Use salt-free margarine. One serving contains 62 milligrams of sodium. Do not use on low-sodium diet because of the natural salt in carrots.

DON'S FAVORITE LANCASTERSHIRE VEGETABLE

Makes 4 servings, 1/2 cup each. One serving equals 1 serving of semistarchy vegetable (or 1/2 slice of bread) and 1/2 teaspoon of fat; contains 50 Calories (P1, F2, C7), no cholesterol.

CARROTS, 1 cup peeled and sliced
RUTABAGAS, 1 cup peeled and diced
MARGARINE, 2 teaspoons. Use corn-oil, soybean-oil or safflower-oil margarine.

SALT, 1/4 teaspoon
PEPPER, 1/16 teaspoon

Put CARROTS in saucepan; add enough water (about 1/2 cup) to prevent burning; cover and cook until tender. Cook RUTABAGAS the same way. Drain both vegetables; discard liquids or save for soup. Combine vegetables; mash thoroughly with potato masher. Blend in MARGARINE, SALT and PEPPER; taste; add seasonings if desired. Serve immediately.

Suggestions: This can be made early and kept covered in the oven for 20 to 30 minutes without changing flavor.

For low-salt diet: Omit salt; use 1/4 teaspoon of salt substitute. One serving contains 17 milligrams of sodium.

HARVARD BEETS

Makes 2 servings. One serving equals 1 serving of semistarchy vegetable (or 1/2 slice of bread) and 1 teaspoon of fat; contains 93 Calories (P1, F5, C11), no cholesterol.

BEETS, 1 cup canned, sliced and drained (save liquid)
LIQUID from beets, plus water to equal 1/2 cup
SUGAR SUBSTITUTE, 1 tablespoon granular; or substitute equal to 2 tablespoons of sugar
CORNSTARCH, 1/2 tablespoon
SALT, 1/8 teaspoon
MARGARINE, 2 teaspoons. Use corn-oil, soybean-oil or safflower-oil margarine.
CLOVES, 4
CIDER VINEGAR, 1-1/2 tablespoons

Combine all ingredients except beets. Cook in double boiler over low heat, stirring frequently to prevent lumps, until liquid turns somewhat clear and thick. Add BEETS; stir gently to coat all slices. Keep warm over hot water at least 15 minutes before serving to allow flavors to penetrate beets.

Suggestions: This recipe can be served cold as an appetizer. Drain off most of the liquid before serving. Tiny whole beets may be used as a finger food.

For low-salt diet: This recipe cannot be made low in salt because of the high natural sodium in beets.

HOT POTATO SALAD

Makes 3 servings. One serving equals 1 slice of bread and 1 teaspoon of fat; contains 129 Calories (P3, F5, C18), no cholesterol.

POTATOES, 1 to 2 (1-1/2 cups)
ONION, 1 tablespoon diced
CELERY, 2 tablespoons diced
GREEN PEPPER, 1 tablespoon diced
OIL, 1 tablespoon corn or soybean
HOT WATER, 2-1/2 tablespoons
CIDER VINEGAR, 2 tablespoons
SUGAR SUBSTITUTE, 1/6 teaspoon granular; or substitute equal to 1/3 teaspoon of sugar
SALT, 1/4 teaspoon
PEPPER, 1/8 teaspoon
DRY MUSTARD, 1/8 teaspoon
BACON BITS, 1 teaspoon imitation
PARSLEY, 1 teaspoon fresh chopped
DILL PICKLE, 2 tablespoons diced
CELERY SEED, 1/4 teaspoon (optional)

Cook POTATOES (do not overcook); peel, dice, measure 1-1/2 cups and keep hot in covered pan. Saute ONION, CELERY and GREEN PEPPER in OIL until slightly brown, stirring to prevent overcooking. To vegetables, add HOT WATER, VINEGAR, SUGAR SUBSTITUTE and SEASONINGS, then BACON BITS and remaining ingredients. Heat to boiling but do not recook. Combine with hot potato; toss with fork to mix gently but well; serve immediately in preheated bowl.

Suggestions: This salad is a good complement for leftover cold meat. It does not reheat well, so plan to use it all at one meal or serve later as a cold salad.

For low-salt diet: Omit salt; use 1/3 teaspoon of salt substitute. Omit imitation bacon bits, which are very high in salt. Omit dill pickle; use 1/2 teaspoon of dill weed, if desired. Omit celery seed. Cook potato in unsalted water. One serving (1/3 recipe) contains 12 milligrams of sodium.

QUICK SCALLOPED POTATOES

Makes 3 servings. One serving equals 1 slice of bread and 1/2 teaspoon of fat; contains 103 Calories (P3, F3, C16), 1 milligram of cholesterol.

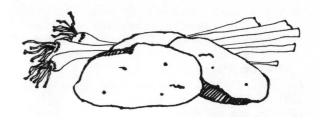

POTATOES, 2 small
ONION, 1/4 small
MARGARINE, 2 teaspoons. Use corn-oil, soybean-oil or safflower-oil margarine.
SKIM MILK, 1/2 cup
BUTTER FLAVORING, 4 drops
SALT, 1/3 teaspoon
PEPPER, 1/8 teaspoon
INSTANT FLOUR, 1 scant tablespoon

Pare and slice POTATOES and ONION thin. Cover with BOILING WATER and let stand about 5 minutes. Melt MARGARINE in MILK; add 1/4 cup of water, FLAVORING, SEASONINGS and FLOUR; stir and cook about 1 minute, until slightly thickened. Drain potatoes and onions (save water for soup pot); pour on sauce; stir to mix. Place in Teflon or lightly oiled baking dish. Bake at 400 degrees until potatoes are fork-tender, about 30 minutes.

Suggestions: If diet permits, sprinkle potatoes lightly with grated cheese before baking. If you use about 1 tablespoon of cheese, you won't have to count its food value. For variety, add 1 tablespoon of imitation bacon bits to potato slices just before adding the sauce. This will make a surprising change in looks and flavor, but not in food value.

For low-salt diet: Cook potatoes and onion in unsalted water. Use salt-free margarine. Omit salt; use 1/3 teaspoon of salt substitute. Do not use grated cheese or imitation bacon bits. One serving (1/3 recipe) contains 29 milligrams of sodium.

MEXICAN TOMATOES WITH CELERY

Makes 5 servings, about 3/4 cup each. One serving equals 1 serving of semistarchy vegetable or 1/2 slice of bread; contains 40 Calories (P2, F0, C8), no cholesterol.

CANNED TOMATOES, 2 cups
CELERY, 1 cup diced medium-size
GREEN PEPPER, 1/3 cup diced
ONION, 1/4 cup diced
SALT, 1/4 teaspoon
TABASCO, 4 to 6 drops
SUGAR SUBSTITUTE, 1/2 teaspoon granular; or substitute equal to 1 teaspoon of sugar
CAYENNE PEPPER, 1/8 teaspoon (optional)

Drain juice from TOMATOES. Add to CELERY, GREEN PEPPER and ONION. Simmer in covered pan until vegetables are tender; add water if needed. Combine vegetables with tomato solids; add SALT, TABASCO, SUGAR SUBSTITUTE and CAYENNE. Heat through to blend flavors. Serve immediately.

Suggestions: This can be simmered until thick, then used on scrambled eggs or for a tasty luncheon dish.

For low-salt diet: This recipe cannot be made low in salt because of the high natural salt in celery.

PENNSYLVANIA DUTCH GREEN BEANS

Makes 4 servings. One serving equals 1 serving of bulky vegetable and 1/2 teaspoon of fat; contains 59 Calories (P2, F3, C6), no cholesterol.

FROZEN GREEN BEANS, 10-ounce package French-cut
ONION, 2 tablespoons diced
OIL, 2 teaspoons corn or soybean
WHITE VINEGAR, 1 tablespoon
SUGAR SUBSTITUTE, 1-1/2 teaspoons granular; or substitute equal to 1 tablespoon of sugar
SALT, 1/4 teaspoon
BACON BITS, 1 teaspoon imitation

Steam GREEN BEANS with minimum amount of water until almost tender; drain but leave about 3 tablespoons of liquid. Saute ONION in OIL until slightly brown; cool a little. Add VINEGAR, SUGAR SUBSTITUTE, SALT and BACON BITS. Add mixture to green beans; toss to mix well. Reheat to serving temperature in tightly covered pan. Time your cooking schedule so beans are still hot when the onion-seasoning mixture is added. Reheating can be avoided and vegetables kept crisp.

Suggestions: If you plan to reheat this dish, save a little cooking liquid from beans to add then. Do not cook long enough that the beans lose their crispness.

For low-salt diet: Use diet-pack green beans, or fresh beans cooked (not overcooked) in unsalted water. Omit salt; use 1/3 teaspoon of salt substitute. Omit imitation bacon bits; they are very high in salt. One serving (1/4 recipe) contains 4 milligrams of sodium.

RICE CURRY - RICE PILAF

Makes 6 servings. One 1/2-cup serving equals 1 slice of bread and 1/2 teaspoon of fat; contains 103 Calories (P2, F3, C17), no cholesterol.

RICE, 2/3 cup uncooked
MARGARINE, 4 teaspoons. Use corn-oil, soybean-oil or safflower-oil margarine.
HOT WATER, 2 cups
CHICKEN BOUILLON, 1 cube
SALT, 1/4 teaspoon
CURRY POWDER, 2/3 teaspoon mild
MUSHROOM PIECES, 1/2 cup cooked (optional)

Stir and brown RICE in MARGARINE. Add WATER, BOUILLON CUBE and SEASONINGS. Cover and cook over low heat until all liquid is absorbed and rice is done, about 20 minutes. Add MUSHROOMS; reheat.

Suggestions: If you like a stronger curry flavor, use more, or use a stronger curry. If you omit the curry powder, you have rice pilaf.

For low-salt diet: Omit salt; use 1/2 teaspoon of salt substitute. Instead of bouillon cube and water, use 2 cups of fat-free chicken broth, homemade without salt (see recipe). Use fresh mushrooms; slice and steam without salt. Use salt-free margarine. One serving (1/6 recipe) contains 3 milligrams of sodium.

SPANISH BAKED EGGPLANT

Makes 6 to 8 servings. One serving (1/6 recipe) equals 1 serving of semistarchy vegetable or 1/2 slice of bread; contains 40 Calories (P2, F0, C8), no cholesterol.

WHOLE STEWED TOMATOES, #303 can containing onion and green pepper; or use 1 can whole tomatoes, 1/4 cup diced green pepper, 1/4 cup diced onion and 1/4 teaspoon of salt
CHILI POWDER, 1/2 teaspoon or more, to taste
CUMIN, small pinch
BUTTER FLAVORING, 6 drops
EGGPLANT, 1 medium
SALTINES, 2, crumbed

If not using canned tomatoes stewed with pepper and onion, combine pepper, onion and salt with whole tomatoes; add 1/4 cup water; simmer until raw vegetables are tender. Add CHILI POWDER, CUMIN and BUTTER FLAVORING to TOMATOES. Wash EGGPLANT; peel if you prefer and slice as for frying; cover with boiling water; cook for 5 minutes; drain well.

Place eggplant slices in greased casserole; pour on hot tomato mixture. Top with crumbed saltines; bake at 375 degrees until eggplant is tender, about 1-1/4 hours.

Suggestions: Use zucchini or yellow squash for this recipe if you prefer; food values remain the same. It can be reheated, but vegetables will get mushy if overcooked.

For low-salt diet: Use fresh or diet-pack tomatoes. If fresh, dip in boiling water for about 30 seconds, peel and chop. Use 1-1/2 to 2 cups of tomatoes, including liquid. Omit salt; use 1/2 teaspoon of salt substitute. Top with crumbs of 1/2 slice of unsalted bread or 2 unsalted crackers. One serving (1/6 recipe) contains 15 milligrams of sodium.

STUFFED BELL PEPPERS

Makes 4 servings. One serving equals 1 slice of bread, 1/2 ounce of meat and 1 serving of bulky vegetable; contains 114 Calories (P5, F2, C19), no cholesterol.

GREEN PEPPERS, 4 medium
POULTRY STUFFING, 1/2 recipe (see recipe)
MUSHROOM PIECES, 1 cup cooked, drained

Core and seed GREEN PEPPERS; blanch in boiling water about 5 minutes; drain and cool. Prepare POULTRY STUFFING without bacon bits; mix in MUSHROOMS. Stuff peppers full; put in greased baking pan. Bake at 350 degrees until top of dressing is brown and peppers are soft (about 20 minutes).

Suggestions: Serve in place of potato or rice as your starch. You may leave out mushrooms and use ordinary poultry stuffing, with or without bacon bits.

For low-salt diet: Make poultry stuffing by low-salt directions. Use fresh mushrooms; saute without salt in a nonstick pan; cover and cook slowly until tender. One serving contains 31 milligrams of sodium.

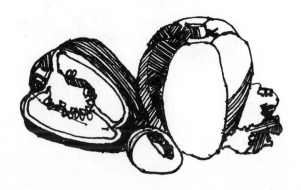

ZUCCHINI CASSEROLE

Makes 6 servings. One serving equals 1 serving of semistarchy vegetable or 1/2 slice of bread; contains 48 Calories (P2, F0, C10), no cholesterol.

ZUCCHINI, 2 cups sliced medium thick
CANNED TOMATOES, 2 cups drained
ONION, 1 tablespoon diced
GREEN PEPPER, 1 tablespoon diced (optional)
PEPPER, 1/16 teaspoon
TABASCO, 2 to 4 drops
SAUERKRAUT, 1 cup
TOAST, 1 slice, cubed small

Cover ZUCCHINI with water and boil 5 minutes; drain; place slices in lightly oiled baking dish. Combine TOMATOES, ONION, GREEN PEPPER, PEPPER and TABASCO. Drain and wash SAUERKRAUT; add to tomatoes and stir; pour over zucchini. (Or layer sauerkraut over zucchini, then pour on tomato mixture.) Top with TOAST CUBES. Bake at 350 degrees until zucchini is soft, about 1 hour and 10 minutes.

Suggestions: This dish reheats well—in fact, it seems better the second time—so plan a leftover.

For low-salt diet: Use fresh or salt-free canned tomatoes. If fresh, dip for 30 seconds in boiling water to loosen skin, peel and chop. Omit sauerkraut; add 3 tablespoons of white vinegar (less if you prefer) to tomato mixture when you add onion and pepper. Add 1/2 teaspoon of salt substitute to tomato mixture. Use 5 unsalted crackers, crumbled, or cube 1 slice of salt-free bread for topping. One serving (1/6 recipe) contains 5 milligrams of sodium.

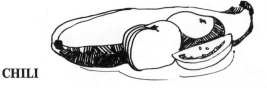

CHILI

Makes 4 servings, about 1 cup each. One serving of vegetable chili equals 1 slice of bread, 1/2 teaspoon of fat and 1 serving of bulky vegetable; contains 103 Calories (P4, F3, C15), no cholesterol. One serving of beef chili equals 3 ounces of meat and 1 slice of bread; contains 213 Calories (P20, F9, C13), 68 milligrams of cholesterol.

PINTO or RED KIDNEY BEANS, 3/4 cup uncooked
ONION, 1/4 cup chopped
GARLIC, 1/4 clove, diced fine
OIL, 1 tablespoon corn or soybean
CANNED TOMATOES, 2 cups
TOMATO LIQUID, 1 cup
OREGANO, 1/8 teaspoon
CUMIN, 1/16 teaspoon
BAY LEAF, 1/2
SALT, 1/2 teaspoon
CHILI POWDER, 1 to 2 teaspoons, to taste
TABASCO, 1/8 teaspoon (optional)
SUGAR SUBSTITUTE, 1-1/2 teaspoons granular; or
substitute equal to 1 tablespoon of sugar
RED FOOD COLORING (optional)

Soak BEANS overnight in cold water; simmer until soft, adding water to cover as needed. Saute ONION and GARLIC in OIL. Add the TOMATOES, TOMATO LIQUID, SEASONINGS and SUGAR SUBSTITUTE. Combine with 2 cups of cooked and drained beans; simmer for at least 40 minutes to blend flavors; if mixture cooks down too much, add hot water to thin; if too pale, add FOOD COLORING. Taste; add more salt and chili powder if desired; serve very hot.

Chili with Beef:
    LEAN GROUND BEEF, 1 pound

Brown the BEEF until well cooked; drain on paper to remove fat; add with beans and tomatoes and proceed. Note change in food values.

Suggestions: This chili reheats well, but may taste too spicy with bay leaf left in, so remove it after the first serving.

For low-salt diet: Use fresh or diet-pack salt-free tomatoes. Dip in boiling water for 30 seconds, peel and chop. Omit salt; use 1/2 teaspoon of salt substitute. Cook beans in unsalted water. Omit Tabasco; add 1/16 teaspoon of cayenne pepper if you want hot chili. With beef, one serving (1/6 recipe) contains 49 milligrams of sodium. When made without beef, one serving (1/5 recipe) contains 5 milligrams of sodium.

Sauces

CRANBERRY SAUCE

Makes about 6 cups. Six tablespoons equal 1/2 cup of fruit; contain 36 Calories (P0, F0, C9), no cholesterol. (You may use 2 tablespoons of this sauce without counting it in your diet.)

PLAIN GELATIN, 1 envelope (1 tablespoon)
WATER, 1-3/4 cups
RAW CRANBERRIES, 4 cups, washed and sorted
SUGAR SUBSTITUTE, 8 tablespoons granular; or substitute equal to 1 cup of sugar
LEMON JUICE, 2 tablespoons
SALT, 2 sprinkles
LIQUID SWEETENER, 1/2 teaspoon
DIETETIC APPLESAUCE, 1/2 cup sweetened

Dissolve GELATIN in 1/4 cup of WATER. Cook BERRIES in 1-1/2 cups of water until very soft; mash with potato masher to open all berries; remove from heat. Add gelatin mixture to hot berries; stir well to dissolve. Add all OTHER INGREDIENTS and mix thoroughly. Pour into sterile jars, cover, and refrigerate or freeze; or pour into canning jars, seal and process in hot-water bath about 30 minutes.

Suggestions: This can be stored in the refrigerator up to 10 days without spoilage. It may be poured into individual molds and served on a lettuce leaf as salad.

For low-salt diet: Omit salt; use sprinkle of salt substitute. Two tablespoons contain 2 milligrams of sodium.

MOCK HOLLANDAISE SAUCE

Makes about 1 cup. One serving (1/3 cup) equals 1 serving of semistarchy vegetable (or 1/2 slice of bread) and 1 teaspoon of fat; contains 81 Calories (P2, F5, C7), 1 milligram of cholesterol.

WATER, 1/2 cup
LEMON JUICE, 1 tablespoon
MARGARINE, 1 tablespoon. Use corn-oil, soybean-oil or safflower-oil margarine.
FLOUR, 2 tablespoons
SALT, 1/3 teaspoon
PAPRIKA, 1/8 teaspoon
DRY MUSTARD, 1/4 teaspoon
SUGAR SUBSTITUTE, 1-1/2 teaspoons granular; or substitute equal to 1 tablespoon of sugar
BUTTER FLAVORING, 8 drops
YELLOW FOOD COLORING, 4 drops. Omit if butter flavoring is colored.
NUTMEG, sprinkle
PLAIN YOGURT, 1/2 cup

Combine FIRST 8 INGREDIENTS; mix well. Cook over low heat until thickened, stirring often to prevent lumps or sticking. Remove from heat; add BUTTER FLAVORING and FOOD COLORING, NUTMEG and YOGURT. Blend well. Serve on vegetables and steamed fish.

Suggestions: You may vary the thickness of this sauce by using less water to make it thicker, or more water to thin it. The food value of the total recipe will be the same, so allow 1/3 of the total volume for 1 serving.

For low-salt diet: Omit salt; use 1/3 teaspoon of salt substitute. Use salt-free margarine. One serving (1/3 recipe) contains 40 milligrams of sodium.

CREAM SAUCE

Makes 1 cup sauce. One-fourth cup equals 1/3 slice of bread and 1/2 teaspoon of fat; contains 50 Calories (P2, F2, C6), 2 milligrams of cholesterol.

MARGARINE, 2 teaspoons. Use corn-oil, soybean-oil or safflower-oil margarine.
FLOUR, 1-1/2 tablespoons
SKIM MILK, 1 cup
SALT, 1/4 teaspoon
PEPPER, sprinkle

Melt MARGARINE; stir in FLOUR; gradually add MILK, stirring constantly. Cook in double boiler until thick. Add SEASONINGS; mix well. Cook about 1 minute longer.

For parsley cream sauce, add:
PARSLEY, 1 tablespoon, chopped fine
ONION, 1/2 teaspoon minced

Add PARSLEY and ONION to Cream Sauce with SEASONINGS. (Vegetables can be a little crisp; they will cook more when sauce is used.)

Suggestions: This goes well with flaked fish, carrots or potatoes.

For low-salt diet: Omit salt; use 1/4 teaspoon of salt substitute. Use salt-free margarine. One-fourth cup contains 33 milligrams of sodium.

Variety is the spice of life—and these fruit dishes are all spicy. Interesting combinations of fruits, and different ways of combining them, offer changes in taste and appearance. These are simple ways of varying the diet to avoid monotony and boredom and increase palatability.

Apples have great sweetening capacity. You will find them in most recipes in this section. Try apples in some favorite recipes you have been unable to adapt to your taste and dietary needs.

BAKED APPLES

Makes 6 servings, each 1/2 apple plus juice. One serving equals 1/2 cup of fruit; contains 48 Calories (P0, F0, C12), no cholesterol.

APPLES, 3 large
SOFT DRINK, 12-ounce can dietetic red-apple
LEMON JUICE, 1 tablespoon
LEMON RIND, 1/2 teaspoon grated
SALT, sprinkle

Cut APPLES in half lengthwise; core; remove stem and blossom end. Place apples, cut side down, in 9-inch-square Teflon pan. Mix SOFT DRINK, LEMON JUICE, LEMON RIND and SALT; pour over apple halves. Bake at 325 degrees until apples wrinkle when touched, about 1 hour. Serve hot or cool, as you prefer.

Suggestions: For nondieters, serve apple half with cut side up and 1 tablespoon of vanilla ice cream in hollow.

For low-salt diet: Omit salt; may use sprinkle of salt substitute. One serving (1/2 apple) contains 11 milligrams of sodium.

SPICY BAKED PEACHES

Makes 3 servings. One serving (2 halves) equals 1/2 cup of fruit and 1 teaspoon of fat; contains 88 Calories (P0, F4, C13), no cholesterol.

PEACH HALVES, 6 dietetic, with juice (about 1/2 cup)
MARGARINE, 3 teaspoons. Use corn-oil, soybean-oil or safflower-oil margarine.
SHERRY or ALMOND EXTRACT, 1/2 teaspoon
LEMON or ORANGE RIND, 1 teaspoon grated
GROUND CLOVES, sprinkle

Drain PEACH HALVES; save juice. Combine melted MARGARINE, JUICE, FLAVORING and RIND. Place peach halves in Teflon pan or pan sprayed with nonstick coating or lightly oiled. Pour juice mixture over peaches so all are covered. Bake at 400 degrees until peaches are steaming hot, about 10 minutes. Sprinkle lightly with GROUND CLOVES and serve as a dessert or as a garnish with meat.

Suggestions: This can be made with pear halves and nutmeg in place of peaches and cloves. For colorful

108   Fruit Dishes

garnishes, try adding food coloring to peaches or pears while still in juice. Allow to stand several hours, so fruit will take up some of the color, then cook as directed. Attractive and tasty!

For low-salt diet: Use salt-free margarine. One serving contains 2 milligrams of sodium.

STAN'S SPICY APPLESAUCE

Makes 7 cups. One serving equals 1/2 cup of fruit; contains 53 Calories (P0, F1, C11), no cholesterol.

APPLES, 8 large. Use Golden Delicious if available.
CORIANDER SEED, 1/2 teaspoon
MARGARINE, 1-1/2 teaspoons. Use corn-oil, soybean-oil or safflower-oil margarine.
BROWN SUGAR SUBSTITUTE, 2-1/2 tablespoons

granular; or substitute equal to 1/3 cup of sugar
GINGER, 1/2 teaspoon
NUTMEG, 1/2 teaspoon
CINNAMON, 1/2 teaspoon
SALT, sprinkle

Peel, core and dice APPLES. Crush CORIANDER SEED and place in spice bag; suspend in heavy saucepan with a tight lid so it can be removed. Place apples, MARGARINE and SUGAR SUBSTITUTE in pot; sprinkle SPICES and SALT on at intervals, so apples and spices are layered. Cook tightly covered over very low heat, without water, until apples are very soft. Remove spice bag with coriander; add water to make 7-cup total. Cool, then refrigerate. If you wish, pack into pint containers and freeze for future use.

Suggestions: Served as a relish, this applesauce is a fine accompaniment for cold meat, such as roast beef or lamb. If apples are quite hard, add 1/4 cup of water before cooking.

For low-salt diet: Omit salt; use sprinkle of salt substitute. Use salt-free margarine. One serving (1/2 cup) contains 1 milligram of sodium.

BERRY APPLESAUCE

Makes 11 servings. A 1/2-cup serving equals 1/2 cup of fruit; contains 48 Calories (P0, F0, C12), no cholesterol.

GREEN APPLES, 4 cups cored and quartered (6 or 7 apples)
BERRIES, 2 cups, cleaned and sliced
LEMON JUICE, 2 tablespoons
SALT, sprinkle
SUGAR SUBSTITUTE, 2 to 4 tablespoons granular; or substitute equal to 1/4 to 1/2 cup of sugar

Core and quarter enough APPLES to make 4 packed cups. Put apples into saucepan with 1-1/2 cups of WATER. Cook, covered, very slowly until tender; stir occasionally to prevent sticking. Remove from heat; put through food mill to remove any lumps or fibers. Set aside. Simmer BERRIES in 1/3 cup of water until soft. Put through food mill to remove any large seeds or fibers. Combine apple and berry pulps; heat to boiling point. Add LEMON JUICE, SALT and SUGAR SUBSTI-TUTE. To preserve more than a few days, freeze or put into sterile jars and process by hot-water bath (see canning instructions).

Suggestions: Use strawberries, raspberries or boysen-berries for a delicious sauce. Taste before adding all the sugar substitute. Very sweet berries or very tart apples will require adjusting the amounts of sweetener and lemon juice.

For low-salt diet: Omit salt; use sprinkle of salt substitute. One serving (1/2 cup) contains 1 milligram of sodium.

RHUBARB APPLESAUCE

Makes about 2-1/2 quarts. One 3/4-cup serving equals 1/2 cup of fruit; contains 44 Calories (P0, F0, C11), no cholesterol.

DRIED APPLE SLICES, 6-ounce package
RHUBARB, 10 to 12 stalks
LEMON JUICE, 4 to 6 teaspoons
SALT, sprinkle
SUGAR SUBSTITUTE, 1/3 to 1/2 cup granular; or substitute equal to 2/3 to 1 cup of sugar

Cover APPLE SLICES with water and soak overnight; if all water is absorbed, add enough to recover and allow to soak longer. Cook apples slowly in at least 1/2 cup of water until tender. Mash apples with potato masher; remove from heat. Slice RHUBARB fine; add 2 tablespoons of water; cover and cook slowly until tender. Remove from heat; add few drops of red food coloring if color is pale. Combine rhubarb and apples; add LEMON JUICE, SALT and SUGAR SUBSTITUTE to taste.

Suggestions: This is delicious as a topping for plain yogurt. It is also good on a biscuit as shortcake.

For low-salt diet: Omit salt; use sprinkle of salt substitute. Use fresh apples, enough to make 6 cups sliced; core and remove blossom end; slice; add 1 cup of water; cook, covered, over low heat until soft; put through food mill to remove skin and fiber. One serving (3/4 cup) contains 1 milligram of sodium.

EVELYN'S HOT FRUIT COMPOTE

Makes 8 servings, each 3/4 cup. One serving equals 3/4 cup of fruit or 1 slice of bread; contains 68 Calories (P1, F0, C16), no cholesterol.

APPLE SLICES, 1 cup diet-pack or unsweetened
DRIED PRUNES, 4, cut in half
DRIED APRICOTS, 8 halves
FROZEN BLUEBERRIES, 2/3 cup; or 1 cup of frozen raspberries
PINEAPPLE CHUNKS, 1/2 cup diet-pack
LEMON RIND, 1/2 teaspoon grated
ORANGE RIND, 1/4 teaspoon grated
MATZO MEAL or FINE BREAD CRUMBS, 3 tablespoons
SALT, sprinkle
BROWN SUGAR SUBSTITUTE, 1/4 cup granular; or substitute equal to 1/2 cup of sugar

Layer FRUITS so colors alternate; save all JUICES in a bowl. Mix RINDS, CRUMBS, SALT and SUGAR SUBSTITUTE; sprinkle on fruit. Pour juice over top; refrigerate for 24 hours. Bake at 250 degrees for 2-1/2 hours. Serve hot.

Suggestions: Serve this compote at the table to keep it very hot. Can be reheated; is good as a cold leftover. The fruits can be varied—peaches, pears, fruit cocktail, for example. Try adding 1/2 teaspoon of sherry flavoring to fruit juice. For nondieters, serve with whipped cream topping.

For low-salt diet: Omit salt; use a sprinkle of salt substitute. Use salt-free crumbs for topping. One serving (1/8 recipe) contains 3 milligrams of sodium.

FRUIT MEDLEY

Makes 5 cups. One serving (1/2 cup) equals 1/2 cup of fruit; contains 48 Calories (P0, F0, C12), no cholesterol.

STRAWBERRIES, 1 cup fresh or frozen; or 2/3 cup of blueberries
DIET PINEAPPLE CHUNKS, 14-ounce can, canned in juice
BANANA, 1 small
APPLE, 1 medium
CANTALOUPE, 1/2 small, peeled and seeded
FRESH MINT, 1 sprig; or 1/4 teaspoon of grated lemon rind (optional)

Wash, hull and slice STRAWBERRIES, or wash blueberries. Drain juice from PINEAPPLE CHUNKS into large bowl. Slice BANANA into juice, stirring to coat all and avoid browning. Peel (if you wish), core and dice APPLE. Add apple to juice, again stirring to coat all and avoid fruit turning brown. Dice MELON into 1/2-inch chunks; add to other fruit. Crush MINT to release flavor and add to fruit, or sprinkle lemon rind over fruit and stir well. Refrigerate in covered plastic container (will keep for about 1 week); stir a few times each day to keep banana and apple coated. Serve chilled.

Suggestions: You may substitute any fruits you wish, as long as you use the pineapple in juice for the basic ingredient. In winter, use frozen berries and substitute diet-pack fruit for the remainder.

For low-salt diet: No changes needed. One serving (1/2 cup) contains 2 milligrams of sodium.

Notes

9. Desserts

Even if you are avoiding sugar or cholesterol, you can have good desserts. Try these and see for yourself. One word of warning, though: Don't change the ingredients, or you might have a flop.

Cakes and other baked goods made with sugar substitute (or egg substitute) tend to be heavier and coarser in texture than those made with natural ingredients. Unusual combinations make acceptable products not so readily compared with the usual cake or pudding-cake.

These desserts are tasty and acceptable in texture, but they will dry out quickly, so use them while fresh or freeze them.

Dietetic cookies dry out very fast. Store them in tight plastic containers and freeze or keep in a very cool place. Do not make large batches ahead.

Even though these cookies are dietetically prepared, they are not free of Calories or carbohydrate. So the "cookie-holic" has to watch the amount consumed. Look for the equivalent value at the top of the recipe and limit your eating accordingly.

Pies and Pie Fillings—Everyone in the family will eat dietetic pies. They're good. Plan to serve them whenever you want a special dessert.

The double-crust pies will freeze well, so you can make more than one at a time and freeze the extras, unbaked. For frozen double-crust pie, allow 20 minutes of baking time at 450 degrees, then 40 to 60 minutes more at 375 degrees until the center of the piecrust is browned.

One-crust pies do not freeze as well, but you can make the shells and freeze them for later use.

Frozen Desserts—Commercially prepared dietetic iced desserts contain sorbitol as the main sweetener. People with hypoglycemia and with elevated triglycerides may find they do not tolerate this additive. Without sorbitol or any of the "fillers" used by creameries, frozen desserts tend to become grainy and unpleasant in texture. You will find that, if the frozen desserts in this chapter are made exactly according to the recipe, this coarse graininess will not develop.

While an ice-cream freezer is not essential for making these desserts, it makes an immensely better-textured product. If you are a real ice-cream addict, you will probably find it worth the money to buy an electric freezer.

The gelatin desserts in this cookbook are appetizing and contain so little of the forbidden Calories or other taboo items (salt, cholesterol) that they can be used frequently.

You can plan on serving the whole family these desserts, as there is nothing to indicate that they are different from the usual gelatin desserts.

Puddings take a little more preparation than the gelatin desserts, but they are also much more filling for the hungry dieter. Whipped cream or ice cream may be added as topping for nondieters.

Sauces—Most conventional dessert sauces are highly sugared. The two here, however, have no sugar, besides being low in saturated fats (butter and eggs). Use them to pamper your palate.

Baked Desserts

APPLE CRUNCH

Makes 9 servings. One serving equals 3/4 cup of fruit (or 1 slice of bread) and 1/2 teaspoon of fat; contains 100 Calories (P1, P4, C15), no cholesterol.

APPLES, 4 medium
BROWN SUGAR SUBSTITUTE, 5 tablespoons granular; or substitute equal to 2/3 cup of sugar
CINNAMON, 1/2 teaspoon
NUTMEG, 1/4 teaspoon
GINGER, 1/8 teaspoon

Topping:
MARGARINE, 3 tablespoons melted. Use corn-oil, soybean-oil or safflower-oil margarine.
LEMON JUICE, 3 tablespoons
BROWN SUGAR SUBSTITUTE, 5 tablespoons granular; or substitute equal to 2/3 cup of sugar
CINNAMON, 1/2 teaspoon
NUTMEG, 1/4 teaspoon
SHREDDED WHEAT, 2 well-crushed biscuits
WATER, 1/4 cup warm

Peel APPLES and slice thin as you would for pie; place in bowl. Spray 9-inch pan with nonstick coating or use Teflon pan. Mix first set of DRY INGREDIENTS and sift over apples; stir to coat all slices well. Arrange in pan.

Melt MARGARINE; mix in LEMON JUICE, SUGAR SUBSTITUTE and SPICES. Add crushed SHREDDED WHEAT to margarine-spice mixture; mix well. Scatter topping evenly over apples. Pour in the WARM WATER at sides of pan, without disturbing the topping. Bake at 350 degrees for 1 hour; serve warm.

Suggestions: If you like a strong lemon flavor, add 1/4 to 1/2 teaspoon of grated lemon rind to topping mixture. This dessert can be made with diet-pack peaches or pears, or a mixture of diet-canned fruit for variety. The food value would be approximately the same.

For low-salt diet: Use salt-free margarine. One serving (1/9 recipe) contains 2 milligrams of sodium.

BREAD PUDDING

Makes 6 servings. One serving, plain, equals 1 ounce of meat and 1/2 cup of fruit; contains 88 Calories (P6, F3, C9), 44 milligrams of cholesterol if made with egg, 2 milligrams of cholesterol if made with egg substitute. One serving with raisins equals 1 ounce of meat and 1 slice of bread; contains 107 Calories (P6, F3, C14).

SKIM MILK, 2 cups, scalded and cooled
EGG, 1; or 1-1/2 ounces of liquid egg substitute
BREAD, 2 slices
MARGARINE, 1 tablespoon. Use corn-oil, soybean-oil or safflower-oil margarine.
BUTTER FLAVORING, 6 drops
BROWN SUGAR SUBSTITUTE, 1/3 cup granular; or substitute equal to 2/3 cup of sugar
SALT, 1/2 teaspoon
VANILLA, 1 teaspoon
CINNAMON, 1/4 teaspoon
NUTMEG, 1/8 teaspoon

GINGER, sprinkle
EGG WHITES, 2
RAISINS, 4 tablespoons, soaked in hot water and drained (optional)

Scald MILK; set aside; when cool, add beaten EGG. Spread BREAD with MARGARINE; cube; add to OTHER INGREDIENTS, except egg whites and raisins. Beat EGG WHITES until stiff; fold into previous mixture. Add RAISINS. Turn into Teflon pan or pan sprayed with nonstick coating. Put pan in hot water; bake at 350 degrees for about 1 hour and 15 minutes. Check by inserting silver knife in center of pudding. If knife comes out clean, pudding is done. Serve warm or cold.

Suggestions: For nondieters, serve warm pudding with a scoop of vanilla ice cream or cool pudding with whipped cream.

For low-salt diet: Use salt-free bread. Use salt-free margarine. Omit salt; use 1/2 teaspoon of salt substitute. Do not use on 400-milligram sodium or 1-gram salt diets. One serving (1/6 recipe) contains 88 milligrams of sodium.

CRUNCHY BANANA BREAD

Makes 16 servings. One serving equals 1 slice of bread and 1 teaspoon of fat; contains 139 Calories (P3, F7, C16), 32 milligrams of cholesterol if made with egg, no cholesterol if made with egg substitute.

MARGARINE, 1/3 cup. Use corn-oil, soybean-oil or safflower-oil margarine.
BROWN SUGAR SUBSTITUTE, 5 tablespoons granular; or substitute equal to 2/3 cup of sugar
VERY RIPE BANANAS, 1-3/4 cups, mashed
EGGS, 2; or 3 ounces of liquid egg substitute
FLOUR, 1-1/2 cups sifted
SALT, 1/2 teaspoon
BAKING POWDER, 2-1/2 teaspoons double-acting
SODA, 1/2 teaspoon
SHREDDED WHEAT, 1 cup crushed biscuits
VANILLA, 1-1/4 teaspoons
WATER, 1-1/2 tablespoons; or plain low-fat yogurt
WALNUTS, 1/2 cup chopped

Cream MARGARINE with SUGAR SUBSTITUTE and mashed BANANAS. Beat EGGS; stir into creamed mixture. Sift FLOUR, SALT, BAKING POWDER and SODA together. With rolling pin, roll SHREDDED WHEAT biscuits until very fine; add to dry ingredients. Combine VANILLA and WATER or yogurt; add alternately with dry ingredients to creamed mixture; mix thoroughly. Add chopped NUTS; mix well. Turn into 9-inch-square Teflon pan or pan sprayed with nonstick coating. Bake at 350 degrees for about 50 minutes. Cool on rack; then cut into 4 parts in each direction (16 total).

Warning: Do not use any but dead-ripe, almost black, bananas for this recipe. Much of the flavor and the sweetening come from the bananas, and unless they are quite ripe, the bread will be poor.

For low-salt diet: Omit salt; use 1/2 teaspoon of salt substitute. Use 3 teaspoons of sodium-free baking powder instead of baking powder and soda. Use water instead of yogurt for liquid. One serving (1/16 recipe) contains 21 milligrams of sodium.

RAISIN-APPLESAUCE CAKE

Makes 16 servings. One serving equals 1 slice of bread and 1 teaspoon of fat; contains 117 Calories (P3, F5, C15), 16 milligrams of cholesterol if made with egg, no cholesterol if made with egg substitute.

SOFT MARGARINE, 1/3 cup. Use corn-oil, soybean-oil or safflower-oil margarine.
BROWN SUGAR SUBSTITUTE, 1/2 cup granular; or substitute equal to 1 cup of sugar
EGG, 1; or 1-1/2 ounces of liquid egg substitute
YOGURT, 2 tablespoons plain low-fat
FLOUR, 2 cups sifted
SODA, 1-1/2 teaspoons
SALT, 1/3 teaspoon
CLOVES, 1/2 teaspoon
CINNAMON, 1 teaspoon
NUTMEG, 1/4 teaspoon
RAISINS, 4 tablespoons
DIET APPLESAUCE, 1 cup sweetened
VANILLA, 1/2 teaspoon (optional)
WALNUTS, 12 medium-size halves

Cream MARGARINE with SUGAR SUBSTITUTE. Add beaten EGG and YOGURT; cream until very smooth and fluffy. Sift DRY INGREDIENTS together. Cut each RAISIN in half; soak at least 5 minutes in hot water; drain well. Add dry ingredients and APPLE-SAUCE, alternately, a little at a time, to creamed mixture; mix well after each addition. Add 1/2 teaspoon of VANILLA, if desired; it will blend nicely with the spices. Add raisins and chopped WALNUTS; mix thoroughly. Pour into 9-inch-square Teflon pan or pan sprayed with nonstick coating. Bake at 350 degrees for 50 minutes, or until toothpick stuck into the middle comes out clean. Cool on rack; serve warm or cold.

Warning: If you use Stan's Spicy Applesauce (see recipe) for this dish, cut the spices in half or omit and use only the vanilla suggested.

For low-salt diet: Use salt-free margarine. Omit salt; use 1/3 teaspoon of salt substitute. Use 1-1/2 teaspoons of sodium-free baking powder in place of soda. Omit yogurt; use 2 tablespoons of skim milk. One serving (1/16 recipe) contains 14 milligrams of sodium.

NEW ENGLAND FLUMMERY

Makes 4 servings. One serving equals 1/2 cup of fruit and 1/2 teaspoon of fat; contains 79 Calories (P1, F3, C12), no cholesterol.

WHITE BREAD, 2 slices
MARGARINE, 2 teaspoons. Use corn-oil, soybean-oil or safflower-oil margarine.
BLUEBERRIES, 1 cup fresh or frozen, unsweetened
LEMON JUICE, 1 teaspoon
LEMON RIND, 1/4 teaspoon grated. Use less if you're lukewarm about lemon.
SUGAR SUBSTITUTE, 1/4 cup granular; or substitute equal to 1/2 cup of sugar
SALT, 1 sprinkle
NUTMEG, 2 sprinkles

Spread BREAD with MARGARINE. Wash and sort BERRIES; place in saucepan with 1-1/2 cups of water. Cook berries over low heat until soft, about 10 minutes. Remove from heat; add LEMON JUICE, LEMON RIND, SUGAR SUBSTITUTE and SALT. Mix well. Spray baking dish with nonstick coating or oil very lightly. Place bread slices in bottom of dish, cutting to fit evenly. Pour cooked berry mixture evenly over bread; sprinkle with NUTMEG. Bake at 350 degrees for about 15 minutes; serve hot or chilled.

Suggestions: Flummery may be made with other berries, but the traditional New England dish is made with blueberries. If the diet allows, top it with 1 tablespoon of dietetic ice cream for extra special flavor.

For low-salt diet: Use salt-free bread. Use salt-free margarine. Omit salt; use a sprinkle of salt substitute. One serving (1/4 recipe) contains 6 milligrams of sodium.

FRUIT BETTY

Makes 4 servings. One serving equals 1/2 cup of fruit and 1 teaspoon of fat; contains 97 Calories (P1, F5, C12), no cholesterol.

CRUSHED PINEAPPLE, 1 cup sweetened dietetic; or another soft fruit, sliced
BREAD, 2 slices, crumbed
BROWN SUGAR SUBSTITUTE, 3 to 4 tablespoons granular; or substitute equal to 1/2 cup of sugar
NUTMEG, 1/8 teaspoon
LEMON JUICE, 1 teaspoon
LEMON RIND, 1/4 teaspoon grated. Use more if you like lemon.
MARGARINE, 4 teaspoons, melted. Use corn-oil, soybean-oil or safflower-oil margarine.
SALT, sprinkle

Drain FRUIT; keep juice for other uses. Combine ALL OTHER INGREDIENTS; mix well. Put fruit into Teflon baking dish or dish sprayed with nonstick coating. Cover with mixture. Bake at 400 degrees until topping looks brown, about 20 minutes. Serve warm, plain or with milk.

Suggestions: For nondieters, add a serving of vanilla ice cream or whipped cream on top.

For low-salt diet: Omit salt; use sprinkle of salt substitute. Use salt-free margarine. Use salt-free bread for crumbs. Use 1-1/2 teaspoons of lemon juice for increased flavor. One serving (1/4 recipe) contains 7 milligrams of sodium.

Cookies

BANANA DROP COOKIES

Makes 50 cookies. One cookie equals 1/4 cup of fruit and 1/2 teaspoon of fat; contains 51 Calories (P1, F3, C5), 10 milligrams of cholesterol if made with egg, no cholesterol if made with egg substitute.

MARGARINE, 1/2 cube (1/4 cup). Use corn-oil, soybean-oil or safflower-oil margarine.
BROWN SUGAR SUBSTITUTE, 8 tablespoons granular; or substitute equal to 1 cup of sugar
VERY RIPE BANANAS, 1-1/2 cups, mashed
EGGS, 2; or 3 ounces of liquid egg substitute
YOGURT, 1/4 cup plain low-fat
BUTTER FLAVORING, 10 drops
OAT FLOUR, 2/3 cup (see recipe)
INSTANT FLOUR, 1 cup
SALT, 1/2 teaspoon
BAKING POWDER, 2 tablespoons double-acting
WALNUTS, 1/2 cup chopped
VANILLA, 1-1/2 teaspoons
BLACK WALNUT FLAVORING, 1 teaspoon

Cream MARGARINE, SUGAR SUBSTITUTE and BANANAS until light and fluffy. Beat EGGS, YOGURT and BUTTER FLAVORING. Add egg mixture to creamed batter; stir until well mixed. Sift DRY INGREDIENTS together and add them to the batter gradually, beating until all lumps are gone. Add WALNUTS and FLAVORINGS; mix well. Drop by teaspoonfuls or small melon scoop onto Teflon baking sheet or sheet sprayed with nonstick coating. Bake at 375 degrees until edges turn brown, about 15 minutes. Cool on rack. Store in a tight container in a cool place, or freeze.

Suggestions: You will find that nondieters also enjoy these cookies. Just be sure the bananas are almost black on the outside, or the cookies will need extra sweetening.

For low-salt diet: Omit salt; use 1/2 teaspoon of salt substitute. Use salt-free margarine. Use 2 tablespoons of sodium-free baking powder. One cookie contains 8 milligrams of sodium.

GRANOLA COOKIES

Makes 64 cookies. Three cookies equal 1/2 cup of fruit and 1 teaspoon of fat; contain 85 Calories (P2, F5, C8), 24 milligrams of cholesterol if made with egg, no cholesterol if made with egg substitute.

MARGARINE, 1/3 cup. Use corn-oil, soybean-oil or safflower-oil margarine.
SUGAR SUBSTITUTE, 6 tablespoons granular; or substitute equal to 3/4 cup of sugar
EGGS, 2; or 3 ounces of liquid egg substitute
YOGURT, 1/2 cup plain low-fat
VANILLA, 1-1/2 teaspoons
BLACK WALNUT FLAVORING, 2/3 teaspoon
BAKING POWDER, 1 teaspoon double-acting
SALT, 2/3 teaspoon
INSTANT FLOUR, 1 cup
DIETETIC GRANOLA, 1 cup (see recipe)

Cream MARGARINE and SUGAR SUBSTITUTE; add beaten EGGS and YOGURT; mix well. Add both FLAVORINGS; mix. Combine BAKING POWDER, SALT and FLOUR; stir thoroughly into first mixture. Add GRANOLA; mix in thoroughly. Drop by teaspoonsful onto Teflon baking sheet or sheet sprayed with nonstick coating. Bake at 375 degrees until edges are light brown, about 15 minutes. Cool on a rack. Store in a tight container in a cool place.

Suggestions: Don't give away the secret of the ingredients and you will puzzle those who eat the cookies. The taste is excellent, the texture quite chewy.

For low-salt diet: Omit salt; use 2/3 teaspoon of salt substitute. Use salt-free margarine. Use 1-1/2 teaspoons of sodium-free baking powder. Follow low-salt instructions for granola (see recipe). One cookie contains 7 milligrams of sodium.

LEMON SPRITZ

Makes 60 cookies the size of a quarter. Three cookies equal 1/2 cup of fruit and 1 teaspoon of fat; contain 77 Calories (P1, F5, C7), 12 milligrams of cholesterol if made with egg, no cholesterol if made with egg substitute.

MARGARINE, 1/2 cup (1 cube). Use corn-oil, soybean-oil or safflower-oil margarine.
BUTTER FLAVORING, 1/4 teaspoon
SUGAR SUBSTITUTE, 7/8 cup granular; or substitute equal to 1-3/4 cups of sugar
EGG, 1; or 1-1/2 ounces of liquid egg substitute
VANILLA, 1-1/2 teaspoons
LEMON JUICE, 2 tablespoons
INSTANT FLOUR, 1-1/2 cups
BAKING POWDER, 3/4 teaspoon double-acting
SALT, 1/3 teaspoon
LEMON RIND, 1-1/2 tablespoons grated
YELLOW FOOD COLORING, few drops (optional)

Cream MARGARINE with BUTTER FLAVORING and SUGAR SUBSTITUTE. Beat EGG lightly; cream into margarine mixture. Combine VANILLA and LEMON JUICE. Sift FLOUR, BAKING POWDER and SALT together. Add dry ingredients alternately with liquid to creamed mixture; beat thoroughly; add LEMON RIND and FOOD COLORING; mix. Form into 2 rolls in wax paper; freeze for about 1 hour, until firm enough to be sliced. Slice into 60 cookies; place on Teflon baking sheet or sheet sprayed with nonstick coating. Bake at 400 degrees until brown on the edges, about 10 minutes. Cool on rack; store in a tight container in a cool place. May be reheated to recrisp.

Suggestions: You may roll the edges of each roll in oatmeal flour before you freeze the dough for a different texture. If you do this, slice the rolls into 65 cookies to compensate for the extra flour.

For low-salt diet: Omit salt; use 1/3 teaspoon of salt substitute. Use salt-free margarine. Use 1-1/8 teaspoons of sodium-free baking powder. One cookie contains 3 milligrams of sodium.

NUT COOKIES

Makes 65 cookies. Three cookies equal 1/2 cup of fruit and 1 teaspoon of fat; contain 90 Calories (P2, F6, C7), 12 milligrams of cholesterol if made with egg, no cholesterol if made with egg substitute.

MARGARINE, 1/2 cup (1 cube). Use corn-oil, soybean-oil or safflower-oil margarine.
BROWN SUGAR SUBSTITUTE, 7 tablespoons granular; or substitute equal to 7/8 cup of sugar
EGG, 1; or 1-1/2 ounces of liquid egg substitute
GROUND WALNUTS, 1/2 cup
YOGURT, 6 tablespoons plain low-fat
MAPLE or BLACK WALNUT FLAVORING, 2/3 teaspoon
VANILLA, 1 teaspoon
INSTANT FLOUR, 1-1/2 cups
SALT, 1/2 teaspoon
BAKING POWDER, 1/2 teaspoon double-acting

Cream MARGARINE with SUGAR SUBSTITUTE. Add beaten EGG, WALNUTS and YOGURT; cream again; add FLAVORINGS. Sift DRY INGREDIENTS together. Gradually add dry ingredients to creamed mixture; beat well. Drop by small spoonfuls onto Teflon baking sheet or sheet sprayed with nonstick coating. Flatten with fork if you wish. Bake at 375 degrees until edges are brown, about 15 minutes. Cool on rack; store in a tight container in a cool place, or freeze.

Suggestions: You may make these into round cookies by flattening them with a greased tumbler dipped into instant flour. You may top each cookie with a walnut half. If you do this, it will add 1/2 teaspoon of fat for each 2 cookies.

For low-salt diet: Omit salt; use 1/2 teaspoon of salt substitute. Use salt-free margarine. Use 3/4 teaspoon of sodium-free baking powder. One cookie contains 4 milligrams of sodium.

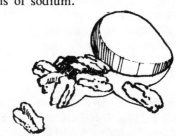

NUTMEG BALLS

Makes 55 cookies. Three cookies equal 1/2 slice of bread and 1-1/2 teaspoons of fat; contain 108 Calories (P1, F8, C8), 21 milligrams of cholesterol if made with egg, no cholesterol if made with egg substitute.

MARGARINE, 1/2 cup (1 cube). Use corn-oil, soybean-oil or safflower-oil margarine.
EGG, 1; or 1-1/2 ounces of liquid egg substitute
BROWN SUGAR SUBSTITUTE, 3/4 cup granular; or substitute equal to 1-1/2 cups of sugar
YOGURT, 1/2 cup plain low-fat
INSTANT FLOUR, 1-1/2 cups
BAKING POWDER, 3/4 teaspoon double-acting
SALT, 1/2 teaspoon
NUTMEG, 3/4 teaspoon
DRY INSTANT COFFEE, 1-1/2 teaspoons, decaffeinated if preferred
VANILLA, 1/2 teaspoon
BUTTER FLAVORING, 1/2 teaspoon
WALNUTS, 1/4 cup chopped
WARM WATER, 2 to 3 tablespoons

Cream MARGARINE with EGG and SUGAR SUBSTITUTE. Add YOGURT; beat well. Combine DRY INGREDIENTS. Add VANILLA, BUTTER FLAVORING and NUTS to creamed mixture. Gradually add dry ingredients, mixing well. Add enough WARM WATER to make consistency suitable for drop cookies. Drop by teaspoonfuls on Teflon baking sheet or sheet sprayed with nonstick coating. Bake at 375 degrees until edges turn slightly brown, 15 to 18 minutes. Cool on rack. Store in a tight container in a cool place, or freeze.

Suggestions: You can make these into flat cookies rather than balls by flattening with greased bottom of a small tumbler, dipped into instant flour. Flatten to about 1/4-inch thickness and allow 10 to 12 minutes for baking.

For low-salt diet: Omit salt; use 1/2 teaspoon of salt substitute. Use salt-free margarine. Use 1-1/8 teaspoons of sodium-free baking powder. One cookie contains 5 milligrams of sodium.

OATMEAL HERMITS

Makes 36 large cookies. One cookie equals 1/2 cup of fruit and 1/2 teaspoon of fat; contains 75 Calories (P2, F3, C10), 7 milligrams of cholesterol if made with egg, no cholesterol if made with egg substitute.

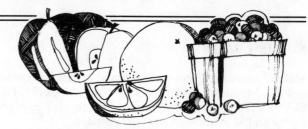

MARGARINE, 1/3 cup. Use corn-oil, soybean-oil or safflower-oil margarine.
BROWN SUGAR SUBSTITUTE, 1/2 cup granular; or substitute equal to 1 cup of sugar
YOGURT, 1/3 cup plain low-fat
EGG, 1; or 1-1/2 ounces of liquid egg substitute
OATMEAL, 2/3 cup quick-cooking
INSTANT FLOUR, 2/3 cup
BAKING POWDER, 2/3 teaspoon double-acting
SALT, 1/4 teaspoon
CINNAMON, 1/2 teaspoon
NUTMEG, 1/4 teaspoon
CLOVES, 1/8 teaspoon
RAISINS, 4 tablespoons, cut in half and soaked in hot water
VANILLA, 2/3 teaspoon
WALNUTS, 12 halves, chopped

Cream MARGARINE with SUGAR SUBSTITUTE until fluffy. Add YOGURT and EGG; mix well. Combine DRY INGREDIENTS; add gradually to creamed mixture. Drain RAISINS well; add raisins, VANILLA and NUTS to creamed mixture. Beat to insure even mixing of nuts and raisins. Drop by teaspoonfuls onto Teflon baking sheet or sheet sprayed with nonstick coating. Bake at 375 degrees until edges are browned, 12 to 14 minutes. Cool on rack; store in tight container in cool place, or freeze.

Suggestions: Make a batch of these and use for lunches and snacks. They will keep fresh longer than most dietetic cookies.

For low-salt diet: Omit salt; use 1/4 teaspoon of salt substitute. Use salt-free margarine. Use 1 teaspoon of sodium-free baking powder. One cookie contains 6 milligrams of sodium.

SHREDDED WHEAT CHEWIES

Makes 36 cookies the size of a half dollar. Two cookies equal 1/2 cup of fruit and 1 teaspoon of fat; contain 106 Calories (P2, F6, C11), 28 milligrams of cholesterol if made with egg, no cholesterol if made with egg substitute.

SHREDDED WHEAT, 1-1/2 cups crushed biscuits
MARGARINE, 1/2 cup. Use corn-oil, soybean-oil or safflower-oil margarine.
BUTTER FLAVORING, 8 drops
BROWN SUGAR SUBSTITUTE, 1 cup granular; or substitute equal to 2 cups of sugar
EGGS, 2; or 3 ounces of liquid egg substitute
INSTANT FLOUR, 1-1/2 cups
BAKING POWDER, 2 teaspoons double-acting
SALT, 1/2 teaspoon
YOGURT, 1/2 cup plain low-fat
VANILLA, 2 teaspoons

Crush SHREDDED WHEAT biscuits. (An easy way is to put biscuits in a plastic bag and roll with rolling pin until evenly fine.) Cream MARGARINE with BUTTER FLAVORING and SUGAR SUBSTITUTE; add EGGS; mix well. Combine FLOUR, BAKING POWDER and SALT. Add YOGURT to creamed mixture; gradually add dry ingredients. Add VANILLA and mix well. Drop onto Teflon baking sheet or sheet sprayed with nonstick coating. Bake at 400 degrees until nicely brown on edges, 14 to 15 minutes. Cool on rack; store in a tight container in a cool place, or freeze.

Suggestions: Chopped walnuts could be added for more chewiness. Use 16 walnut halves, chopped medium-fine. Allow 1/2 teaspoon of fat extra for each 2 cookies. No additional cholesterol.

For low-salt diet: Omit salt; use 1/2 teaspoon of salt substitute. Use salt-free margarine. Use 1 tablespoon of sodium-free baking powder. One cookie contains 12.5 milligrams of sodium.

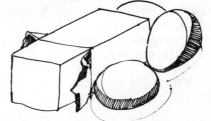

SOFT GINGER DROPS

Makes 60 cookies. One cookie equals 1/2 teaspoon of fat and 1/4 cup of fruit; contains 42 Calories (P1, F2, C5), 4 milligrams of cholesterol if made with egg, no cholesterol if made with egg substitute.

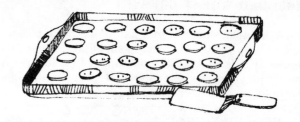

MARGARINE, 1/2 cup (1 cube). Use corn-oil, soybean-oil or safflower-oil margarine.
BROWN SUGAR SUBSTITUTE, 1 cup granular; or substitute equal to 2 cups of sugar
EGG, 1, and 2 EGG WHITES; or 3 ounces of liquid egg substitute
STRONG COFFEE, 3/4 cup, decaffeinated if preferred
YOGURT, 1/4 cup plain low-fat
BAKING POWDER, 3/4 teaspoon double-acting
CINNAMON, 1 teaspoon
CLOVES, 1 teaspoon
GINGER, 1-1/2 teaspoons
SALT, 1 teaspoon
BAKING SODA, 3/4 teaspoon
INSTANT FLOUR, 3-1/4 cups

Cream MARGARINE with SUGAR SUBSTITUTE until light and fluffy. Beat EGG lightly; add to creamed mixture. Combine COFFEE and YOGURT. Sift DRY INGREDIENTS together. Add liquid and dry ingredients alternately to creamed mixture, beating thoroughly after each addition. Drop by rounded teaspoonfuls onto Teflon baking sheet or sheet sprayed with nonstick coating. Bake at 375 degrees until edges are browned, 18 to 20 minutes. Cool on rack; store in tight containers in cool place, or freeze.

For low-salt diet: Omit salt; use 1 teaspoon of salt substitute. Use salt-free margarine. Use 1-3/4 teaspoons of sodium-free baking powder and omit both regular baking powder and soda. One cookie contains 5.5 milligrams of sodium.

Pies and Pie Fillings

PIECRUST

Makes two 8-inch double-crust pies or 3 pie shells. One-eighth portion of an 8-inch pie with top crust (but not including filling) equals 1 slice of bread and 2 teaspoons of fat; contains 153 Calories (P3, F9, C15), no cholesterol. One-eighth of a single crust pie shell equals 2/3 slice of bread and 1 teaspoon of fat; contains 106 Calories (P2, F6, C11), no cholesterol. **Note:** Figures given for the pie recipes include piecrust.

FLOUR, 3 cups sifted
SALT, 1 teaspoon
MARGARINE, 3/4 cup (1-1/2 cubes). Use corn-oil, soybean-oil or safflower-oil margarine.
COLD WATER, 2/3 cup

Sift FLOUR and SALT together. With pastry blender, cut MARGARINE into flour until fat is like coarse crumbs. Work in WATER gradually, adding only enough to make mixture stick together. The amount will vary with room temperature. Form dough into balls, 3 equal balls for one-crust pies, 2 large and 2 smaller for double-crust pies. Wrap in plastic wrap or waxed paper; refrigerate for 15 to 20 minutes. Using pastry cloth and rolling-pin cover to avoid using too much flour, roll crusts out on lightly floured board; roll into thin circle about the size of the pie plate. Fit crust into plate, rolling edge a bit to be sure it is not stretched too thin.

For shell only: Flute edge or firm with a fork. Bake at 450 degrees for about 15 minutes.

For filled pie: Place filling in bottom shell; spread evenly. If you wish, fruit may be heaped slightly in center of pie. Roll out top crust from smaller ball of dough; cut slits about 2 inches in from edge to let steam escape during baking. Moisten edge of lower shell; put on top crust to overlap all around; flute edges together or press with fork. Trim all around with sharp knife. Bake at 450 degrees for 15 minutes, then follow individual recipe.

For frozen pie: Allow 20 minutes at 450 degrees, then 40 to 60 minutes at 375 degrees, until center of piecrust is lightly browned.

For low-salt diet: Omit salt; use 1 teaspoon of salt substitute. Use salt-free margarine. One-eighth of the piecrust contains 1 milligram of sodium.

APPLE-RAISIN PIE

Makes filling for two 8-inch double-crust pies. One serving (1/8 pie) equals 1-1/3 slices of bread, 1/2 cup of fruit and 2 teaspoons of fat; contains 226 Calories (P4, F10, C30), no cholesterol.

PIECRUST, 1 recipe
RAISINS, 4 tablespoons, soaked in hot water and drained
APPLES, 6 large, sliced thin (6 generous cups)
LEMON JUICE, 2 to 4 tablespoons. Use larger amount with sweeter apples.
SUGAR SUBSTITUTE, 6 to 8 tablespoons granular; or substitute equal to 3/4 to 1 cup of sugar
INSTANT FLOUR, 1/4 cup
CINNAMON, 1/2 teaspoon
NUTMEG, 1/4 teaspoon
GINGER, 1/8 to 1/4 teaspoon (optional)
SALT, sprinkle
MARGARINE, 1 tablespoon soft-type. Use corn-oil, soybean-oil or safflower-oil margarine.

Prepare PIECRUST (see recipe); refrigerate. Soak RAISINS in hot water. Peel and slice APPLES thin; pour LEMON JUICE on them. Combine DRY INGREDIENTS in bowl; sift them over apples so all are covered; let stand at least 10 minutes, stirring occasionally to keep slices covered evenly. Roll out bottom crusts, according to directions. Drain raisins; combine with apples; divide fruit mixture into equal parts. Fill each shell with half of mixture. Divide MARGARINE into 2 equal parts; from each part, dab about 6 tiny pieces on top of fruit mixture so it will melt into fruit as evenly as possible. Roll out top crusts and put on pie as directed in recipe, cutting air vents and sealing edges. Bake at 450 degrees for 15 minutes, then at 375 degrees for 40 to 50 minutes, until center of pie is nicely browned. Cool on rack. Do not cut until fairly cool, or filling will be runny.

Suggestions: Second pie may be frozen, unbaked, for later use.

For low-salt diet: Omit salt; use sprinkle of salt substitute. Use salt-free margarine. Make piecrust according to low-salt directions. One-eighth of pie contains 3.5 milligrams of sodium.

BERRY PIE

Makes one 8-inch pie filling. One serving (1/8 pie) equals 1 slice of bread, 1/2 cup of fruit and 2 teaspoons of fat; contains 219 Calories (P4, F11, C26), no cholesterol.

PIECRUST, 1/2 recipe
BERRIES, 3 cups strawberries or raspberries, sliced if large
LEMON JUICE, 1 to 2 tablespoons, depending on sweetness of berries
SUGAR SUBSTITUTE, 4 tablespoons granular; or substitute equal to 1/2 cup of sugar
SALT, 2 sprinkles
INSTANT FLOUR, 3 tablespoons
MARGARINE, 1 tablespoon soft-type. Use corn-oil, soybean-oil or safflower-oil margarine.

For blueberry pie:
NUTMEG, 1/4 teaspoon

For boysenberry pie:
LEMON EXTRACT, 1/4 teaspoon; or 1 teaspoon grated lemon rind

Make PIECRUST (see recipe); refrigerate. Wash and sort BERRIES. Pour LEMON JUICE over berries. Mix so it covers all of them evenly. Combine SUGAR SUBSTITUTE, SALT and FLOUR. Sift dry ingredients over berries; let stand about 10 minutes, stirring occasionally to keep berries covered. Roll out bottom crust; place in pie plate. Spread berry mixture evenly in bottom crust. Dab MARGARINE over fruit. Roll out top crust, make steam vents, place and seal as directed. Bake at 425 degrees for 15 minutes, then at 350 degrees until middle of crust is lightly browned, 45 to 50 minutes. Cool on rack. Do not cut until cold, or it will be runny.

Suggestions: You may combine apples with berries for a good variation. Such combinations may require added spices, such as nutmeg or cinnamon. Use half of each fruit and adjust the flavoring accordingly.

For low-salt diet: Omit salt; use 2 sprinkles of salt substitute. Use salt-free margarine. Make crust by salt-free directions. One-eighth of pie contains 3.5 milligrams of sodium.

CHEESE PIE

Makes one 8-inch pie filling. One serving (1/8 pie) equals 2/3 slice of bread (or 1/2 cup of fruit) and 2 ounces of meat. Contains 195 Calories (P13, F11, C11), 101 milligrams of cholesterol if made with egg, 2 milligrams of cholesterol if made with egg substitute.

PIE SHELL, 1, unbaked
EGGS, 3; or 4-1/2 ounces of liquid egg substitute
SKIM MILK, 3 tablespoons
COTTAGE CHEESE, 1 pint
INSTANT FLOUR, 1 tablespoon
BROWN SUGAR SUBSTITUTE, 1/2 cup granular; or substitute equal to 1 cup of sugar
SALT, 1/8 teaspoon
VANILLA, 1/2 teaspoon
LEMON RIND, 1/2 teaspoon grated
CINNAMON, sprinkle

Make PIE SHELL (see recipe). Beat EGGS well; add MILK. Put COTTAGE CHEESE and 1/2 egg mixture into blender; blend for 1 minute. Add blended mixture to remainder of egg; add FLOUR, SUGAR SUBSTITUTE, SALT, VANILLA and LEMON RIND; mix well. Pour into pie shell; sprinkle generously with CINNAMON. Bake at 475 degrees for 10 minutes, then at 375 degrees until filling is set (test with silver knife blade), about 35 minutes. Cool on rack. Do not cut while still very warm, or it may be soft and runny.

For low-salt diet: One-eighth pie contains 188 milligrams of sodium. This is obviously not a low-salt recipe, and it cannot be made low in salt because of the high natural sodium content of eggs, milk and cottage cheese. Do not use it in low-salt or low-sodium diets.

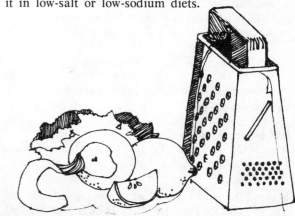

MINCE PIE

Makes two 8-inch pies. One serving (1/8 pie) equals 1 slice of bread, 2 teaspoons of fat and 1 cup of fruit; contains 233 Calories (P3, F9, C35), no cholesterol.

PIECRUST, 1 recipe
APPLE PULP, 3 cups ground medium coarse (about 5 medium-large apples)
SEEDLESS RAISINS, 1 cup ground coarse
LEMON, 1/2 large including skin, ground coarse
CURRANTS, 1 cup
CINNAMON, 2 teaspoons
NUTMEG, 3/4 teaspoon
CLOVES, 3/4 teaspoon
ALLSPICE, 3/4 teaspoon (optional)
SALT, 1/2 teaspoon
INSTANT FLOUR, 2 tablespoons
BROWN SUGAR SUBSTITUTE, 1/3 to 1/2 cup granular; or substitute equal to 2/3 to 1 cup of sugar
BRANDY, 1/3 cup; or 1-1/2 teaspoons of rum flavoring

Make PIECRUST (see recipe). Quarter and core APPLES, but do not peel; grind with coarse blade. Grind RAISINS and LEMON (remove seeds); add to apples. Add CURRANTS, SPICES and other DRY INGREDIENTS; mix well. Add BRANDY; stir well to blend. Allow to stand at least 1 hour. This improves with age, so it may be made and refrigerated the day before needed. Roll out bottom crusts; put into pie plates; spread half of filling evenly on each crust. Prepare, put on and seal top crusts as directed. Bake at 475 degrees for 15 minutes, then at 375 degrees until center of top crust is nicely browned, about 50 minutes. Cool on rack. Do not cut until cool, or it will be soft and runny.

Suggestions: If you like mincemeat less spicy, cut spice amounts by a third or a half. The alcohol in the brandy evaporates during cooking and does not have to be counted.

For low-salt diet: Omit salt; use 1/2 teaspoon of salt substitute. Make crust by salt-free directions. Do not use on 400-milligram sodium or 1-gram salt diets. One-eighth of pie contains 42 milligrams of sodium.

PEACH CUSTARD PIE

Makes filling for one 8-inch pie. One serving (1/8 pie) equals 1 slice of bread and 1-1/2 teaspoons of fat; contains 147 Calories (P4, F7, C17), 32 milligrams of cholesterol if made with egg, 1 milligram of cholesterol if made with egg substitute.

PIE SHELL, 1, unbaked
FRESH PEACHES, 1-1/2 cups sliced; or drained dietetic peaches
SUGAR SUBSTITUTE, 2-1/2 tablespoons granular; or substitute equal to 1/3 cup of sugar
INSTANT FLOUR, 1 tablespoon; or quick-cooking tapioca
SKIM MILK, 1 cup
EGG, 1, and 1 EGG WHITE; or 2-1/4 ounces of liquid egg substitute
SALT, 1/4 teaspoon
ALMOND EXTRACT, 1/3 teaspoon
VANILLA, 1/4 teaspoon
NUTMEG, sprinkle
CINNAMON, sprinkle

Make PIE SHELL according to recipe. (If using frozen pie shell, allow to stand at room temperature while preparing filling to prevent sogginess.) Peel and slice FRESH PEACHES, or drain CANNED SLICES. For fresh peaches or unsweetened slices, sprinkle with 1-1/2 tablespoons of SUGAR SUBSTITUTE and mix well. Add FLOUR to MILK; let stand at least 10 minutes. Add beaten EGG or egg substitute to milk mixture. Add SALT, EXTRACTS, and 1 tablespoon of SUGAR SUBSTITUTE. Arrange peaches evenly in shell; sprinkle lightly with NUTMEG and CINNAMON. Cover peaches with egg-milk mixture; sprinkle top with spices, as before. Bake at 425 degrees until custard is set and fruit seems to separate slightly from custard, about 45 minutes. Cool on rack. Do not cut until cool, or it will be too soft.

Suggestions: You may substitute other canned fruit for the peaches, using the spices that best complement the fruit.

For low-salt diet: Omit salt; use 1/4 teaspoon of salt substitute. Make crust by salt-free directions. Do not use on 400-milligram sodium or 1-gram salt diets. One-eighth of a pie contains 42 milligrams of sodium.

PUMPKIN PIE OR CUSTARD

Makes two 8-inch pie fillings or 8 servings of custard. One serving (1/8 pie) equals 1 slice of bread and 1-1/2 teaspoons of fat; contains 147 Calories (P4, F7, C17), 32 milligrams of cholesterol if made with egg, 2 milligrams of cholesterol if made with egg substitute. One serving (1/2 cup) of custard equals 1/2 ounce of meat and 1/2 cup of fruit or 1/2 slice of bread; contains 49 Calories (P3, F1, C7), 37 milligrams of cholesterol if made with egg, 2 milligrams of cholesterol if made with egg substitute.

PIE SHELLS, 2, unbaked (optional)
SQUASH, 1-1/2 cups cooked; or pumpkin or pureed carrots
EGGS, 2; or 3 ounces of liquid egg substitute
EVAPORATED SKIM MILK, 1-1/2 cups
INSTANT FLOUR, 1/4 cup
BROWN SUGAR SUBSTITUTE, 4 tablespoons granular; or substitute equal to 1/2 cup of sugar. Use 6 tablespoons of sugar substitute with pumpkin or carrot.
GINGER, 1/2 teaspoon
CINNAMON, 1/2 teaspoon
NUTMEG, 1/2 teaspoon
CLOVES or ALLSPICE, 1/4 teaspoon
SALT, 1/4 teaspoon
VANILLA, 1/3 teaspoon

Make PIE SHELLS (see recipe). Add well-beaten EGGS to SQUASH; mix well. Stir in MILK. Combine DRY INGREDIENTS and add to mixture. Add VANILLA. For PIE pour into unbaked SHELLS; bake at 425 degrees for 15 minutes, then at 350 degrees for 45 minutes. Check with silver knife blade; it should come out clean if filling is done. For CUSTARD, spray baking dish with nonstick coating; pour in custard. Place dish in pan of hot water and bake at 350 degrees for about 1 hour. Test with knife blade, as above. Cool pie or custard on rack. Do not serve until at least lukewarm.

For low-salt diet: Omit salt; use 1/4 teaspoon of salt substitute. Make piecrust by salt-free directions. Do not use this recipe on a 400-milligram sodium or 1-gram salt diet. One-eighth of pie contains 45 milligrams of sodium.

RHUBARB PIE

Makes filling for one 8-inch pie. One serving (1/8 pie) equals 1 slice of bread, 1/2 cup of fruit and 2 teaspoons of fat; contains 211 Calories (P4, F11, C24), no cholesterol.

PIECRUST, 1/2 recipe
RHUBARB, 3-1/2 cups sliced 1/2-inch thick
APPLES, 1-1/2 cups peeled and diced
RED FOOD COLORING, 5 to 6 drops
INSTANT FLOUR, 1-1/2 tablespoons; or quick-cooking tapioca
LEMON JUICE, 2 tablespoons
SALT, sprinkle
SUGAR SUBSTITUTE, 1/2 cup granular; or substitute equal to 1-1/2 cups of sugar. Use more if you like it sweet.
MARGARINE, 1 tablespoon. Use corn-oil, soybean-oil or safflower-oil margarine.

Make PIECRUST (see recipe). Dice RHUBARB; add 1/3 cup of water; cover and cook until slightly soft. Drain in colander and save liquid. Dice APPLES small (dried apples should be soaked 24 hours in water); add 3/4 cup water; cover and simmer until slightly soft; remove from heat. Add RED FOOD COLORING to make apple as red as the rhubarb. Drain apples in colander; add liquid to rhubarb liquid. Add FLOUR, LEMON JUICE, SALT and SUGAR SUBSTITUTE to liquid; mix well. Add to fruit; stir to blend; set aside. Roll out bottom crust as directed; spoon in filling; smooth out. Dab MARGAR-INE onto fruit as evenly as possible. Add top crust. Bake at 475 degrees for 15 minutes, then at 375 degrees until center of top crust is well browned, about 45 minutes. Cool on rack. Do not cut until well cooled, or filling will be runny.

For low-salt diet: Omit salt; use salt substitute. Use salt-free margarine. Make crust by salt-free directions. One-eighth of pie contains 5 milligrams of sodium.

LEMON PIE OR PUDDING

Makes about 3 cups, enough for one 8-inch pie. One-half cup of filling equals 1/2 ounce of meat, 1 teaspoon of fat and 1/2 cup of fruit; contains 102 Calories (P4, F6, C8), 84 milligrams of cholesterol if made with egg, no cholesterol if made with egg substitute. One serving (1/8 pie) including crust and filling equals 1/2 ounce of meat, 2 teaspoons of fat and 1 slice of bread. Contains 183 Calories (P5, F11, C16), 63 milligrams of cholesterol if made with egg, no cholesterol if made with egg substitute.

PIE SHELL, 1, baked and cooled (optional)
INSTANT FLOUR, 1/3 cup
WATER, 1-1/4 cups
SALT, 2 sprinkles
LEMON JUICE, 1/4 cup plus 1 tablespoon
EGGS, 2; or 3 ounces of liquid egg substitute
MARGARINE, 2 tablespoons. Use corn-oil, soybean-oil or safflower-oil margarine.
SUGAR SUBSTITUTE, 4-1/2 teaspoons granular; or substitute equal to 3 tablespoons of sugar
DIET APPLESAUCE, 1/2 cup, artificially sweetened
LEMON RIND, up to 1 tablespoon
EGG WHITES, 2

Make SHELL for pie (see recipe). Mix FLOUR with WATER to make smooth paste; add SALT. Cook in double boiler, stirring constantly, until slightly thick. Remove from heat; add LEMON JUICE; cool slightly; add beaten EGGS, stirring well to prevent curdling. Add REMAINING INGREDIENTS, except lemon rind and egg whites. Return to heat in double boiler; cook, covered, about 10 minutes. Remove from heat; add LEMON RIND; set aside to cool. Beat EGG WHITES until very stiff; fold into cooked mixture, being gentle so the whites keep their lightness. Pour into baked pie shell; put into freezer to set firm. For pudding, spoon into parfait glasses and refrigerate until firm. Top with small sprigs of mint for garnish (optional).

For low-salt diet: Omit salt; use 2 sprinkles of salt substitute. Use salt-free margarine. Make crust by salt-free directions. Do not use on 400-milligram sodium or 1-gram salt diets. One-eighth of pie contains 52.5 milligrams of sodium. One serving (1/2 cup) of pudding contains 60 milligrams of sodium.

CHERRY TARTS

Makes 8 tarts. Half a tart equals 1/2 cup of fruit, 1/2 slice of bread and 1 teaspoon of fat; contains 155 Calories (P2, F7, C21), no cholesterol.

PIECRUST, 1/2 recipe
RED PIE CHERRIES, 2-1/2 cups (#2 can)
CORNSTARCH, 2-1/2 tablespoons
MARGARINE, 2 teaspoons. Use corn-oil, soybean-oil or safflower-oil margarine.
SALT, sprinkle
SUGAR SUBSTITUTE, 1/2 cup granular; or substitute equal to 1 cup of sugar
ALMOND EXTRACT, 1/2 to 3/4 teaspoon

Make PIECRUST (see recipe); roll thin; cut out tart shells and fit into pans; prick shells (especially the edges) with fork. Bake at 425 degrees until lightly browned, 10 to 12 minutes; allow to cool. Drain CHERRIES, saving liquid. Mix CORNSTARCH, MARGARINE, SALT and SUGAR SUBSTITUTE with CHERRY LIQUID. Cook slowly, stirring constantly, until thick. Remove from heat; add ALMOND EXTRACT and cherries; cool slightly. Pour cooled fruit mixture into cooled shells; allow to set at least 2 hours before serving. For faster thickening, let set in refrigerator.

Suggestions: If dieter's Calorie and fat allowances permit, serve with a tablespoon of vanilla ice cream (see recipe) for topping.

For low-salt diet: Omit sprinkle of salt; use salt substitute. Use salt-free margarine. Make piecrust by salt-free directions. One tart contains 3 milligrams of sodium.

Frozen Desserts

BUTTERMILK ICED DESSERT

Makes 8 servings, 1/2 cup each. One serving equals 1/2 cup of nonfat milk; contains 40 Calories (P4, F0, C6), 1 milligram of cholesterol.

BUTTERMILK, 3 cups
LEMON JUICE, 1/2 cup
LEMON RIND, 1 teaspoon grated
SUGAR SUBSTITUTE, 1/2 cup granular; or substitute equal to 1 cup of sugar
EGG WHITES, 2
SALT, 1/8 teaspoon
YELLOW FOOD COLORING, few drops

Combine BUTTERMILK, LEMON JUICE and RIND and SUGAR SUBSTITUTE; taste to be sure it is sweet enough. It is meant to be rather tart. Put in freezer and allow to chill until almost set. Remove from freezer; add EGG WHITES and SALT. Beat with rotary beater or mixer until very fluffy; add FOOD COLORING for a pale lemon color. Freeze in covered plastic container. Remove from freezer at least 15 minutes before serving.

For low-salt diet: This recipe cannot be made low in salt because of the natural sodium in the buttermilk and egg whites.

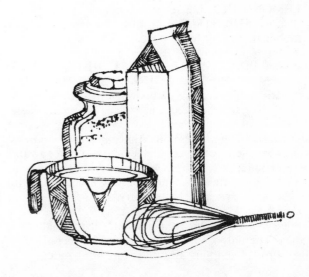

FRUIT POPSICLES

Makes 6 popsicles. One popsicle equals 1/2 cup of fruit; contains 40 Calories (P0, F0, C10), no cholesterol.

PINEAPPLE JUICE, 2 cups unsweetened
LEMON-LIME POP, 2 cups dietetic
LEMON RIND, 1/2 teaspoon grated
SUGAR SUBSTITUTE, up to 1 tablespoon granular (optional)

Combine PINEAPPLE JUICE and DIETETIC POP; add LEMON RIND and SUGAR SUBSTITUTE to taste; stir well to remove carbonation in the soft drink. Pour into popsicle molds, about 3/4 cup per mold; freeze.

Suggestions: You may use other juice-pop combinations, such as raspberry soda with diet lemonade (no food value there at all!), or root beer with apple juice. Use your imagination and experiment. You might come up with the flavor discovery of the century.

For low-salt diet: This recipe is fairly low in salt as it stands. The only sodium comes from the dietetic pop. One popsicle contains 16 milligrams of sodium.

BASIC VANILLA ICE CREAM

Makes 10 servings, 1/2 cup each. One serving equals 1/2 cup of fruit and 2 teaspoons of fat; contains 123 Calories (P3, F11, C13), 26 milligrams of cholesterol if made with egg, 1 milligram of cholesterol if made with egg substitute.

SKIM MILK, 2 cups
CORN OIL or SOYBEAN OIL, 1/2 cup
BUTTER FLAVORING, 16 drops
PLAIN GELATIN, 1 envelope (1 tablespoon)
WATER, 1/2 cup
EGG, 1; or 1-1/2 ounces of liquid egg substitute
SUGAR SUBSTITUTE, 1/2 cup granular; or substitute equal to 1 cup of sugar
VANILLA, 2 teaspoons
SALT, 1/2 teaspoon

Put MILK, OIL and BUTTER FLAVORING in blender; blend at top speed for 2 minutes to emulsify fat into milk. Add GELATIN to WATER; heat gently to dissolve. Add to milk. Beat EGG and add SUGAR SUBSTITUTE, VANILLA and SALT; combine with milk mixture; stir well. Place in electric ice-cream freezer and mix until almost hard according to instructions for your freezer. Put into covered plastic container and place in freezer to set until hard. Remove from freezer at least 15 minutes before serving.

Suggestions: If there is no cholesterol restriction, use 2-1/2 cups of half-and-half instead of milk, oil and butter flavoring; skip blender step. Calories and replacements are the same, except for cholesterol content. This basic ice cream can be varied by adding chopped fresh fruit or various flavorings. Add 2 tablespoons of unsweetened chocolate extract to 1/3 of the recipe, then streak it through the vanilla ice cream. No extra Calories need be counted for the chocolate.

For low-salt diet: Omit salt; use 1/2 teaspoon of salt substitute. Do not use this recipe for a 400-milligram sodium or 1-gram salt diet. One serving (1/2 cup) contains 35 milligrams of sodium.

VANILLA ICED MILK

Makes about 6 half-cup servings. One serving equals 1/2 cup of fruit and 1 ounce of meat; contains 64 Calories (P8, F0, C8), 3 milligrams of cholesterol.

SKIM MILK, 2 cups
SKIM MILK POWDER, 2/3 cup
PLAIN GELATIN, 1 envelope (1 tablespoon)
SUGAR SUBSTITUTE, 3 tablespoons granular; or substitute equal to 6 tablespoons of sugar
EGG WHITES, 2
LEMON RIND, 1 tablespoon grated
LEMON JUICE, 3 tablespoons
VANILLA, 1 tablespoon

In saucepan, dissolve MILK POWDER in LIQUID MILK; beat until smooth. Add GELATIN; stir; heat gently, stirring constantly, to dissolve gelatin. Remove from heat; add SUGAR SUBSTITUTE. Pour into freezer tray; freeze until frozen about 1 inch in from edges. Into mixer bowl put EGG WHITES, LEMON RIND and JUICE, and VANILLA; add milk mixture; beat at high speed for 2 minutes, until light and fluffy. Store in covered plastic container in freezer. Remove 15 minutes before serving.

For low-salt diet: This recipe cannot be made low in salt because of the natural sodium in the milk. Do not use on 400-milligram or 1-gram salt diets. One serving (1/2 cup) contains 95 milligrams of sodium.

COFFEE ICE CREAM

Makes about 5 cups. One serving (1/2 cup) equals 1/4 cup of fruit and 2 teaspoons of fat; contains 114 Calories (P3, F10, C3), 22 milligrams of cholesterol if made with egg, 1 milligram of cholesterol if made with egg substitute.

SKIM MILK, 2 cups
CORN OIL or SOYBEAN OIL, 1/2 cup
BUTTER FLAVORING, 16 drops
PLAIN GELATIN, 1 envelope (1 tablespoon)
WATER, 1/2 cup
EGG, 1; or 1-1/2 ounces of liquid egg substitute
SUGAR SUBSTITUTE, 1/2 cup granular; or substitute equal to 1 cup of sugar
DRY INSTANT COFFEE, 3-1/2 teaspoons, decaffeinated if preferred
SALT, 1/3 teaspoon
VANILLA, 1 teaspoon

Put MILK, OIL and BUTTER FLAVORING into blender; blend at top speed for 2 minutes to emulsify fat into milk. Dissolve GELATIN in WATER; heat gently to dissolve completely; add to milk mixture. Beat EGG well; add SUGAR SUBSTITUTE, COFFEE, SALT and VANILLA; mix well; add to milk mixture. Place in ice-cream freezer and mix until firm, following instructions for your freezer. When very firm, store in freezer. Be sure container is airtight to help prevent formation of crystals. Remove from freezer at least 15 minutes before serving.

Suggestions: If there is no cholesterol restriction, use 2-1/2 cups of half-and-half in place of the skim milk, oil and butter flavoring; skip the blender step.

For low-salt diet: Omit salt; use 1/3 teaspoon of salt substitute. Do not use this recipe for a 400-milligram sodium or 1-gram salt diet. One serving (1/2 cup) contains 35 milligrams of sodium.

MAPLE NUT ICE CREAM

Makes about 5-1/2 cups. One serving (1/2 cup) equals 1/4 cup of fruit and 2 teaspoons of fat; contains 132 Calories (P3, F12, C3), 22 milligrams of cholesterol if made with egg, 1 milligram of cholesterol if made with egg substitute.

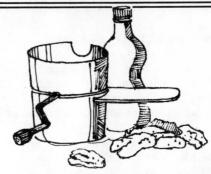

SKIM MILK, 2 cups
CORN OIL or SOYBEAN OIL, 1/2 cup
BUTTER FLAVORING, 16 drops
PLAIN GELATIN, 1 envelope (1 tablespoon)
WATER, 1/2 cup
EGG, 1, well beaten; or 1-1/2 ounces of liquid egg substitute
SUGAR SUBSTITUTE, 1/2 cup granular; or substitute equal to 1 cup of sugar
VANILLA, 2/3 teaspoon
MAPLE FLAVORING, 2-1/2 teaspoons
SALT, 1/2 teaspoon
WALNUTS, 1/2 cup chopped

Put MILK, OIL and BUTTER FLAVORING in blender; blend at top speed for 2 minutes to emulsify fat into milk. Add GELATIN to WATER; heat gently to dissolve. Add ALL INGREDIENTS except nuts to the milk; stir well. Put in electric freezer and mix until almost firm, using instructions for your freezer. Add NUTS; continue to freeze until very hard. Store in freezer in covered plastic containers. Remove from freezer at least 15 minutes before serving.

Suggestions: If there is no cholesterol restriction, use 2-1/2 cups of half-and-half in place of skim milk, oil and butter flavoring; skip the blender step.

For low-salt diet: Omit salt; use 1/2 teaspoon of salt substitute. Do not use this recipe for a 400-milligram sodium or 1-gram salt diet. One serving (1/2 cup) contains 35 milligrams of sodium.

RASPBERRY ROYAL ICE CREAM

Makes 11 servings, 1/2 cup each. One serving equals 1/4 cup of fruit and 2 teaspoons of fat; contains 135 Calories (P3, F11, C6), 24 milligrams of cholesterol if made with egg, 1 milligram of cholesterol if made with egg substitute.

SKIM MILK, 2 cups
CORN OIL, 1/2 cup
BUTTER FLAVORING, 16 drops
PLAIN GELATIN, 1 envelope (1 tablespoon)
WATER, 1/2 cup
EGG, 1, well beaten; or 1-1/2 ounces of liquid egg substitute
SUGAR SUBSTITUTE, 1/2 cup granular; or substitute equal to 1 cup of sugar
VANILLA, 1-1/2 teaspoons
SALT, 1/4 teaspoon
RASPBERRIES, 1-1/2 cups

Put MILK, OIL and BUTTER FLAVORING in blender; blend at top speed for 2 minutes to emulsify fat into milk. Add GELATIN to WATER; heat gently to dissolve. Add gelatin to milk; add OTHER INGREDI-ENTS except fruit. Mash half the BERRIES; add to milk mixture. Put in ice cream freezer and freeze until almost hard. Add whole berries; continue to freeze until hard. Store in covered plastic containers in freezer. Remove from freezer at least 15 minutes before serving.

Suggestions: Instead of raspberries, use strawberries, or blueberries with 2 sprinkles of nutmeg. If there is no cholesterol restriction, use 2-1/2 cups of half-and-half in place of milk, oil and butter flavoring; skip blender step.

For low-salt diet: Omit salt; use 1/4 teaspoon of salt substitute. Do not use on a 400-milligram sodium or 1-gram salt diet. One serving (1/2 cup) contains 30 milligrams of sodium.

REFRIGERATOR CHEESECAKE

Makes 8 servings. One serving equals 1-1/2 ounces of meat, 1 slice of bread and 1 teaspoon of fat; contains 207 Calories (P12, F11,C15), 6 milligrams of cholesterol.

FILLED MILK, 1 cup (see recipe)
DIETETIC PEARS, 10-1/2-ounce can, artificially sweetened
JUICE from pears
PLAIN GELATIN, 2 envelopes (2 tablespoons)
SALT, 1/2 teaspoon
SUGAR SUBSTITUTE, 1/2 cup granular; or substitute equal to 1 cup of sugar
COTTAGE CHEESE, 2 cups, drained
LEMON JUICE, 1 to 1-1/2 tablespoons
LEMON RIND, 1-3/4 tablespoons grated
EGG WHITES, 2
VANILLA, 1/3 teaspoon
SUGAR SUBSTITUTE, 2 tablespoons granular; or substitute equal to 1/4 cup of sugar

Crust:
RICE CHEX, 1 cup, crushed fine; Rice Krispies or shredded wheat
MARGARINE, 3 teaspoons. Use corn-oil, soybean-oil or safflower-oil margarine.

Prepare FILLED MILK (see recipe). Chill until very cold. Drain PEARS; put JUICE into saucepan and heat. Add GELATIN to warm juice; stir to dissolve completely.

Add SALT and 1/2 cup of SUGAR SUBSTITUTE to gelatin; stir well; add to filled milk. Chill well; remove from refrigerator and whip until thick. Put PEARS and COTTAGE CHEESE through food mill to remove any lumps; add to LEMON JUICE and RIND. Combine with gelatin-milk mixture; fold in gently. Whip EGG WHITES until very dry; add VANILLA and 2 tablespoons of sugar substitute. Fold in egg whites, gently. Grease deep pie plate with MARGARINE; coat lightly with crushed CEREAL. Pour in filling; allow to set until firm, about 1 hour, in refrigerator or freezer. It will set very hard in freezer. Serve cold in wedges.

Suggestions: You may make an excellent topping for this cheesecake with 4 tablespoons of diet orange marmalade. Thin with hot water to a good spreading consistency; spread on top of frozen pie; chill until topping gets hard. You do not have to allow extra Calories for the topping.

For low-salt diet: This recipe cannot be made low in salt because of the high natural sodium in the cottage cheese, filled milk and egg whites.

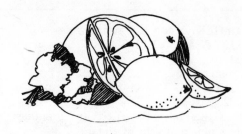

MOCK ORANGE SHERBET

Makes 4 servings, 1/2 cup each. One serving equals 1/2 cup of fruit; contains 24 Calories (P2, F0, C4), no cholesterol.

PLAIN GELATIN, 1 envelope (1 tablespoon)
WATER, 1-1/2 cups
LEMON JUICE, 2 teaspoons
LEMON or ORANGE RIND, 1-1/2 to 2 teaspoons grated
FROZEN ORANGE JUICE CONCENTRATE, 1/2 cup
SUGAR SUBSTITUTE, 1-1/2 teaspoons granular; or substitute equal to 1 tablespoon of sugar
SALT, sprinkle

Dissolve GELATIN in WATER; heat gently to complete dissolving. Add LEMON JUICE and RIND (use less to make it less lemony), ORANGE JUICE, SUGAR SUBSTITUTE and SALT. Mix well. Pour into loaf pan and allow to set in refrigerator or freezer until firm. Slice and serve as a frozen sherbet, or in parfait dishes as a gelatin dessert. (Allow frozen sherbet to stand at room temperature for 15 minutes before trying to cut it.)

Suggestions: You can make miniature Dixie Cups from this sherbet and freeze them for summer treats. Use colorful cups to make them attractive as well as tasty.

For low-salt diet: Omit salt; use sprinkle of salt substitute. One serving (1/4 recipe) contains 4 milligrams of sodium.

Gelatin Desserts

COFFEE JELLY

Makes 4 servings. No replacement. One serving (1/2 cup) contains 8 Calories (P2, F0, C0), no cholesterol.

PLAIN GELATIN, 1 envelope (1 tablespoon)
COLD WATER, 1/4 cup
COFFEE, 1-3/4 cups strong, decaffeinated if preferred
SUGAR SUBSTITUTE, 3 teaspoons granular; or substitute equal to 2 tablespoons of sugar
VANILLA, 1/2 teaspoon
SALT, sprinkle
CINNAMON, sprinkle (optional)

Dissolve GELATIN in 1/4 cup cold WATER; heat gently to dissolve completely. Add COFFEE, SUGAR SUBSTITUTE, VANILLA, SALT and CINNAMON; mix well. Pour into molds or bowl; refrigerate to set.

Suggestions: If diet allows, serve this with 1 teaspoon of diet ice cream as a topping; use regular ice cream or whipped cream for nondieters. As a variation, use 1 cup of double-strength instant coffee and 3/4 cup of juice from canned peaches or pears; omit vanilla and use slightly more cinnamon. This too can be used, up to 1/2 cup at a time, without replacement.

For low-salt diet: Omit salt; use sprinkle of salt substitute. Be sure to use a sprinkle of cinnamon; it will help the taste when made without salt. One serving (1/2 cup) contains 3 milligrams of sodium.

LEMON WHIP

Makes 6 servings, 1/2 cup each. One serving equals 1/4 cup of fruit; contains 24 Calories (P2, F0, C4), no cholesterol.

PLAIN GELATIN, 1 envelope (1 tablespoon)
WATER, 3/4 cup
DIET APPLESAUCE, 1/2 cup
SALT, 2 sprinkles
LEMON JUICE, 7 tablespoons
LEMON RIND, 1 tablespoon grated
YELLOW FOOD COLORING, 3 to 4 drops
SUGAR SUBSTITUTE, 1/4 cup granular; or substitute equal to 1/2 cup of sugar
EGG WHITE, 1 chilled

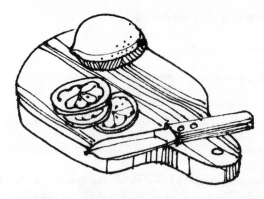

Dissolve GELATIN in WATER; warm gently to dissolve completely. Add APPLESAUCE, SALT, LEMON JUICE and RIND; mix well. Add enough FOOD COLORING to give lemon color. Taste; add SUGAR SUBSTITUTE to suit; if applesauce is fairly sweet, you will need as little as 2 teaspoons (equivalent to 1-1/2 tablespoons of sugar). Chill until thick and syrupy. Beat chilled EGG WHITE until very stiff; fold into chilled gelatin, using wire whip. Pile into parfait or sherbet glasses; chill until set; serve, perhaps with a thin twist of lemon on top for color.

Suggestions: Do not get this too sweet, or it will lose some of its appeal. The lemon rind flavor develops as it stands and will be considerably stronger the day after the dish is made.

For low-salt diet: Omit salt; use 2 sprinkles of salt substitute. One serving (1/2 cup) contains 4 milligrams of sodium.

FRUITED GELATIN

Makes 5 servings, 1/2 cup each. One serving equals 1/2 cup of fruit; contains 44 Calories (P1, F0, C10), no cholesterol.

PLAIN GELATIN, 1 envelope (1 tablespoon)
WATER, 1 cup
DIET-PACK PEACHES, 1/2 cup drained
DIET-PACK PINEAPPLE, 1/2 cup drained
JUICE, 1/2 cup from peaches and pineapple
LEMON JUICE, 1-1/2 tablespoons
LEMON RIND, 1/2 teaspoon (optional)
SUGAR SUBSTITUTE, 1-1/2 teaspoons granular; or substitute equal to 1 tablespoon of sugar
SALT, sprinkle
RED FOOD COLORING

Add GELATIN to WATER; let stand a few minutes, then heat gently to complete dissolving; set aside to cool. Slice or dice FRUIT into bite-size pieces. To 1/2 cup combined PEACH and PINEAPPLE JUICES, add LEMON JUICE and RIND, SUGAR SUBSTITUTE, SALT and FOOD COLORING to make a cherry color. Add juice to gelatin; add more coloring if needed to make color deep enough. Add diced fruit; pour into large mold or 5 individual molds; chill.

Suggestions: To change the appearance of this dessert, use pears in place of peaches and green food coloring instead of red, perhaps with 1/4 to 1/2 teaspoon of spearmint extract for flavor.

For low-salt diet: Omit salt; use sprinkle of salt substitute. One serving (1/5 recipe) contains 3 milligrams of sodium.

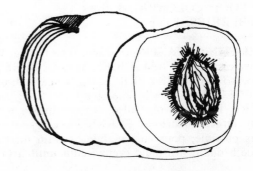

RASPBERRY MOLD

Makes 6 servings, about 3/4 cup each. One serving equals 1/2 cup of fruit; contains 48 Calories (P2, F0, C10), no cholesterol.

PLAIN GELATIN, 1 envelope (1 tablespoon)
WATER, 1/3 cup
ORANGE JUICE, 2/3 cup
LEMON JUICE, 1 tablespoon
SUGAR SUBSTITUTE, 3 tablespoons granular; or substitute equal to 6 tablespoons of sugar
SALT, sprinkle
RASPBERRIES, 1 cup pureed
RED FOOD COLORING, 4 drops
RASPBERRIES, 1 cup

Add GELATIN to WATER; let stand, then heat gently to dissolve completely. Add JUICES, SUGAR SUBSTI-TUTE, SALT and BERRY PUREE; stir to mix well; add FOOD COLORING to get a pleasing pink. Chill until fairly thick. Pour half of chilled mixture into a mold (5-cup or larger); distribute BERRIES over gelatin as evenly as possible; pour on remaining gelatin mixture and smooth out to fill mold evenly; chill until firm.

Suggestions: Strawberries would be as good for this dish, and less seedy. You can make this in winter with frozen berries. If using frozen whole berries, do not thaw before adding. Serve on a bed of washed maple, apple or other leaves.

For low-salt diet: Omit salt; use sprinkle of salt substitute. One serving (3/4 cup) contains 3 milligrams of sodium.

Puddings

BERRY PARFAIT

Makes 4 servings. One serving equals 1/2 cup of fruit and 1/2 ounce of meat; contains 66 Calories (P2, F2, C10), 2 milligrams of cholesterol.

BERRIES, 1 cup fresh. Use strawberries, raspberries or boysenberries.
SKIM MILK, 1 cup
CORNSTARCH, 2 tablespoons
MARGARINE, 2 teaspoons melted. Use corn-oil, soybean-oil or safflower-oil margarine.
SALT, 1/8 teaspoon
SUGAR SUBSTITUTE, 1-1/2 tablespoons granular; or substitute equal to 3 tablespoons of sugar
VANILLA or ALMOND EXTRACT, 1/8 teaspoon

Slice 1/2 cup of BERRIES; puree 1/2 cup of berries; keep out 4 small, perfect berries for garnish. Add CORNSTARCH to MILK; stir well; add melted MARGARINE. Add OTHER INGREDIENTS; stir to mix completely. Cook in double boiler, stirring constantly, until fairly thick. Remove from heat; add pureed berries and sugar substitute to taste; cool. Put sliced berries in bottoms of 4 parfait glasses; spoon in cooked and cooled mixture; top each with a whole berry. Serve very cold.

For low-salt diet: Omit salt; use 1/8 teaspoon of salt substitute. Use salt-free margarine. Do not use on 400-milligram sodium or 1-gram salt diets. One serving contains 52 milligrams of sodium.

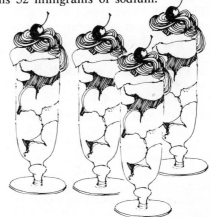

FRUIT COCKTAIL PUDDING

Makes 3 servings. One serving equals 1/2 cup of fruit; contains 36 Calories (P0, F0, C9), no cholesterol.

DIETETIC FRUIT COCKTAIL, 2 cups sweetened
CORNSTARCH, 1-1/2 tablespoons
SALT, 1/8 teaspoon
LEMON JUICE, 1 tablespoon
LEMON RIND, 1/3 teaspoon grated

Drain FRUIT COCKTAIL, saving juice; add water to juice to make total of 2/3 cup of liquid. Mix CORNSTARCH, SALT and LEMON JUICE into liquid. Cook slowly, stirring frequently, until thick. Remove from heat; add fruit cocktail and LEMON RIND. Cool before serving.

Suggestions: This pudding, layered alternately with Vanilla Cornstarch Pudding (see recipe) in parfait glasses, makes an excellent dessert. If combining in equal parts, 1 serving equals 1 slice of bread.

For low-salt diet: Omit salt; use 1/8 teaspoon of salt substitute. One serving contains 7 milligrams of sodium.

DOUBLE CHOCOLATE PUDDING

Makes 4 servings. One serving, plain, equals 1/2 cup of fruit and 1 teaspoon of fat; contains 85 Calories (P3, F4, C9), no cholesterol. One serving with raisins equals 1 slice of bread and 1 teaspoon of fat; contains 105 Calories (P3, F4, C14), no cholesterol.

COCOA, 1-3/4 to 2 tablespoons, to taste
CORNSTARCH, 2 tablespoons
INSTANT COFFEE GRANULES, 1/8 teaspoon, decaffeinated if preferred
SALT, 1/8 teaspoon
WATER, 1 cup
SKIM MILK, 1 cup
MARGARINE, 1 tablespoon. Use corn-oil, soybean-oil or safflower-oil margarine.
RAISINS, 2 tablespoons, soaked in hot water (optional)
SUGAR SUBSTITUTE, 1/2 cup granular; or substitute equal to 1 cup of sugar
VANILLA, 2 teaspoons
CINNAMON, 1/8 teaspoon
CHOCOLATE EXTRACT, 1/2 teaspoon unsweetened

Mix COCOA, CORNSTARCH, COFFEE GRANULES, SALT and WATER in top of double boiler; add MILK. Cook, stirring frequently, until it starts to thicken. Add MARGARINE; continue cooking and stirring until thick. Remove from heat; add RAISINS. Add SUGAR SUBSTITUTE, VANILLA, CINNAMON and CHOCOLATE EXTRACT; mix well. Pour into 4 serving dishes. Allow to cool before serving.

Suggestions: For nondieters, serve with a topping of whipped cream or vanilla ice cream. For the dieter, serve plain or with skim milk.

For low-salt diet: Omit salt; use 1/8 teaspoon of salt substitute. Use salt-free margarine. Use breakfast cocoa or just plain, old-fashioned cocoa. Do not use Dutch-process cocoa. Do not use on 400-milligram sodium or 1-gram salt diets. One serving contains 36 milligrams of sodium.

MARBLED BERRY-TAPIOCA PUDDING

Makes 6 servings. One serving (1/2 cup) equals 1/2 ounce of meat and 1/2 cup of fruit; contains 76 Calories (P5, F1, C12), 37 milligrams of cholesterol if made with egg, 1 milligram of cholesterol if made with egg substitute.

TAPIOCA, 3 tablespoons quick-cooking
EGG, 1; or 1-1/2 ounces of liquid egg substitute
SKIM MILK, 2-3/4 cups
SUGAR SUBSTITUTE, 2-1/2 tablespoons granular; or substitute equal to 1/3 cup of sugar
VANILLA, 1/4 teaspoon
SALT, 1/2 teaspoon
BERRY JAM, 3 tablespoons dietetic

In top of double boiler put TAPIOCA, beaten EGG and MILK; stir; let stand at least 15 minutes to moisten tapioca. Heat to boiling point, stirring constantly; boil for 1 minute; remove from heat. Add SUGAR SUBSTITUTE, VANILLA and SALT; stir well; drop BERRY JAM on by spoonfuls, then use a knife to streak jam through the pudding. Spoon equally into 6 individual serving dishes. Cool before serving.

For low-salt diet: Omit salt; use 1/4 teaspoon of salt substitute. This recipe cannot be made low in sodium. Do not use on 400-milligram sodium or 1-gram salt diets. One serving contains 85 milligrams of sodium.

PEANUT BUTTER TAPIOCA PUDDING

Makes 6 servings. One serving (about 1/2 cup) equals 1 ounce of meat and 1 slice of bread; contains 155 Calories (P8, F7, C15), 40 milligrams of cholesterol if made with egg, about 4 milligrams of cholesterol if made with egg substitute.

TAPIOCA, 3 tablespoons quick-cooking
EGG, 1; or 1-1/2 ounces of liquid egg substitute
SKIM MILK, 2-3/4 cups
PEANUT BUTTER, 5 tablespoons old-fashioned
SUGAR SUBSTITUTE, 3 tablespoons granular; or substitute equal to about 1/3 cup of sugar
SALT, 1/4 teaspoon
VANILLA, 1/2 teaspoon
NUTMEG, sprinkle (optional)

In top of double boiler put TAPIOCA, beaten EGG and MILK; stir well; allow to stand at least 15 minutes to moisten tapioca. Heat to boiling, stirring often to prevent sticking; boil 1 minute; remove from heat. Add PEANUT BUTTER; stir well; add SUGAR SUBSTITUTE and FLAVORINGS; stir again. Portion equally into 6 individual serving dishes; cool before serving.

Suggestions: Peanut-butter lovers will prefer this dish with crunchy-style peanut butter. Be sure to use the old-fashioned style, with no sugar or corn syrup added.

For low-salt diet: Omit salt; use 1/3 teaspoon of salt substitute. Use salt-free peanut butter. This recipe cannot be made low in sodium because of the high natural sodium content of egg or egg substitute and milk. Do not use on 400-milligram sodium or 1-gram salt diets. One serving (1/6 recipe) contains about 90 milligrams of sodium.

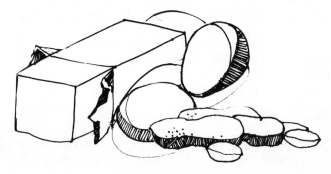

DOUBLE CHOCOLATE TAPIOCA PUDDING

Makes 6 half-cup servings. One serving equals 1/2 ounce of meat and 1/2 cup of fruit; contains 69 Calories (P4, F1, C11), 37 milligrams of cholesterol if made with egg, 1 milligram of cholesterol if made with egg substitute.

TAPIOCA, 3 tablespoons quick-cooking
BREAKFAST COCOA, 1-1/2 tablespoons
INSTANT COFFEE GRANULES, 1/8 teaspoon for mocha taste (optional)
SALT, 1/8 teaspoon
SKIM MILK, 2 cups
WATER, 3/4 cup
EGG, 1 well beaten, or 1-1/2 ounces of liquid egg substitute
SUGAR SUBSTITUTE, 4-1/2 tablespoons granular; or substitute equal to 9 tablespoons of sugar
VANILLA, 1-1/4 teaspoons
CHOCOLATE EXTRACT, 1/2 teaspoon unsweetened

Put TAPIOCA, COCOA, INSTANT COFFEE and SALT into top of double boiler. Add MILK, WATER and beaten EGG; stir well. Let stand at least 15 minutes to moisten tapioca. Bring slowly to boil, stirring frequently; boil for 1 minute. Remove from heat; add SUGAR SUBSTITUTE, VANILLA and CHOCOLATE EXTRACT. Mix well. Pour equal portions into 6 serving dishes; cool before serving.

Suggestions: For nondieters, serve with a topping of whipped cream or vanilla ice cream.

For low-salt diet: Omit salt; use 1/8 teaspoon of salt substitute. Use plain or breakfast cocoa, not Dutch-process cocoa. Do not use on 400-milligram sodium or 1-gram salt diets. One serving contains 70 milligrams of sodium.

TAPIOCA CREAM

Makes 4 servings. One serving equals 1/2 cup of fruit and 1/2 ounce of meat; contains 68 Calories (P5, F0, C12) and 3 milligrams of cholesterol if made with egg white, 77 Calories (P5, F1, C12) and 0 milligrams of cholesterol if made with egg substitute.

SKIM MILK, 2 cups
TAPIOCA, 3 tablespoons quick-cooking
BUTTER FLAVORING, 4 drops
EGG WHITE, 1; or 3/4 ounce of liquid egg substitute
SALT, 1/4 teaspoon
SUGAR SUBSTITUTE, 2-1/2 tablespoons granular; or substitute equal to 1/3 cup of sugar
VANILLA, 1 teaspoon

Soak TAPIOCA in 1/2 cup of MILK. Scald remaining milk; cool slightly. Add BUTTER FLAVORING and tapioca to WARM MILK; add EGG SUBSTITUTE, if using. Cook in double boiler, stirring constantly until fairly thick; remove from heat (the mixture will thicken more as it cools). Add SALT, SUGAR SUBSTITUTE and VANILLA; mix well. If using EGG WHITE, beat until stiff and fold into tapioca mixture. Cool and serve.

Suggestions: Add diet-pack diced pineapple to tapioca just before serving. Use 1/2 cup of fruit and make 5 servings. No change in food value.

For low-salt diet: Omit salt; use 1/4 teaspoon of salt substitute. Do not use on 400-milligram sodium or 1-gram salt diets. One serving contains 76 milligrams of sodium.

FRUIT RICE PUDDING

Makes 6 servings. One serving equals 1 slice of bread and 1/2 ounce of meat; contains 83 Calories (P3, F3, C11), 32 milligrams of cholesterol if made with egg, 1 milligram of cholesterol if made with egg substitute.

COOKED RICE, 1 cup (1/3 cup raw)
EGG, 1; or 1-1/2 ounces of liquid egg substitute
SKIM MILK, 1 cup
DATES, 2, chopped
WALNUTS, 8 halves, chopped
RAISINS, 2 tablespoons cut in half
SUGAR SUBSTITUTE, 2-1/2 tablespoons granular; or substitute equal to 5 tablespoons of sugar
CINNAMON, 1/2 teaspoon
NUTMEG, 1/8 teaspoon
SALT, 1/4 teaspoon
WATER, 1/2 cup

Cook 1/3 cup of RICE until tender; drain and set aside. Beat EGG; add to MILK. Chop DATES, NUTS and RAISINS. Add DRY INGREDIENTS to milk-egg mixture; add WATER; add rice; mix well. Put into lightly oiled baking dish; put dish in pan of hot water; bake at 325 degrees until browned on top, about 1 hour. Divide into 6 equal portions.

Suggestions: This pudding may be made with 4 tablespoons of raisins instead of half dates and half raisins.

For low-salt diet: Omit salt; use 1/4 teaspoon of salt substitute. Do not salt the cooking water for the rice. Do not use on 400-milligram sodium or 1-gram salt diets. One serving contains 48 milligrams of sodium.

VANILLA CORNSTARCH PUDDING

Makes 5 servings. One serving equals 1/2 cup of fruit and 1/2 ounce of meat; contains 74 Calories (P4, F2, C10), 52 milligrams of cholesterol if made with egg, 2 milligrams of cholesterol if made with egg substitute.

SKIM MILK, 2 cups
CORNSTARCH, 3-1/2 tablespoons
SALT, 1/4 teaspoon
EGG, 1; or 1-1/2 ounces of liquid egg substitute
BUTTER FLAVORING, 6 drops
MARGARINE, 1 teaspoon. Use corn-oil, soybean-oil or safflower-oil margarine.
VANILLA, 1 teaspoon

Add enough MILK to CORNSTARCH to make smooth paste; stir in rest of milk. Add SALT; cook in double boiler, stirring frequently, until it starts to thicken; cover; turn down heat; let cook for about 10 minutes. Remove from heat; cool slightly. Add part of mixture to beaten EGG, beating well to avoid lumps; add BUTTER FLAVORING and MARGARINE; return to cooking pot; cook about 2 minutes longer. Remove from heat; add VANILLA. Divide into 5 equal servings; chill.

Suggestions: Add sliced banana for banana-cream pudding or pie filling. Or add drained fruit cocktail, mixed in or as topping. Allow extra food value for added fruit.

For low-salt diet: Omit salt; use 1/4 teaspoon of salt substitute. Use salt-free margarine. Do not use on a 400-milligram sodium or 1-gram salt diet. One serving contains 82 milligrams of sodium.

Dessert Sauces

DOUBLE CHOCOLATE SAUCE

Makes about 2 cups. One-fourth cup equals 1/4 cup of fruit; contains 33 Calories (P1, F1, C5), no cholesterol.

BREAKFAST COCOA, 1-1/2 to 2-1/2 tablespoons, depending on how strong you like chocolate
CORNSTARCH, 1-1/4 tablespoons
SALT, 1/8 teaspoon
INSTANT COFFEE GRANULES, 1/4 teaspoon, decaffeinated if preferred (optional)
WATER, 1 cup
SKIM MILK, 1 cup
VANILLA, 2 teaspoons
SUGAR SUBSTITUTE, 1/2 cup granular; or substitute equal to 1-1/3 cups of sugar. Use 2/3 cup for 2-1/2 tablespoons of cocoa.
CHOCOLATE EXTRACT, 1/2 teaspoon unsweetened (optional)

In saucepan combine COCOA, CORNSTARCH, SALT and COFFEE GRANULES; gradually add enough WATER to make a paste, then remainder of water. Add MILK; stir well. Cook over low heat, stirring constantly until thickened. Remove from heat; add REMAINING INGREDIENTS; mix well. Serve hot on pudding or dietetic ice cream, or refrigerate for later use cold.

For low-salt diet: Use old-fashioned plain cocoa, if you can find it; if not, use breakfast cocoa powder but not Dutch-process cocoa. Omit salt; use 1/8 teaspoon of salt substitute. One-quarter cup contains 17 milligrams of sodium.

FRUIT SAUCE

Makes 1 cup. One serving (1/8 cup) equals 1/4 cup of fruit; contains 20 Calories (P0, F0, C5), no cholesterol.

JUICE, 1 cup, blended from diet-pack peaches and pears, or other fruits
CORNSTARCH, 1 tablespoon
LEMON JUICE, 3 tablespoons
SALT, sprinkle
LEMON RIND or ORANGE RIND, 1/4 teaspoon grated
SUGAR SUBSTITUTE, 1 tablespoon granular; or substitute equal to 2 tablespoons of sugar

Save JUICE from canned dietetic peaches and pears until you have 1 cup. Blend CORNSTARCH with LEMON JUICE to make smooth paste; stir into fruit juice. Add SALT. Cook in double boiler until mixture thickens and becomes somewhat clear, about 5 minutes. Cover and cook about 10 minutes more, stirring occasionally. Remove from heat; add LEMON RIND and SUGAR SUBSTITUTE; stir well. Serve hot on biscuit or hot apple pie. For pie topping, add cinnamon if desired.

Suggestions: Add 1/4 cup of fruit to each 1/4 cup of sauce, allowing 1/2 cup of fruit per serving. For pie topping, add 1/4 teaspoon of cinnamon just before covering for final cooking.

For low-salt diet: Omit salt; use sprinkle of salt substitute. Be sure to use grated rind for extra flavoring. One-fourth cup contains 1 milligram of sodium.

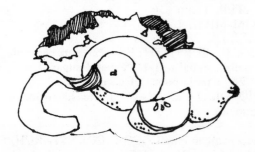

10. Snacks & Spreads

The snack foods are often not allowed on diets, and finding interesting sandwich spreads for the dieter is always a problem. The recipes given here are low in cholesterol and moderate in Calories. Don't be dismayed by the combinations of ingredients. Try them—you may find you really like them.

FRUIT SQUARES

Makes 25 squares. Two squares equal 1 slice of bread and 1 teaspoon of fat; contain 91 Calories (P3, F3, C13), no cholesterol.

DRIED FRUIT, 6 ounces. Use apples, apricots, peaches and pears, or prunes.
WATER, 2 cups
CORNSTARCH or INSTANT FLOUR, 1 tablespoon
LEMON JUICE, 1 tablespoon
SALT, 1/8 teaspoon
PLAIN GELATIN, 2 envelopes (2 tablespoons)
LEMON EXTRACT or RIND, 1/4 teaspoon
WALNUTS, 1/2 cup, chopped into eighths
SUGAR SUBSTITUTE, to taste, about 1-1/2 teaspoons granular; or substitute equal to 1 tablespoon of sugar

Cook DRIED FRUIT in WATER until tender; add a little more water if it gets too dry to prevent sticking and scorching. Puree in food mill to remove any skins or fibers. Add CORNSTARCH, LEMON JUICE, SALT and enough water to prevent sticking. Cook slowly until the cornstarch is cooked and the color clears, stirring often. Dissolve GELATIN in hot mixture; stir well to blend. Remove from heat; add LEMON, WALNUTS and SUGAR SUBSTITUTE. Mix well; pour into 8- or 9-inch square pan lined with wax paper or foil. Cool until firm. Cut into 25 parts, 5 each way in the pan. Optional: Sift 1 tablespoon of cornstarch over squares to keep them from sticking together; turn them to cover all sides.

Suggestions: You can vary these greatly by changing the fruit used. Equal parts of apple, apricot and pear make a very good combination. Prunes make the least attractive color. It is better to use prunes by themselves or with apple only.

For low-salt diet: Omit salt; use 1/8 teaspoon of salt substitute. One square contains 2 milligrams of sodium.

Using fine grater, grate RINDS onto Teflon cookie sheet; spread over sheet, avoiding large clumps. Place on top rack of oven preheated to 200 degrees; turn heat control to 150 degrees; leave in oven for 1-1/2 hours, or until completely dry; remove and let cool. Crush any lumps with bottom of tumbler or rolling pin covered with waxed paper. Store in airtight container. Do not leave in bright sunlight or some color will be lost. Refrigeration not needed.

Suggestions: Most, if not all, dried fruit rind on the market has been sugared. Read the label and you will see that dextrose is a principal ingredient. Make your own to have something you can safely use—and save money. Use slightly more orange than lemon rind for a less bitter flavor; use grapefruit rind in the same proportion as lemon. You will not usually notice the difference in a recipe. About 3 tablespoons of wet ingredients yield 1-1/2 tablespoons of dry material. Use about half the fresh amount called for in a recipe. If you wish, add a small amount of liquid to the dry rind and allow to remoisten before using.

For low-salt diet: Sodium content is negligible; no changes are required.

GRATED FRUIT RIND

No substitution required. Calories negligible.

CITRUS FRUIT, 1 or 2 lemons or oranges, 1 grapefruit, or all three mixed

VEGETABLE NIBBLERS

Makes about 2 quarts of vegetables. One cup equals 1 serving of semistarchy vegetable; contains 28 Calories (P0, F0, C7), no cholesterol. No allowance need be made for the marinade.

Marinade:
  WATER, 4 cups
  SUGAR SUBSTITUTE, 1/4 cup granular; or substitute equal to 1/2 cup of sugar
  SALT, 1/4 cup
  WHITE VINEGAR, 1/2 cup
Vegetables:
  CELERY sticks
  CARROT sticks
  CAULIFLOWER buds
  GREEN PEPPER sections
  SMALL ONIONS, or sections of larger onions or onion slices
  TOMATO wedges
  TURNIP or RUTABAGA slices
  OTHER RAW VEGETABLES to suit your taste

Prepare MARINADE; mix well to dissolve all solids. Pour over RAW VEGETABLES; let stand overnight in refrigerator. Serve in marinade, or drain and serve.

Suggestions: An excellent nibbling food for the cocktail hour, low-Calorie and appetizing.

For low-salt diet: Omit salt; use salt substitute. Omit celery and turnip; use fewer carrot sticks, which are high in sodium. One-half cup contains 6 to 12 milligrams of sodium, depending upon vegetables used.

FILLED MILK (Imitation Half-and-Half)

Makes about 2-1/2 cups. Two tablespoons equal 1/4 slice of bread and 1 teaspoon of fat; contain 70 Calories (P1, F6, C3), 3 milligrams of cholesterol.

  SKIM MILK, 2 cups
  CORN OIL or SOYBEAN OIL, 4 ounces
  BUTTER FLAVORING, 16 drops
  SALT, sprinkle

Put ALL INGREDIENTS into blender bowl. Blend at top speed for 2 minutes to emulsify oil with milk. Refrigerate to keep stable.

Suggestions: This milk can be substituted for cream in any recipe. It is almost equivalent to half-and-half but has practically no cholesterol.

For low-salt diet: Omit sprinkle of salt; use salt substitute. One ounce contains 14 milligrams of sodium.

HOLIDAY SNACK MIX

Makes about 10 cups. One-half cup equals 1/2 slice of bread and 2 teaspoons of fat; contains 121 Calories (P2, F9, C8), no cholesterol.

SHREDDED WHEAT, 3 cups miniature biscuits
PUFFED WHEAT or PUFFED RICE, 3 cups
THIN PRETZELS, 3 cups
WALNUTS, 1 cup of halves, broken into quarters or eighths
MARGARINE, 2/3 cup melted. Use corn-oil soybean-oil or safflower-oil margarine.

ONION POWDER, 1/2 teaspoon
GARLIC POWDER, 1/3 teaspoon
WORCESTERSHIRE SAUCE, 1 teaspoon
SALT, 1/2 teaspoon (optional)

Combine CEREALS, PRETZELS and NUTS in a large bowl. Melt MARGARINE and add all SEASONINGS. Pour margarine mix over cereals; stir well to coat all. Spread on baking sheet; put into oven at 200 degrees for about 20 minutes; stir every 5 minutes to brown evenly. Cool; store in airtight container in cool place. Will keep well for about 2 weeks.

Suggestions: You may vary the ingredients, but only the dry cereals listed are completely sugar-free and fat-free. If you want more margarine, double the amount and allow twice as much fat—3 teaspoons of fat per 1/2 cup of mix.

For low-salt diet: Omit salt; use 1/2 teaspoon of salt substitute. Use salt-free margarine. Omit pretzels; use 4-1/2 cups of miniature shredded wheat and 4-1/2 cups of puffed wheat, or 3 cups each of shredded wheat, puffed wheat and puffed rice. One-half cup contains 3 milligrams of sodium.

LEMON GINGER DRINK

Makes 3 servings, poured over crushed ice. One serving equals 1/2 cup of fruit; contains 32 Calories (P0, F0, C8), no cholesterol.

ORANGE JUICE, 1/2 cup; or 1/3 cup of unsweetened pineapple juice
LEMON JUICE, 1/2 cup
SUGAR SUBSTITUTE, 1-1/2 tablespoons granular; or substitute equal to 3 tablespoons of sugar
GINGER ALE, 2 cups dietetic
ICE CUBES, crushed
GARNISH, slices of lemon or orange, or a sprig of mint

Combine ORANGE JUICE and LEMON JUICE. Add SUGAR SUBSTITUTE; stir well. Combine with GINGER ALE; mix gently to avoid losing the carbonation. Pour over CRUSHED ICE in tall glasses; GARNISH with slice of fruit.

Suggestions: This can be made a little ahead of time, but not long. A sprig of peppermint or spearmint, if available, will give a faint mint flavor.

For low-salt diet: This recipe cannot be made lower in salt because of the diet ginger ale. Do not use on 400-milligram sodium or 1-gram salt diets. One serving contains 34 milligrams of sodium.

MOCK SOUR CREAM

Makes about 1-1/2 cups. Three tablespoons equal 1/2 ounce of meat; contain 29 Calories (P4, F1, C1), 1 milligram of cholesterol. You may use 1-1/2 tablespoons without substitution.

LIQUID PECTIN, 4 to 6 tablespoons
COTTAGE CHEESE, 1 cup low-fat
LEMON JUICE, 2 tablespoons
SKIM MILK, 1 tablespoon

Put 4 tablespoons of PECTIN and OTHER INGREDIENTS into blender jar; blend at high speed for 1 minute. Check for smoothness; if some graininess still shows, add 2 tablespoons of pectin and blend 1 minute longer at highest speed. Store covered in refrigerator. Will usually keep about 10 days without separating.

Suggestions: Use as a sour cream substitute on baked potato or in stroganoff, for example. Use as a dip for raw vegetables (see Party Dip recipe). Use with sugar substitute for fruit dressing (1/4 teaspoon of liquid sugar substitute, 1/2 teaspoon of celery seed and 1/2 cup of Mock Sour Cream, with 1/2 teaspoon of lemon juice to thin). Use with 2 teaspoons of imitation bacon bits and 1 teaspoon of chopped chives for fancier baked potato dressing.

For low-salt diet: Wash cottage cheese with cold water until water runs clear to remove salt added in processing. One tablespoon contains about 31 milligrams of sodium. Do not use on 400-milligram sodium or 1-gram salt diets. If you can find unsalted cottage cheese, it has about 1/3 less sodium content.

TASTY PARTY DIP

Makes about 1-1/2 cups. Three tablespoons equal 1/2 ounce of meat; contain 29 Calories (P4, F1, C1), no cholesterol. You may use 1-1/2 tablespoons without substitution.

MOCK SOUR CREAM, 1-1/2 cups (see recipe)
GARLIC, 1/2 teaspoon finely minced
PARSLEY, 1/2 teaspoon diced fresh
DRY MUSTARD, 1/4 teaspoon; or 6 drops of Worcestershire sauce
HORSERADISH, 1/2 teaspoon
TABASCO, 3 to 4 drops
THYME, pinch
SALT, to taste
LEMON JUICE, about 1 tablespoon (optional)

Make MOCK SOUR CREAM (see recipe). Mix OTHER INGREDIENTS except lemon juice, together; stir gently into Mock Sour Cream. Taste; add SALT if desired; thin with LEMON JUICE if needed.

Suggestions: This dip is delicious served on a tray with a variety of raw vegetables for dipping. It is especially good on raw cauliflower, turnip or rutabaga. Experiment!

For low-salt diet: Omit salt; use salt substitute to taste. Make Mock Sour Cream by low-salt directions. Do not use on 400-milligram sodium or 1-gram salt diets. One tablespoon contains 40 milligrams of sodium.

CHRISTINE'S DIETETIC GRANOLA

Makes about 9 cups. One serving (1/4 cup) equals 1 slice of bread and 1 teaspoon of fat; contains 130 Calories (P4, F6, C15), no cholesterol.

OATMEAL, 4 cups (not instant)
4-GRAIN CEREAL, 2 cups
WHEAT GERM, 1/2 cup
SESAME SEEDS, 3 tablespoons
SUNFLOWER KERNELS, 1/2 cup
PECAN CHIPS, 1-5/8-ounce package
WALNUT or ALMOND CHIPS, 1-5/8-ounce package
SALT, 1/2 teaspoon
MARGARINE, 1/3 cup. Use corn-oil, soybean-oil or safflower-oil margarine.
BROWN SUGAR SUBSTITUTE, 1/3 cup granular; or substitute equal to 2/3 cup of sugar
RAISINS, 3/4 cup

Combine DRY INGREDIENTS except sugar substitute and raisins. Melt MARGARINE and dribble over dry ingredients; mix well. Sprinkle SUGAR SUBSTITUTE over all; mix again; add RAISINS. Spread on baking pan; bake at 300 degrees, stirring every 5 minutes until slightly browned, 20 to 25 minutes. Remove from oven and let cool; stir occasionally to speed cooling. Pack in covered containers and store in cool place.

Suggestions: The raisins will be quite different in texture if you add them after baking, rather than before. See granola cookie recipe for a very special cookie made from this mixture.

For low-salt diet: Omit salt; use 1/2 teaspoon of salt substitute. Use salt-free margarine. One-fourth cup contains 3 milligrams of sodium.

CHEESE AND PICKLE SPREAD

Makes 1 to 2 servings. One serving (1/2 recipe) equals 1 ounce of meat; contains 80 Calories (P5, F5, C2), 12 milligrams of cholesterol.

LOW-FAT CHEESE, 2 ounces, 5% butterfat or less
EXTENDED MAYONNAISE, 1 tablespoon (see recipe)
DILL PICKLE, 1 to 2 tablespoons minced
DILL WEED, sprinkle (optional)

Allow CHEESE to soften to room temperature; with large spoon or spatula, mash into an even, soft pile. Add MAYONNAISE, PICKLE and DILL WEED; cream well. Spread on bread or crackers.

Suggestions: Bread that has been spread may become soggy, so keep refrigerated until eaten. If leftover spread weeps, recream.

For low-salt diet: This recipe cannot be made low in salt.

CHICKEN OR TURKEY SALAD SPREAD

Makes 1 to 2 servings. One-half recipe equals 1 ounce of meat; contains 73 Calories (P7, F5, C0), 32 milligrams of cholesterol.

CHICKEN or TURKEY, 2 ounces without skin, chopped or coarse-ground
CELERY, 1 tablespoon diced
CHIVES, 1/2 teaspoon minced
GREEN PEPPER or PIMENTO, 1/2 teaspoon diced
MAYONNAISE, 1 teaspoon
YOGURT, 1 tablespoon plain low-fat
CIDER VINEGAR, 1/4 teaspoon
SALT, PEPPER and PAPRIKA, sprinkles

Put MEAT into mixing bowl; add VEGETABLES; mix well. Combine MAYONNAISE, YOGURT, VINEGAR and SEASONINGS; add to first mixture; mix thoroughly. Taste; add seasonings to suit.

For low-salt diet: Cook chicken or turkey without salt. Use salt-free mayonnaise. Omit salt; use sprinkle of salt substitute. One-half recipe contains about 24 milligrams of sodium.

FISH SALAD SPREAD

Makes 1 to 2 servings. One-half recipe equals 1 ounce of meat; contains 85 Calories (P7, F6, C1), about 30 milligrams of cholesterol.

TUNA, 2 ounces water-pack; or flaked white fish such as halibut or sole
CELERY, 1 teaspoon finely chopped
ONION, 1/2 teaspoon minced
DILL PICKLE, 1 teaspoon minced
EXTENDED MAYONNAISE, 1 tablespoon (see recipe)
PEPPER, sprinkle
CIDER VINEGAR, 1/2 to 1 teaspoon, to taste

Flake TUNA in mixing bowl; add VEGETABLES and MAYONNAISE. Sprinkle on PEPPER and 1/2 teaspoon of VINEGAR; mix well; taste; add more vinegar and seasonings if desired. Spread it on either bread or crackers.

Suggestions: You will want more spices if you use a bland white fish. Try a sprinkle of garlic powder and a pinch of sweet basil for variety.

For low-salt diet: Use salt-free water-pack tuna or fresh fish cooked without salt. Omit pickle; use sprinkle of dill weed. Use mayonnaise extended by salt-free directions. One-half recipe contains 20 milligrams of sodium.

JANE'S FAVORITE SPREAD

Makes 1 serving. One serving equals 1 ounce of meat and 1/4 cup of fruit; contains 60 Calories (P8, F3, C4), about 6 milligrams of cholesterol.

COTTAGE CHEESE, 1/4 cup low-fat
BERRY JAM or JELLY, 2 teaspoons dietetic
LEMON RIND, sprinkle
CINNAMON, sprinkle (optional)

In sieve or colander, wash COTTAGE CHEESE in cold water to remove any fat or liquid. Dry cottage cheese on paper towel. Mix cheese with JAM; add LEMON RIND. Spread on bread, crackers or hot toast. Top with a light sprinkle of CINNAMON if you wish.

Suggestions: Make this spread just before using it; it does not hold well when spread.

For low-salt diet: This recipe cannot be made low in sodium because of the natural sodium in cottage cheese. One recipe contains about 128 milligrams of sodium.

LOW-CHOLESTEROL EGG SALAD SPREAD

Makes 3 portions. One portion (1/3 recipe) equals 1 ounce of meat and 1/2 teaspoon of fat; contains 105 Calories (P7, F8, C0), 8 milligrams of cholesterol.

LIQUID EGG SUBSTITUTE, 1/2 cup
EGG, 1 hard-cooked
EXTENDED MAYONNAISE, 1 tablespoon (see recipe)
PREPARED MUSTARD, 1/4 teaspoon
CIDER VINEGAR, 1/2 teaspoon
ONION, 1/3 teaspoon finely minced
SALT, 1/4 teaspoon
PEPPER, 1/8 teaspoon

Into top of double boiler sprayed with nonstick coating, put EGG SUBSTITUTE; place over boiling water; cook for 5 minutes; turn off heat and let stand for 5 minutes; remove from heat; allow to cool slightly. Turn out egg substitute into small mixing bowl; mince with fork until evenly broken and fairly fine; add hard-cooked EGG WHITE (discard yolk); mince to same consistency. Add MAYONNAISE, MUSTARD, VINEGAR, ONION and SEASONINGS. Mix thoroughly; taste; add more seasonings if you wish. Divide into 3 equal portions and use as spread.

Suggestions: If the dieter has enough fat allowance, mince stuffed olives into this for a change. Do not use olives if diet limits salt or sodium intake.

For low-salt diet: Omit salt; use 1/4 teaspoon of salt substitute. Omit prepared mustard; use 1/16 teaspoon of dry mustard dissolved in the vinegar; add a few drops of water to make a paste, which will blend with the other ingredients. Use salt-free mayonnaise, extended by salt-free instructions. Do not use on a very low-sodium diet, because it cannot be made low enough in sodium. One serving (1/3 recipe) contains 137 milligrams of sodium.

PEANUT BUTTER SPREAD

Makes 2 servings. One serving equals 1 ounce of meat, 1 teaspoon of fat and 1/4 cup of fruit; contains 143 Calories (P6, F12, C6), about 2 milligrams of cholesterol.

PEANUT BUTTER, 3 tablespoons old-fashioned
YOGURT, 2 tablespoons plain low-fat
LIQUID SWEETENER, 1 to 3 drops
NUTMEG, sprinkle or two

In small bowl, mix PEANUT BUTTER and YOGURT; cream with spoon or spatula until smooth. Add SWEETENER and SPICE; blend thoroughly. Spread on crackers or bread.

Suggestions: This spread keeps well, so may be made ahead of time. It makes an excellent stuffing for celery.

For low-salt diet: Use salt-free peanut butter. One-half recipe contains about 10 milligrams of sodium.

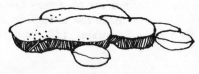

SMOKY CHEESE SPREAD

Makes 2 servings. One serving (1/2 recipe) equals 1 ounce of meat and 1/2 teaspoon of fat; contains 107 Calories (P6, F8, C2), about 12 milligrams of cholesterol.

LOW-FAT CHEESE, 2 ounces with 5% butterfat or less
EXTENDED MAYONNAISE, 1 tablespoon (see recipe)
YOGURT, 1 tablespoon plain low-fat
GARLIC POWDER, sprinkle
BACON BITS, 1 teaspoon imitation

Allow CHEESE to soften to room temperature; with large spoon or spatula, mash into an even, soft pile. Add MAYONNAISE, YOGURT and GARLIC POWDER; cream thoroughly. Stir in imitation BACON BITS. Taste; add more seasonings if you wish. Spread on bread or crackers.

Suggestions: Because this is a soft spread, it is best refrigerated until eaten.

For low-salt diet: This recipe cannot be made low in salt.

11. Canning, Freezing & Pickling

With the cost of dietetic foods being so high, those who have the time and inclination can save a lot of money by doing their own processing when the fruit and vegetables are ripe and available on the market at a good price.

It is best to process fruits in small jars so you don't have to eat a large amount of one kind before they spoil. Care must be taken that the canning is done properly because spoilage can take place if the lid is not sealed or there is any air leak. In the case of vegetables, tomatoes are the only ones we would suggest you can. The danger of botulism from home canned vegetables, other than tomatoes, is too high.

If you do can fruits or vegetables, discard any suspicious can or jar that looks even a little questionable. If the vegetables are to be combined with other foods and thoroughly cooked (30 minutes or more at temperatures above boiling) they need not be reheated to destroy any contaminating bacteria.

Canning Fruit

Preparation of Fruit

Be sure fruit is ripe enough to eat. Pick over to be sure all is firm and unbruised; use only fruit at its peak of condition for best results. Wash in cold water to remove any dust or dirt. Drain on several layers of paper towels to remove excess water.

For soft fruits, peel, core or remove pits. You may want to dip fruit to be peeled in boiling water for a minute to make it easier to remove the peel. When peeled, drop fruit into a solution that contains 3 tablespoons of lemon juice per quart of water. This will prevent browning until you can get fruit into jars.

For berries, merely pick over and remove any stems or overripe fruit. If whole berries are to be canned, prick each with a fork so the liquid will reach the inside of the berries while cooking.

Preparation of Syrup

Bring water to a boil. Using the following chart, add sweetening to the strength you desire. Taste the fruit to see how sweet it is and judge accordingly. If syrup is to be made ahead, store in sterilized jar in refrigerator and reboil just before using.

Sweetener
Granular type substitute
1 teaspoon per cup of fruit for light sweetening
2 teaspoons per cup of fruit for medium sweetening
3 teaspoons per cup of fruit for extra heavy sweetening
Liquid type substitute
1/3 teaspoon per cup of fruit for light sweetening
1/2 teaspoon per cup of fruit for medium sweetening
2/3 teaspoon per cup of fruit for extra heavy sweetening

Important: It is better to under-sweeten than to use too much. More sugar substitute can be added to opened jar just before use. If you will allow the fruit with added sweetener to stand 15-20 minutes before using, the flavor will penetrate the fruit. Allowing longer time gives even better penetration for thicker pieces.

Preparation of Jars and Lids

Be sure jars are clean and lids are the proper type for the jars. Fill canning boiler with water, add jars and fill with water until tops are completely covered. Boil for at least 5 minutes; start timing after water comes to a vigorous boil. Boil lids and rings in a separate pan, covering with water and timing the same as for jars.

Drain jars, pack with fruit to within 3/4 inch of top. Fill with hot syrup. Use tongs to remove lids from hot water. Place on jars and fasten down with rings. Be careful that no fruit gets on the rims or the lid will fail to seal when processed.

Canning Directions

Only acid fruits may be processed in a boiling water bath. These are: apples, apricots, berries, peaches, pears, pineapple, plums, rhubarb and tomatoes. ALL OTHERS MUST BE PRESSURE COOKED for safety.

Fill boiler with boiling water to almost jar height. Place a rack in the boiler so the jars will not sit directly on the bottom of the pan. Place jars (with lids screwed down tight) on rack, leaving 2 inches between jars. Add more boiling water to cover the tops of the jars by at least 1 inch. Process by cooking 25 minutes from the time the water reboils after adding jars. Add more boiling water if needed to keep jar tops well covered.

Remove jars from boiler with tongs. Cool in upright position for 12 hours. Then check for seal by tapping jar lids with a metal spoon. You will get a ringing note from properly sealed jars. If the sound is dull and hollow, reprocess or use immediately. Store jars of fruit in a cool

(45 to 60 degrees), dark place to avoid color fading and prevent spoilage.

Tricks to Improve Flavor

Following are a few ideas for variety.

In apricots, peaches and other pitted fruits, leave a few pits in the fruit so that each jar has 1 or 2. The oil in the pit will give an almond flavor to the fruit.

In apple slices, peaches and pears, add a stick of cinnamon (or part of one) to each jar of fruit. In apricots, pears and plums, add a few cloves to each jar.

Add a sprinkle of salt (or salt substitute) to each jar before you put the lid on. This helps bring out the natural sweetness of the fruit.

Combine fruits to make interesting mixtures; apple slices, apricots and plums, for example.

Cook fruit in the juice from a different fruit; use pineapple juice with pears, for example. You then have to count the juice as an extra fruit serving but if you use a smaller portion (1/3 less) it comes out to the same Calories.

For low-salt diet: All natural fruit is low in sodium. Canning does not alter this so fruit may be eaten safely without concern about its sodium content.

Freezing Fruit

Preparation of Fruit

Pick over fruit to be sure all is firm and unbruised. Wash in cold water to remove any dust or dirt. Drain on several layers of paper towels to absorb all water left on fruit.

Peel, core or remove pits of soft fruits. You may want to dip fruit to be peeled in boiling water for a minute to make it easier to remove the peel. When fruit is peeled, drop it into a solution that contains 3 tablespoons of lemon juice per quart of water. If you wish, you may add sugar substitute to this liquid and use for freezing the fruit.

Berries need only be picked over to remove stems and bruised fruit. (Canning berries changes the texture but freezing does not.) When drained of wash water, pack berries into containers and place in freezer. If whole strawberries are packed, prick each with a fork before freezing. This is supposed to release any trapped air and to give a finer end product.

Preparation of Syrup for Soft Fruits

Bring water to boil. Remove from heat and add sugar substitute (see chart, page 176). When syrup is cooled, add 3 tablespoons of lemon juice per quart. Do not reheat or the blanching action of the lemon juice will be destroyed.

Cool syrup until very well chilled. It can be made the day before and kept in a sterile container in the refrigerator.

Packing Fruit

Use a container large enough to hold the amount of fruit to be eaten at one meal, or two meals at the most. (Frozen fruit loses much of its appetizing qualities when left too long after it is thawed.)

Pack fruit into containers leaving 1 to 1-1/2 inches of space at the top for expansion. In the case of soft fruits, cover with prepared syrup, again leaving space at the top. If the soft fruit will not stay below the liquid, use a piece of crumpled wax paper in the top of the container. This can be left in and discarded when the fruit is thawed. Cover with lid; sharp-freeze.

NOTE: Apple slices, cherries, peaches and pears will give a superior frozen product if you blanch them before you put them into the syrup. (You may use the blanching liquid to make syrup so it saves the juice which comes out in blanching.) Process for about 1-1/2 minutes of steam from the time blanching liquid boils after adding fruit. Use a basket so fruit is not in direct contact with the boiling water for best results.

For low-salt diet: These fruits are low-sodium as packed.

Jams, Jellies and Relishes

Most people find the dietetic jams on the market expensive, and often they don't find their favorite varieties at all. The recipes given here are easy to make, and the unusual combinations make meals more appetizing.

Cooked jams are generally superior to frozen jams made with sugar substitute, as large ice crystals tend to form in the frozen jam. This makes the fruit somewhat tough.

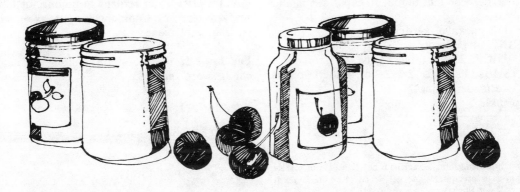

BASIC RECIPE FOR COOKED JAM

Makes approximately 9-1/2 cups. One tablespoon may be eaten without replacement.

Equipment needed: At least a 5-quart kettle, big enough to allow about 3 quarts of contents to come to a rolling boil. Canning jars and lids which can be processed to seal. Water bath deep enough to cover jars completely during boiling process.

FRESH FRUIT, 5 pounds (about 10 cups), stems and pits removed
PECTIN, 1/2 package powdered
GLYCERINE, 4 tablespoons*
LEMON JUICE, 2 to 3 tablespoons
SUGAR SUBSTITUTE, 2-1/2 to 4 tablespoons liquid. Taste to determine
SALT, sprinkle

Sort and cut FRUIT; put in large kettle with 1 tablespoon of water per cup of cut fruit; bring to boil; cover; simmer until soft. Time will vary from 8 to 10 minutes for berries to 15 minutes for plums. Add PECTIN, GLYCERINE and LEMON JUICE; stir well; bring to a full, rolling boil; boil for exactly 1 minute; remove from heat; add SUGAR SUBSTITUTE to taste. Pack into sterile jars, leaving 1/2 to 3/4 inch at top for expansion; sprinkle with SALT. Put on sterilized lids and rings; tighten. Put into boiling water bath so jars are completely covered through processing. Process for 20 minutes after water returns to boiling, or longer, if you like jam very soft. Cool; check seals, as on canned fruit; store in cool place.

For low-salt diet: Sodium content is negligible; no changes are required.

*USP grade glycerine (drugstore). Glycerine is not digested but merely thickens the jam as it precipitates the gel. If no glycerine is used, sugarless jams will not thicken.

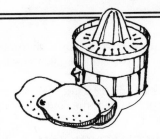

APPLE-BERRY JAM

Makes 9-1/2 to 10 cups. One tablespoon may be eaten without replacement. Six tablespoons equal 1/2 cup of fruit; contain 40 Calories (P0, F0, C10), no cholesterol. One tablespoon contains 6 Calories; may be eaten without replacement.

BERRIES, 5 cups. Use strawberries, raspberries or boysenberries, mashed or chopped.
APPLES, 5 cups peeled and sliced. Yellow transparent are best.
PECTIN, 1/2 package powdered
GLYCERINE, 4 tablespoons
LEMON JUICE, 3 to 5 tablespoons, depending on sweetness of apples
SUGAR SUBSTITUTE, 2-1/2 to 4 tablespoons liquid. Taste to determine amount.
SALT, sprinkle

Wash, sort and measure FRUIT; put into large kettle; add 1 tablespoon of water for each cup of fruit, more if fruit is not juicy. Bring to a boil; turn heat down; cover kettle. Simmer until fruit is soft, 8 to 12 minutes or up to 15 minutes if apples were firm. Remove from heat; add PECTIN, GLYCERINE and LEMON JUICE—5 tablespoons if apples are sweet, 3 tablespoons for tart apples; stir until well dissolved. Return to heat; bring to a full, rolling boil; boil for exactly 1 minute. Remove from heat; add 1/2 of the SWEETENER or less; taste; add more if needed, remembering that it will taste sweeter when cool. Pour into sterile jars, leaving 1/2 to 3/4 inch at top for expansion; sprinkle with SALT; put on caps and rings; tighten. Put into boiling water bath so jars are completely covered through processing; process for 20 minutes after water returns to boiling. Add water as needed to keep jars well covered. Cool; check seals as on canned fruit; store in a cool place.

Suggestions: This jam can be made with slices of apples and whole berries for a conserve, or mashed and blended for the usual jam appearance.

For low-salt diet: Omit salt; use sprinkle of salt substitute. Sodium content is negligible.

APPLE BUTTER

Makes about 6 cups. Three tablespoons equal 1/2 cup of fruit; contain 40 Calories (P0, F0, C9), no cholesterol. One teaspoon may be eaten without replacement.

APPLES, 6 cups diced
APPLE JUICE or CIDER, 6 cups
LEMON JUICE, 6 tablespoons
CINNAMON, 1 tablespoon
NUTMEG, 1 teaspoon
GROUND CLOVES, 1 teaspoon
SALT, 1/8 teaspoon
SUGAR SUBSTITUTE, 8 to 10 teaspoons granular; or substitute equal to 6 tablespoons of sugar

---

Peel and core APPLES; remove stems and blossom ends; put in large kettle; add APPLE JUICE and LEMON JUICE; cook over low heat until volume is reduced to about half; if not thick, cool to consistency of applesauce. Add SPICES and SALT; mix to blend well; heat about 1 minute. Taste; if sweet enough, omit SUGAR SUBSTITUTE; if not, add up to 10 teaspoons—a little at a time. Freeze in small, tight containers, or put into sterilized canning jars and process as for cooked jams (see recipe).

Suggestions: You may wish to vary the amounts of spices used. If you add smaller amounts, then taste.

Low-salt diet: Omit salt; use 1/8 teaspoon of salt substitute. Sodium content is negligible.

APRICOT-LEMON JAM

Makes 9-1/2 cups. Four and one-half tablespoons equal 1/2 cup of fruit; 1 tablespoon contains 10 Calories (P0, F0, C2.5), no cholesterol. One tablespoon may be eaten without replacement.

APRICOTS, 9 cups fresh, quartered
LEMON, 1 large, sliced paper-thin
LEMON JUICE, 2 to 3 tablespoons
PECTIN, 1 package powdered
GLYCERINE, 6 tablespoons
SALT, sprinkle
SUGAR SUBSTITUTE, 4 tablespoons granular; or substitute equal to 1/2 cup of sugar
ALMOND EXTRACT, 1/4 to 1/2 teaspoon
PLAIN GELATIN, 1 envelope (1 tablespoon), dissolved in 1/4 cup of water

---

Pit and quarter APRICOTS; slice LEMONS (remove seeds); put apricots, lemon, LEMON JUICE and 2 tablespoons of water into kettle; cook until tender, about 20 minutes. Add PECTIN, GLYCERINE and SALT; stir well; return to heat; bring to full rolling boil; boil exactly 1 minute. Remove from heat; add SUGAR SUBSTITUTE and ALMOND EXTRACT; taste; add more sugar if desired; add GELATIN; stir well. Pack in sterile jars and process for 20 minutes in hot water bath. Cool; check seals; store in cool, dark place.

For low-salt diet: Omit sprinkle of salt; use salt substitute. Sodium content is negligible.

GRAPEFRUIT-ORANGE MARMALADE

Makes approximately 10 cups. One tablespoon contains 8 Calories (P0, F0, C2), no cholesterol. One tablespoon may be eaten without replacement.

GRAPEFRUIT, 3 large
ORANGES, 15 large
LEMON, 1 large
PECTIN, 1 package powdered

GLYCERINE, 6 tablespoons
SALT, sprinkle
SUGAR SUBSTITUTE, 4 to 5 tablespoons liquid.
PLAIN GELATIN, 1 envelope (1 tablespoon), dissolved in 1/4 cup of water

Section GRAPEFRUIT and ORANGES; retain juice with fruit. Should be 9 cups total. Using coarsest blade, grind 1 grapefruit rind, 2 orange rinds and the whole LEMON (remove the seeds), or chop rinds very fine instead of grinding. Add to fruit. Cook until fruit is tender and rind is firm but not hard. Add PECTIN, GLYCERINE and SALT; bring to boil; cook exactly 1 minute at rolling boil; remove from heat. Add SUGAR SUBSTITUTE to taste (keep it slightly tart); add GELATIN; mix well. Pack in sterile jars; process for 20 minutes in hot water bath; cool, check seals. Store in cool, dark place.

Suggestions: You may vary the proportions of the fruit, using less or more grapefruit or lemon. Chop the sectioned fruit if smaller pieces are preferred.

For low-salt diet: Omit salt; use salt substitute. Sodium content is negligible.

MIXED SOFT FRUIT JAM

Makes approximately 9-1/2 cups. Five tablespoons equal about 1/2 cup of fruit; 1 tablespoon contains about 8 Calories (P0, F0, C2), no cholesterol. One tablespoon may be eaten without replacement.

FRUIT, 10 cups diced apricots, peaches, pears or combination
WATER, 10 tablespoons
PECTIN, 1 package powdered
GLYCERINE, 6 tablespoons
SALT, sprinkle
LEMON JUICE, 5 tablespoons
SUGAR SUBSTITUTE, 2 to 3 tablespoons liquid (optional)

Peel and chop FRUIT; retain any juice and include with total volume. Put fruit into large kettle; add WATER, more if fruit is not juicy. Bring to boil; cover, lower heat and cook until fruit is soft, 10 to 15 minutes. Remove from heat; add PECTIN, GLYCERINE, SALT and LEMON JUICE; stir well. Return to heat; bring to full rolling boil; boil exactly 1 minute. Remove from heat; add SUGAR SUBSTITUTE to taste. Pack into sterilized jars, seal and process in hot water bath for 30 minutes after bath returns to boiling. Cool; check seals. Store in cool place.

Suggestions: This jam can be made with the fruit in slices, ground into very small pieces, or chopped as for marmalade. If you like, add 1/4 teaspoon of almond extract to each jar just before filling. This will not give a strong almond flavor, but will add to the appeal.

For low-salt diet: Omit salt; use salt substitute. Sodium content is negligible.

PLUM JAM

Makes 9-1/2 to 10 cups. About 5 tablespoons equal 1/2 cup of fruit; 1 tablespoon contains 8 Calories (P0, F0, C2), no cholesterol. One tablespoon may be eaten without replacement.

PLUMS, 10 cups ripe, stemmed, pitted and quartered
LEMON JUICE, 5 tablespoons
LEMON RIND, about 1-1/2 tablespoons finely grated (optional)
PECTIN, 1 package powdered
GLYCERINE, 6 tablespoons
SALT, sprinkle
SUGAR SUBSTITUTE, 2 to 4 tablespoons liquid.

Wash and sort PLUMS. Remove stems and pits; cut into quarters. Put into kettle; add 1 tablespoon of WATER per cup of fruit, or 1-1/2 tablespoons if fruit is not juicy. Bring to a boil; lower heat; cover and simmer until fruit is soft, 12 to 14 minutes. Remove from heat; add LEMON JUICE and RIND, PECTIN, GLYCERINE and SALT; stir well. Return to heat; bring to full rolling boil; boil for exactly 1 minute. Remove from heat; add SUGAR SUBSTITUTE to taste. If fruit is very ripe, you may need none. Put into sterilized jars; seal and process for 30 minutes (20 minutes if you want firm fruit) in hot water bath as for cooked jams (see recipe). Cool; check seals; store in cool, dark place.

Suggestions: For plum preserve, add 1/2 cup of finely chopped (not ground) walnuts and seeded coarse-ground orange to fruit after adding sugar substitute. Five tablespoons equal 1/2 cup of fruit and 1 teaspoon of fat.

For low-salt diet: Omit salt; use salt substitute. May use 1 tablespoon of this jam without counting it. Sodium content is negligible.

BASIC RECIPE FOR FROZEN JAM

Makes approximately 10-1/2 cups. One tablespoon contains approximately 4 Calories (P0, F0, C1), no cholesterol. One tablespoon may be eaten without replacement.

Equipment needed: Approximately a 3-quart kettle, big enough to allow about 1-1/2 quarts of contents to come to a rolling boil. Jars with tight lids for freezing. Either use lids that can be boiled to sterilize or use disposable containers.

FRESH FRUIT, 10 cups, stems and pits removed
LEMON JUICE, 2 tablespoons
PECTIN, 1 package powdered
GLYCERINE, 5 tablespoons
SALT, 1/8 teaspoon
PLAIN GELATIN, 2 envelopes (2 tablespoons)
COLD WATER, 1/2 cup
SUGAR SUBSTITUTE, 3 tablespoons liquid; or substitute equal to 3/4 to 1-1/4 cups of sugar

Mash half the FRUIT, add LEMON JUICE, PECTIN, GLYCERINE and SALT; bring to a hard boil for 1 minute, stirring constantly. Remove from heat; add remainder of fruit—whole berries, halves or mashed—as you prefer. Add GELATIN to WATER; allow to stand about 5 minutes, then heat gently to completely dissolve; add to berry or fruit mixture. Add SUGAR SUBSTITUTE to taste; cool. Place slightly cooled mixture in jars or freezer cartons. Leave 1/2 inch at top for fruit to expand when freezing. Cover and place in coldest part of freezer to freeze quickly. Store in freezer; to thaw, place in refrigerator for 24 hours before using. Use within 10 days of thawing to prevent spoiling.

Important: The jam will be all hard crystals when frozen. It cannot be used directly from the freezer. In ordinary frozen jam the sugar and corn syrup keep the ice crystals from becoming solid, so it can be kept semiliquid and can be used directly. This recipe will make a fairly soft jam, but by keeping it in the refrigerator until just before using it, it will be similar in consistency to ordinary freezer jam.

For low-salt diet: Omit salt. Use 1/8 teaspoon of salt substitute. Sodium content is negligible.

FROZEN BOYSENBERRY JAM

Makes approximately 10-1/2 cups. Eight tablespoons equal 1/2 cup of fruit; 1 tablespoon contains approximately 6 Calories (P0, F0, C1.5), no cholesterol. One tablespoon may be used without replacement.

BOYSENBERRIES, 10 cups, washed and hulled
LEMON JUICE, 3 tablespoons
LEMON RIND, 2 tablespoons grated
PECTIN, 1 package powdered
GLYCERINE, 5 tablespoons
SALT, sprinkle
PLAIN GELATIN, 2 envelopes (2 tablespoons)
COLD WATER, 1/2 cup
SUGAR SUBSTITUTE, 2 to 4 tablespoons liquid or substitute equal to 3/4 to 1-1/4 cups of sugar

Mash or crush half the BOYSENBERRIES, place in a kettle; add LEMON JUICE, LEMON RIND, PECTIN, GLYCERINE and SALT. Bring to a full rolling boil for exactly 1 minute, stirring constantly. Remove from heat; add the remainder of the berries (whole or crushed, as you prefer). Add the GELATIN to 1/2 cup of COLD WATER; allow to stand about 5 minutes, then warm to dissolve completely; add to the berry mixture. Sweeten with SUGAR SUBSTITUTE to suit your taste. (Remember that the jam will taste sweeter when cold.) Allow to cool slightly before packaging. Pour into jars or freezer containers, leaving 1/2 to 3/4 inch for expansion when the fruit freezes. Cover. Place in coldest area of freezer to allow quick freezing. Keep frozen until ready for use. Place in refrigerator 24 hours before using to thaw slowly. Use within 10 days of thawing to prevent spoiling.

For low-salt diet: Omit salt; use sprinkle of salt substitute. Sodium content is negligible.

FROZEN STRAWBERRY JAM

Makes approximately 10-1/2 cups. Ten tablespoons equal 1/2 cup of fruit; 1 tablespoon contains 5 Calories (P0, F0, C1), no cholesterol. Two tablespoons of jam may be used without replacement.

STRAWBERRIES, 10 cups, washed and hulled
LEMON JUICE, 2 tablespoons
PECTIN, 1 package powdered
GLYCERINE, 5 tablespoons
SALT, sprinkle
PLAIN GELATIN, 2 tablespoons; or 2 packages of strawberry flavor dietetic gelatin
COLD WATER, 1/2 cup
SUGAR SUBSTITUTE, 3 to 4 tablespoons liquid, 6 to 8 tablespoons granular, or substitute equal to approximately 1 cup of sugar

Mash half the BERRIES after cleaning and culling any that are overripe or green; place in a kettle with LEMON JUICE, PECTIN and GLYCERINE; sprinkle SALT on top. Bring to a full rolling boil for 1 minute, stirring constantly. Remove from the heat. Add the remainder of the berries (diced, sliced or whole, as you prefer).

Combine GELATIN with 1/2 cup of COLD WATER; allow to stand 5 minutes, then heat gently to dissolve. Add to berries; add SUGAR SUBSTITUTE. Stir well to mix. Allow to cool slightly before packing into jars. Pour into jars or freezer cartons. Cover. Place on coldest shelf in freezer to allow quick freezing. Store in freezer until time of use. Allow 24 hours thawing time in the refrigerator before using. Use within 10 days of thawing to prevent spoiling.

Note: If fruit is not sweet and ripe it will not make good jam. Be sure not to over-sweeten as it is our experience that it tastes sweeter when cold than when warm and first cooked.

For low-salt diet: Omit salt; use salt substitute. Sodium content is negligible.

FRUIT RELISH

Makes 2-1/8 cups. Ten tablespoons equal 1/2 cup of fruit; 1 tablespoon contains 5 Calories (P0, F0, C1), no cholesterol. One tablespoon may be eaten without replacement.

APPLESAUCE, 2 cups sweetened dietetic
HORSERADISH, 2 tablespoons prepared
LEMON JUICE, 1 tablespoon
LEMON RIND, 1/4 teaspoon (optional)
SALT, sprinkle

Mix well to blend flavors. Pack in jars or containers for freezing, leaving 1/2- to 3/4-inch space for contents to expand when freezing. Cover; freeze in coldest part of freezer. Keep frozen until needed.

Suggestions: This can be made at canning time and frozen for later use or may be made up as wanted during the year. You may color this green or red for special occasions. It is best not to try to freeze it after it has been colored as it may develop an odd appearance and become unappetizing.

For low-salt diet: Omit salt; use salt substitute. One tablespoon contains less than 1 milligram of sodium.

Pickles and Seasoning Sauces

When these items are made with sugar substitute they have very little food value. Accordingly, they can be used in reasonable amounts without giving up anything else.

Some of these recipes are listed as ingredients in other recipes in the various chapters of this cookbook. For example, the Tomato Sauce is used in the Spaghetti Sauce; the Ketchup is the basis for the barbecued salmon recipe. So if you think that you have no interest in these items, it will be a limiting factor in making other things in the book.

Many of these recipes cannot be made salt-free or even low in salt, due to the use of salt solution in making pickles. Substituting potassium chloride for sodium chloride results in a very strong and somewhat bitter pickle. We do not recommend that you try this.

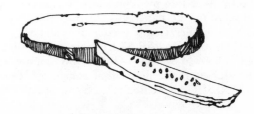

BREAD AND BUTTER PICKLES

Makes approximately 4 pints. One serving (1/4 cup) contains 8 Calories (P0, F0, C2), no cholesterol. May be used without replacement.

CUCUMBERS, 9 large or 12 medium
ONIONS, 2 small or 8 pickling size
PICKLING SALT, 1/4 cup coarse
VINEGAR, 1 cup
WHOLE MUSTARD SEED, 2/3 teaspoon
SUGAR SUBSTITUTE, 10 tablespoons granular; or substitute equal to 1-1/4 cups of sugar
CELERY SEED, 1/2 teaspoon
PEPPER, 1 teaspoon
TUMERIC POWDER, scant 1/2 teaspoon

Score CUCUMBERS lengthwise all around with tines of sharp fork. Slice into medium slices (5 to 6 per inch or less), discarding the hard ends. Slice ONIONS equally thin or even thinner. Combine cucumber and onion slices and cover with COARSE SALT; mix so all slices are covered; allow to sit for 1/2 hour to remove excess moisture. Discard the liquid that comes off. Combine VINEGAR, SUGAR SUBSTITUTE and SEASONINGS in a nonaluminum kettle; add the cucumber and onion slices. Heat to boiling; boil for about 5 minutes until the slices look a little transparent. Pack immediately in hot sterilized jars; seal with sterilized lids. Process in water bath 20 minutes after water returns to boiling. Store in cool, dark area until you wish to use them.

Suggestions: You may pickle other vegetables in this type of liquid. Cucumbers, cauliflower, celery, carrots and green peppers all make fine pickles. Leave the pieces larger and process for a little longer to be sure the vinegar has penetrated the vegetables thoroughly.

For low-salt diet: This recipe cannot be made low in salt.

CHRISTINE'S MUSTARD PICKLES

Makes approximately 8 quarts, depending upon size you make the vegetable pieces. One-quarter cup equals 1 serving of bulky vegetable; contains 16 Calories (P0, F0, C4), no cholesterol. May be used without replacement.

CUCUMBERS, 2 quarts tiny (2 inches long or smaller)
PEARL ONIONS, 2 quarts tiny white
GREEN BEANS, 2 quarts, ends trimmed and beans cut in halves or thirds
GREEN TOMATOES, 2 quarts quartered
CAULIFLOWER, 2 heads, cut into buds (approximately 1-inch)
WHITE CABBAGE, 1 small head, coarsely chopped (optional)
GREEN PEPPERS, 6 small, coarsely chopped
PICKLING SALT, 1/4 cup coarse
TUMERIC POWDER, 1 ounce
WHOLE MUSTARD SEED, 2 tablespoons
CELERY SEED, 2 tablespoons
CLOVES, 1/2 tablespoon
WHOLE ALLSPICE, 1 tablespoon
DRY MUSTARD, 2/3 cup
CIDER VINEGAR, to completely cover vegetables
FLOUR, 1/2 cup
SUGAR SUBSTITUTE, 3/4 to 1 cup granular, or substitute equal to 2 cups of sugar

Place chopped VEGETABLES in nonaluminum kettle and cover with PICKLING SALT, mix well so salt covers all the vegetables. Place a plate over the vegetables so they stay down in the kettle and allow to stand 24 hours. Drain and discard the liquid that comes off. Place vegetables and SEASONINGS, with VINEGAR to cover, over heat and bring to a boil. Boil for 5 minutes, or until vegetables are soft but not mushy. Leave a little crisp, if you prefer them chewy. Drain off liquid and save. Make a thin paste with FLOUR, SUGAR SUBSTITUTE and a little water. Add to the liquid and cook until it is slightly thick. Add vegetables to thickened liquid. Heat through. Pack in sterilized jars while still very hot. Seal with sterilized lids. Process 15 minutes in boiling water bath to insure seal. Cool. Store in cool, dark place.

Suggestions: You can pickle almost any vegetable in this mixture. Try zucchini or broccoli. It makes excellent yellow wax bean pickles mixed with small onions.

For low-salt diet: This recipe cannot be made low in salt.

CELERY CHUTNEY

Makes approximately 3 pints. Two tablespoons equal 1 serving of bulky vegetable; contain 16 Calories (P0, F0, C4), no cholesterol. May be eaten without replacement.

CELERY, 3 cups diced fairly fine
TOMATOES, 6 cups chopped. If you use canned tomatoes, omit 2 teaspoons of the salt.
GREEN PEPPER, 1/4, diced fine
ONION, 1 medium, diced
GARLIC, 1 clove, diced
CIDER VINEGAR, 1/2 cup
SUGAR SUBSTITUTE, 1/3 cup granular; or substitute equal to 2/3 cup of sugar
SALT, 1 tablespoon. Use 1 teaspoon with canned tomatoes.
PEPPER, 1/2 teaspoon
CELERY SEED, 1 teaspoon

Sterilize the jars and keep them hot. Combine chopped VEGETABLES in large nonaluminum kettle; add VINEGAR and OTHER INGREDIENTS. Mix well. Simmer over low heat until the volume is reduced and the mix looks quite thick. Do not allow chutney to cool but pack it in hot jars while it is boiling hot. Top with sterilized lids and tighten rings firmly. Process in water bath (water must cover jars completely) for 15 minutes to sterilize and seal the jars. Cool. Store in cool, dark place until you wish to use them. Refrigerate after opening to prevent spoiling.

Suggestions: This is particularly good with cold meat or cold fish. Use it to give color and interest to a meal of leftovers.

For low-salt diet: This recipe cannot be made low in salt because of the natural high salt content of the celery.

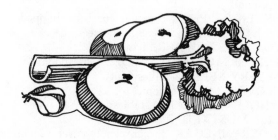

BARBECUE SAUCE

Makes 2-1/2 cups. One-half cup equals 1/2 slice of bread; contains 36 Calories (P2, F0, C7), no cholesterol. (You may use 2 tablespoons of this sauce without counting it in your diet.)

TOMATO SAUCE, 1 pint. See recipe or substitute the following ingredients for the same Calories: 2 cups of tomato puree, 1 tablespoon of granular sugar substitute or substitute equal to 2 tablespoons of sugar, 1/4 teaspoon of onion powder, 1/16 teaspoon of allspice, 1/16 teaspoon of garlic powder.
RED WINE VINEGAR, 1/2 cup
WORCESTERSHIRE SAUCE, 1/2 teaspoon
For hot barbecue sauce, add:
TABASCO, 1/2 teaspoon
CAYENNE PEPPER, 1/4 to 1/2 teaspoon

Mix ALL INGREDIENTS; stir to blend well. Taste; add salt and pepper if you think they are needed. Use to baste barbecued or baked meat, fish or poultry.

For low-salt diet: Use Tomato Sauce recipe made according to low-salt directions. If substitute ingredients listed here are used instead, be sure tomato puree is labeled salt-free. Use salt-free soy sauce instead of Worcestershire sauce. Two tablespoons contain 14 milligrams of sodium.

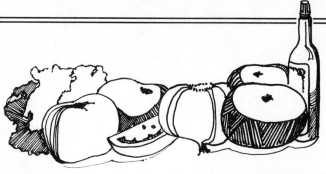

SPANISH BARBECUE SAUCE

Makes about 1-1/2 pints. One tablespoon contains 4 Calories (P0, F0, C1), no cholesterol. A 1/4-cup serving may be eaten without replacement.

TOMATOES, 1 quart
ONION, about 1/3 cup finely chopped
DRY MUSTARD, 1/2 teaspoon
SALT, 1 teaspoon
SUGAR SUBSTITUTE, 1 tablespoon granular; or substitute equal to 2 tablespoons of sugar
TABASCO, 1/16 to 1/8 teaspoon, to taste
CAYENNE PEPPER, several sprinkles

Puree TOMATOES in food mill or grind in meat grinder. Put ALL INGREDIENTS into large non-aluminum kettle; simmer about 15 minutes, until mixture begins to look thick. If sauce is not to be used soon, pack into sterilized jars, cover with sterilized lids, and process for 15 minutes in boiling water bath (see instructions for canning fruit).

Suggestions: This sauce may be used as a topping for meat, for meat balls or with other dishes. It is very hot, so a little goes a long way. For a milder sauce, cut the cayenne and Tabasco to half or less.

For low-salt diet: Omit salt; use 1 teaspoon of salt substitute. Cut Tabasco to 6 drops or less. One tablespoon contains 2 milligrams of sodium.

TOMATO KETCHUP

Makes 3-1/2 pints. One tablespoon contains 4 Calories (P0, F0, C1), no cholesterol. A 1/4-cup serving may be eaten without replacement.

TOMATOES, 8 cups fresh, peeled and quartered, or drained canned tomatoes
ONIONS, 2 medium, chopped
GREEN PEPPER, 1, chopped
GARLIC, 4 small cloves, minced
CELERY, 2 large stalks, diced
CIDER VINEGAR, 1 cup
SUGAR SUBSTITUTE, 1/2 cup granular; or substitute equal to 1 cup of sugar
GROUND CLOVES, 1/2 teaspoon
DRY MUSTARD, 1 teaspoon
CINNAMON, 1 teaspoon
MACE, 1/2 teaspoon
GROUND ALLSPICE, 1 teaspoon
TABASCO, 1/4 teaspoon (optional)
SALT, 1 tablespoon
PEPPER, 1/2 teaspoon

Prepare VEGETABLES; combine ALL INGREDIENTS in large nonaluminum kettle. Cook slowly over low heat until vegetables are very soft; do not allow to boil. Remove from heat; put through food mill or blend to break up any hard fibers. Return to heat and bring to boiling point. Bottle in sterilized jars; seal with sterilized lids; process in hot water bath for 15 minutes (see instructions for canning fruit). Store in cool, dark place to prevent color loss.

Suggestions: You may want to use less spice than the recipe calls for. It makes a spicy, hot ketchup.

For low-salt diet: Use fresh or diet-pack tomatoes. Omit salt; use 1 tablespoon of salt substitute. One tablespoon contains 1 milligram of sodium.

TOMATO SAUCE

Makes about 3 pints. One tablespoon contains 4 Calories (P0, F0, C1), no cholesterol. A 1/4-cup serving may be eaten without replacement.

TOMATOES, 8 cups, peeled and quartered; or tomato puree
ONIONS, 2 medium, chopped
GREEN PEPPER, 1, chopped
GARLIC, 1 large clove, minced
CIDER VINEGAR, 2/3 cup
GROUND ALLSPICE, 1/2 teaspoon
SALT, 1 tablespoon
PEPPER, 1/4 teaspoon
SUGAR SUBSTITUTE, 1/2 cup granular; or substitute equal to 1 cup of sugar

Prepare VEGETABLES; combine in large non-aluminum kettle; add ALL INGREDIENTS except sugar substitute and tomato puree (if used). Cook over low heat until all vegetables are very soft and volume is reduced about 1/3; remove from heat; add SUGAR SUBSTITUTE. Put through food mill to remove seeds and any other firm material. Return to heat; add tomato puree (if used) and bring to boil. Pack in sterilized jars; seal with sterilized lids; process for 15 minutes in hot water bath (see canning instructions). Cool; store in cool, dark place.

For low-salt diet: Omit salt; use 1 tablespoon of salt substitute. Use diet-pack or fresh tomatoes, or salt-free tomato puree. One tablespoon contains 0.5 milligrams of sodium.

12. Eating Out

One of the worst problems with trying to stick to a diet is the temptation offered when you have to eat away from home. It can be discouraging and alarming to read a menu and find nothing on it that you should be eating.

This chapter is meant to start you thinking about how to cope without getting into too much trouble. If you are new to special dieting, it will show you how to plan; even old hands may find new ideas. One meal off the diet will not cause serious problems for most people. However, once you allow yourself to break the routine, it becomes easier to do it another time. If you need to be on a diet for medical reasons, then you should try to stick to it carefully unless the circumstances are most unusual.

Read the suggestions carefully. Try the meal replacements and practice until the items are familiar to you. Then try the next time you are away from home. We predict that your choices will be wise and close to what you should be having for that meal—and you will be very pleased with yourself for having learned to eat away from home without too much difficulty.

If you're on a low-salt diet, you will be sure to get more salt than you should have unless you pick very carefully. Even at best there are sources of sodium that you may not know about. Plan on being very careful for the following several days to make up for the extra salt in restaurant food.

General Rules for Eating Out

Menus in restaurants aren't planned to fit a diet. If you try, often you can find items that will fit your needs both in type of food and size of portion—unless you're on a low-salt diet. It is not usually possible to follow a restricted salt menu in a restaurant. Picking foods that require a minimum of preparation (baked potato, broiled meat, poultry or fish), avoiding canned vegetables and asking that no salt be added in cooking gives the best results. If you continually eat in the same places, they will probably try harder to fix the food as you request.

For other diets, try to replace each item of your normal meal with what is available on the menu. If you use the items from the replacement lists that follow this chapter, you should do quite well. But eating out is not ideal, and you will do better at home or where the cook understands your diet restriction.

Replacements

Here's how to figure a whole meal easily.

1. Write down your meal plan. Leave space alongside for replacements.

2. Take each item and look it up in the groups given in the replacement lists. Pick something you would be apt to find in a restaurant and write it down beside what you would normally have.

3. Consider what else you have picked for replacement so you have an appetizing meal—and when you are done, congratulate yourself on not letting dieting be dull.

Sample Dinner Plan

Diet Plan	Replacement
3 meat servings	1 slice of roast beef (lean only)
2 starch servings	1/2 of a large baked potato and 3 ounces of dry wine, or 1 roll
1 to 2 vegetable servings	green salad with oil and vinegar dressing, and frozen peas
1 fruit serving	2/3 of a roll or 1/3 more baked potato
1 fat serving	oil in salad dressing

While this doesn't look the same, your body will get just about the same nourishment from the two meals. Depending on your choice, you may not be as satisfied because the replacement isn't as bulky. (For a low-cholesterol replacement, a poultry or fish entree is your best choice.)

Practice

Write down a favorite restaurant meal—one that you often ate in predieting days. Now try to see how much of it you can eat on your diet. Try to replace with similar items if possible.

You may be pleasantly surprised to find that you can eat almost everything except the dessert. You may have to take meat home in a doggie bag and eat it for lunch the next day, but many people do. In fact, some restaurants have people bags—and call them that.

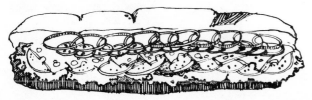

Banquets and Dinner Parties

There you are, captive for a meal. Do you make a big scene and show all around that you are dieting? Or do you try to be selective and follow your pattern as well as you can with what is available? For the least fuss, try the following:

If you can find out ahead of time what the menu will be, replacement will be much easier. Then plan ahead at home as explained under the general rules for eating out. You will have to skip the dessert, sweet salads such as gelatin, and gravy. Make up for these with additional bread or starchy vegetables to fill the holes in your diet pattern. (Nobody will think you are on a special diet if you eat both the bread and potato. What they won't know is that one replaces your usual dessert of fruit.)

If you don't know the menu, it is much harder to plan. Perhaps ahead of the main dish you can ask the waitress what is coming. If you find the dessert is fresh fruit—a welcome but rare occasion—you can save for it. If it is the usual sweet, gooey dish, plan to have more starch at the earlier courses and skip the dessert. Again, use the substitutions given in the replacement lists.

If you can't find out anything ahead, then assume the worst and act as if you knew you could not eat the dessert. Eat the main course as both entree and dessert. If they bring you dessert, put it aside and ignore it or even offer it to a neighboring diner. (Since they saw you eating all that starch, they will just think you are full and don't want it.) Avoid making yourself conspicuous. Your table companions aren't interested in your diet and it gets old very quickly as a main subject of conversation.

Regarding alcohol, if you plan to have a drink, remember that 1 ounce of alcohol (or 3 ounces of dry wine) replaces 1 serving of starch. You probably can't have both a before-dinner drink and dry wine with dinner. Choose what you want and then don't fudge and have both. Some diets totally forbid the use of alcohol, and if your doctor says that you can't have any, then don't. Chances are there is a sound medical reason and drinking could delay your recovery of good health.

Do the best you can and then forget about it.

Drive-Ins

Drive-ins are not for low-sodium dieters.
The only place you can find to eat is a drive-in . . . or you like to eat at drive-ins . . . or all the others want to go to a drive-in to eat. Whatever the cause, you are there, and now what can you eat? Following is a suggested replacement meal. For other replacement values, check the replacement lists (information very handy to carry with you if you eat out often).

Your Usual Meal	Your Drive-In Choice
2 slices of bread	Hamburger bun (both halves)
2 ounces of low-fat meat	Fish square (if too large, leave some uneaten)
1 fruit serving	2/3 of a small bag of potato chips or 1/3 of a cup of French fries Coffee, tea, diet pop
2 fat servings	1 teaspoon of tartar sauce and fat in the potatoes

Picnics

What can you take on a picnic and still follow your diet? Recipes for the following items are all in this cookbook. They will keep without refrigeration for a reasonable time, and most are items that the whole family will eat without complaining.

Main Dishes and Salads
Meat Loaf Sandwiches
Chicken Italienne or Chicken Bavarian
Patrick's Shrimp Dish (very good cold)
Three-Bean Salad with Tuna or Chicken
Hot Potato Salad (good cold, too)
Coleslaw
Cabbage Fruit Salad
Carrot and Onion Puree (good cold)
Vegetable Potpourri
Tomato Madrilene Soup (good chilled)

Desserts
Crunchy Banana Bread
Fruit Betty
Raisin-Applesauce Cake
Fruit Medley
Apple-Raisin Pie
Berry Pie
Rhubarb Pie
Cookies

Travel Meals

By Car

Travel by car requires only a little planning ahead.

Take along a small polyfoam ice chest. Prepare your own breakfast and lunch and eat only your dinner meal out. If it happens that at lunch time there is a nice restaurant on the road, stop and eat there. If all that is available is a greasy spoon, find a park and picnic.

Low-fat cheese or cottage cheese can be satisfactory breakfast items. They are the easiest things to carry, provided you have an ice chest, and will allow you to have the protein at breakfast that will stick with you through the morning.

By Airplane

If you can eat on the ground before boarding the plane, it will simplify things aboard. Then you can skip or pick items from the meal served without too much hunger.

It is possible to order special diet meals on an airplane if you notify the airline about 24 hours ahead of time. However, airlines often offer a choice of meat or fish/poultry, so you could select the one you should have without making a special order. Avoid the breading and sauces; eat only the meat. Then you won't have to allow any extra for the cooking method. Use the methods suggested earlier under "Banquets and Dinner Parties."

By Bus

Most bus meal-stops are not fancy. You may have to fall back on the drive-in menu selection. Try not to take a long trip without making a stop for a night's sleep and some more appropriate meals. For the first day you can pack a lunch from the picnic items. Beyond that you are on your own; do the best you can.

Rule

The real success is when you manage to follow your diet under difficult circumstances. Then you can be proud of yourself!

Table I.   Restaurant Food Replacements

Each food listed here is measured not in Calories but in equivalent servings of bread, meat, fruit or fat. This is done so that you can easily make trades between the restaurant menu and your usual diet. Choose either the food listed to the left or the equivalent serving of bread, meat, fruit or fat listed at the right. With a little juggling, you should be able to assemble a restaurant meal that won't wreck your diet.

All food values are approximate.

†Much of the carbohydrate in bulky raw vegetables is not digestible and need not be counted. In a salad, however, there will usually be at least 1 teaspoon of salad dressing (1 fat serving) and perhaps a half cup or more.

BREAKFAST FOODS

Don't eat pastry, sweet rolls, butterhorns or doughnuts. Do use dietetic syrup (in reasonable amounts) on the French toast, pancakes and waffles.

Grapefruit half	¼ of a large cantaloupe small glass of fruit juice 1 fruit serving ⅔ bread serving
Cereal, unsweetened, ½ cup	1 bread serving
Scrambled eggs (usually 2 eggs)	2 meat servings

Omelette (usually 3 eggs)	3 meat servings
Bacon, 1 crisp slice	1 fat serving
Canadian bacon, 2 thin slices	1 meat serving
Sausage, 2 small links	1 meat + 3 fat servings
French toast, 1 slice	1 bread + ½ meat serving
Pancake, 3-inch	1 bread serving
Waffle, 3½-inch square	1 bread serving
Fruit muffin, 1 small	1 bread + 1 fruit serving

BEVERAGES

Black coffee or tea	free; no replacement needed
Whole milk (4% fat), 8 ounces	1 bread + 1 meat + 1 fat serving
Skim or buttermilk, 8 ounces	1 bread + 1 meat serving
Beer (3.2%), 8 ounces (7 grams of alcohol)	dry wine, 3 ounces (11 grams of alcohol) whiskey, gin, vodka, 1 ounce (12 grams of alcohol) 1 bread serving

BREAD AND CEREAL

Bread, 1 slice	1 medium roll 5 salted crackers 1 small potato ½ cup of rice or noodles 1 bread serving
Cereal (unsweetened) or starch, ½ cup	1 bread serving
Salted crackers, 5	1 bread serving
French toast, 1 slice	1 bread + ½ meat serving

Pancake, 3-inch	1 bread serving
Waffle, 3½-inch square	1 bread serving
Fruit muffin, 1 small	1 bread + 1 fruit serving

SOUP

Thin, watery, 6-ounce cup	½ bread serving
Average, 6-ounce cup	1 bread serving
Thick, 6-ounce cup	1¼ to 1½ bread servings

SALAD

Raw mixed vegetables†, 1 cup	free except for dressing; no replacement needed
Cottage cheese and fruit (1/2 cup of cottage cheese and 2 pieces of sweetened, canned fruit)	2 meat + 2 fruit servings

Starchy (potato, macaroni), 1 cup	2 bread + fat allowance for salad dressing†
Meaty (chicken, seafood), 1 cup	{ 3 to 4 meat servings { + fat allowance for salad dressing†
Salad dressing†, 1 tablespoon	oil or mayonnaise, 1 teaspoon 1 fat serving

MEATS

Fish:

1 ounce	1 meat serving
1 medium fish steak (4 ounces)	3 to 4 meat servings

Poultry:

1 ounce	1 meat serving
½ chicken breast (4 ounces)	1 chicken drumstick and 1 thigh 3 to 4 meat servings

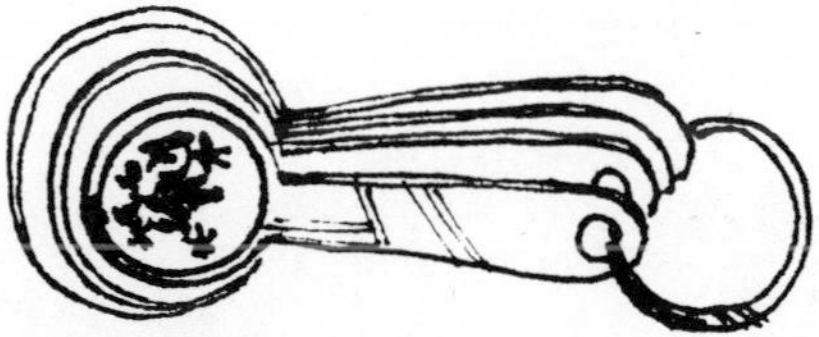

Beef, pork, lamb, veal:

1 ounce

1 meat serving

2 ounces

1 small meat patty
1 small chop
2 eggs
½ cup of creamed cottage cheese
2 meat servings

4 ounces

1 large meat patty
center of lean rib steak
1 cup of cottage cheese
4 meat servings

Casserole:

Meaty, 1 cup

1 bread + 2 to 3 meat servings

Starchy, 1 cup

1½ bread + 1 to 2 meat servings

Breakfast meat:

Bacon, 1 crisp slice

1 fat serving

Canadian bacon, 2 thin slices

1 meat serving

Sausage, 2 small links

1 meat + 3 fat servings

EGGS AND CHEESE

Egg, 1 medium	1 meat serving
Eggs, scrambled (usually 2 eggs)	2 meat servings
Omelette (usually 3 eggs)	3 meat servings
Cottage cheese, ¼ cup	low-fat cheese, 1 slice (1 ounce) 1 meat serving

VEGETABLES

Bulky vegetables (cauliflower, celery, tomato, cucumber, etc.) raw†, 1 cup	{ cooked, ½ cup { free except for dressing; no replacement needed
Semistarchy vegetables, raw or cooked: (beets, carrots, green peas, mixed vegetables, onions, rutabagas, turnips, winter squash), ½ cup	½ bread serving
Starchy vegetables, cooked: (Beans, potatoes, etc.), ½ cup	Corn, ⅓ cup Parsnips, ⅔ cup 1 bread serving

FRUIT DISHES

Grapefruit half	¼ of a large cantaloupe small glass of fruit juice, ½ cup (except grape or prune juice, ¼ cup) 1 fruit serving ⅔ bread serving
Bulky fruit (melon, berries), 1 cup	1 fruit serving ⅔ bread serving
Average fruit (apples, apricots, grapefruit, oranges, peaches, pears, plums), ½ cup	1 fruit serving ⅔ bread serving
Sweet fruit (bananas, cherries, dried fruits, grapes), ¼ cup	1 fruit serving ⅔ bread serving

DESSERTS
Unless fresh fruit is available, skip dessert and have more starch with the main course.

Fruit, 1 serving	⅔ bread serving
Dietetic gelatin	free; no replacement needed

FATS

Salad dressing†, 1 tablespoon	oil or mayonnaise†, 1 teaspoon margarine, 1 teaspoon 6 peanuts 5 olives 4 walnut halves 1 fat serving

DRIVE-IN FOOD

Hot dogs and hamburgers are both high in fat and high in cholesterol. Fish, on the other hand, is low in cholesterol and moderate in fat. Each half of a hamburger bun is 1 bread serving; if you can eat your hamburger or fish sandwich without the lid, you can save one bread serving. And since hot dogs are never as large as hot dog buns, the value given in this table is based on the assumption that you'll only eat the ⅔ of the bun that the hot dog fills. Also, the tomatoes and pickles† are free, as long as the pickles aren't sweet.

Hot dog, 1 large	1 bread + 1½ to 2 meat servings
Hamburger (on a bun), regular size	2 bread + 2 meat servings
Hamburger deluxe (on a bun), ¼ pound, with tomato and pickle†	2 bread + 4 meat servings
Fish sandwich	2 bread + 3 meat servings

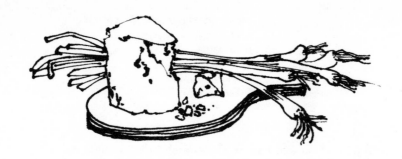

Potato chips, 1 small bag (1 cup)	1 bread + 1 to 2 fat servings
Potato chips, ⅔ of a small bag	1 fruit + 1 fat serving
French fries, ½ cup	1 bread + 2 fat servings
French fries, ⅓ cup	1 fruit + 1 fat serving
Pizza, 1 wedge	1 bread + 1 meat serving
Coleslaw, ½ cup	1 bulky vegetable† (free) + 1 to 2 fat servings (fat is in dressing)

Table II. Average Food Values

All food values are approximate.
*Cal = Calories. P, F and C = protein, fat and carbohydrate, in grams. These values are expressed in a similar way in recipes throughout the book.

†Much of the carbohydrate in bulky raw vegetables is not digestible and need not be counted. In a salad, however, there will usually be at least 1 teaspoon of salad dressing (1 fat serving) and perhaps a half cup or more.

Food and Amount	Food Values*			
	Cal	P	F	C
BEVERAGES				
Coffee (without sugar)	7 to 9	0	0	1
Tea (without sugar)	0	0	0	0
Milk, 8 ounces:				
Skim	84	9	0	12
2%-fat	125	8	5	12
Whole (4%-fat)	170	8	10	12
Buttermilk	84	9	0	12
Beer (3.2%), 8 ounces (7 grams of alcohol)	81	1	0	8
Wine, dry red or white, 3 ounces (11 grams of alcohol)	81	0	0	1

Food and Amount	Food Values*			
	Cal	P	F	C
Whiskey, gin or vodka, 1 ounce (12 grams of alcohol)	80	0	0	0
BREAD AND CEREAL				
Bread, 1 slice	68	2	0	15
Roll, 1 medium	68	2	0	15
Salted crackers, 5	68	2	0	15
Cereal or starch, ½ cup	68	2	0	15
French toast, 1 slice	107	5	3	15
Pancake, 3-inch	72	3	2	13
Waffle, 3½-inch square	84	3	3	15
Fruit muffin, 1 small	135	3	4	22
SOUP				
Thin, watery, 6-ounce cup	54	1	2	8
Average, 6-ounce cup	86	2	2	15

Food and Amount	Food Values*				Food and Amount	Food Values*			
	Cal	P	F	C		Cal	P	F	C
Thick, 6-ounce cup	93 to 136	3 to 5	1 to 4	18 to 20	Meaty (chicken, seafood—includes 1 tablespoon of salad dressing†), 1 cup	313	16	21	15
SALAD					Salad dressing†, 1 tablespoon in each cup of potato, macaroni, chicken or seafood salad	135	0	15	0
Raw mixed vegetables†, 1 cup	12 to 28	1 to 2	0	3 to 5	**MEATS**				
Cottage cheese and fruit (½ cup of cottage cheese and 2 pieces of canned fruit):					**Fish:**				
					1 ounce	55	7	3	0
Unsweetened fruit at home	154	15	6	10	Fish steak, 1 medium (4 ounces)	220	28	12	0
Sweetened fruit in restaurant	194	15	6	20	**Poultry:**				
Starchy (potato, macaroni— includes 1 tablespoon of salad dressing†), 1 cup	271	4	15	30	1 ounce	55	7	3	0
					Chicken breast, ½ large (4 ounces)	220	28	12	0
					Chicken, 1 drumstick and 1 thigh	220	28	12	0
					Beef, pork, lamb, veal:				
					1 ounce	73	7	5	0
					2 ounces (1 small meat patty or 1 small chop)	146	14	10	0

Food and Amount	Food Values*				Food and Amount	Food Values*			
	Cal	P	F	C		Cal	P	F	C
4 ounces (1 large meat patty or center of lean rib steak)	292	28	20	0	**VEGETABLES**				
					Bulky vegetables (cauliflower, celery, tomato, cucumber, etc.): Raw†, 1 cup, or cooked, ½ cup	12 to 28	1 to 2	0	3 to 5
Casserole:									
Meaty, 1 cup	214	16	10	15					
Starchy, 1 cup	177	10	5	23					
Breakfast meat:					Semistarchy vegetables, raw or cooked (beets, carrots, green peas, mixed vegetables, onions, rutabagas, turnips, winter squash), ½ cup	36	2	0	7
Bacon, 1 crisp slice	45	0	5	0					
Canadian bacon, 2 thin slices	73	7	5	0					
Sausage, 1 small link	104	3½	10	0					
EGGS AND CHEESE					Starchy vegetables, cooked:				
Egg, 1 medium	73	7	5	0	Beans, potatoes, etc., ½ cup	68	2	0	15
Cottage cheese, ¼ cup	55	7	3	0	Corn, ⅓ cup	68	2	0	15
Low-fat cheese, 1 slice (1 ounce)	55 to 66	7	3 to 5	0	Parsnips, ⅔ cup	68	2	0	15

Food and Amount	Food Values*				Food and Amount	Food Values*			
	Cal	P	F	C		Cal	P	F	C
FRUIT DISHES					**FATS**				
Use fresh fruit if possible, or unsweetened diet-pack fruit.					Diluted fats (French or Italian salad dressing†), 1 tablespoon	45	0	5	0
Grapefruit half	40	0	0	10					
¼ of a large cantaloupe	40	0	0	10					
Fruit juice, ½ cup (except grape or prune juice, ¼ cup)	40	0	0	10					
Bulky fruit (melon, berries), 1 cup	40	0	0	10					
Average fruit (apples, apricots, grapefruit, oranges, peaches, pears, plums), ½ cup	40	0	0	10					
Sweet fruit (bananas, cherries, dried fruits, grapes), ¼ cup	40	0	0	10					
DESSERTS									
Unless fresh fruit is available, skip dessert and have more starch with the main course.					Concentrated fats (oil†, mayonnaise†, margarine), 1 teaspoon	58	0	5	0
Fruit, 1 serving	40	0	0	10	Nuts (6 peanuts, 5 olives or				
Dietetic gelatin	7	7	7	0	4 walnut halves)	45	0	5	0

Table III.   Food Replacements for Diabetics

If you are a diabetic on insulin or for some other reason need to eat an exact amount of carbohydrate (even if you feel nauseated), this table will show you how to replace the carbohydrate in foods left uneaten.

All food values are approximate.

*1 ounce of milk is equivalent to 1 scant ounce of grapefruit or orange juice or 3/4 ounce of apple juice.

†Much of the carbohydrate in bulky raw vegetables is not digestible and need not be counted. In a salad, however, there will usually be at least 1 teaspoon of salad dressing (1 fat serving) and perhaps a half cup or more.

Food and Amount	Grams of carbohydrate	Ounces of milk or juice to replace carbohydrate*		
		Milk	Orange	Apple
BEVERAGES				
Black coffee or tea	0	0	0	0
Milk, 8 ounces	12	8	7	6
BREAD AND CEREAL				
Bread, 1 slice	15	8	7	6
Roll, 1 medium	15	8	7	6
Salted crackers, 5	15	8	7	6
Cereal or starch, 1/2 cup	15	8	7	6
SOUP 6-ounce cup:				
Thin, watery, 6-ounce cup	8	4	3	2
Average, 6-ounce cup	15	8	5	4
Thick, 6-ounce cup	20	Too variable to calculate		

Food and Amount	Grams of carbohydrate	Ounces of milk or juice to replace carbohydrate*		
		Milk	Orange	Apple
SALAD				
Raw mixed vegetables†, 1 cup (Free except for dressing; no replacement needed.)	5	0	0	0
Starchy (potato, macaroni), 1 cup	30	16	11	8
Meaty (chicken, seafood), 1 cup	15	12	8	6
Salad dressing†, 1 tablespoon	0	0	0	0
Oil or margarine†, 1 teaspoon	0	0	0	0
MEATS				
Fish:				
1 ounce	0	2	1	1
1 medium fish steak (4 ounces)	0	7½	5	4
Poultry:				
1 ounce	0	2	1	1
½ large chicken breast (4 ounces)	0	7½	5	4
1 chicken drumstick and 1 thigh	0	7½	5	4
Beef, pork, lamb, veal:				
1 ounce	0	2	1	1
2 ounces (1 small meat patty or 1 small chop)	0	4	2	2
4 ounces (1 large meat patty or center of lean rib steak)	0	8	4	4

Food and Amount	Grams of carbohydrate	Ounces of milk or juice to replace carbohydrate*		
		Milk	Orange	Apple
Casserole:				
Meaty, 1 cup	15	10	8	6
Starchy, 1 cup	23	13	9	7
Breakfast meat:				
Bacon, 1 crisp slice	0	0	0	0
Canadian bacon, 2 thin slices	0	2	1	1
Sausage, 1 small link	0	2	1	1
EGGS AND CHEESE				
Egg, 1 medium	0	2	1	1
Cottage cheese, ¼ cup	0	2	1	1
Low-fat cheese, 1 slice (1 ounce)	0	2	1	1
VEGETABLES				
Bulky vegetables (cauliflower, celery, cucumber, tomato, etc.) Free except for dressing; no replacement needed.				
Raw†, 1 cup	5	0	0	0
Cooked, ½ cup	5	0	0	0

Food and Amount	Grams of carbohydrate	Ounces of milk or juice to replace carbohydrate*		
		Milk	Orange	Apple
Semistarchy vegetables, raw or cooked (beets, carrots, green peas, mixed vegetables, onions, rutabagas, turnips, winter squash), ½ cup	7	3½	2½	2
Starchy vegetables, cooked:				
Beans, potatoes, etc., ½ cup	15	7	5	4
Corn, ⅓ cup	15	7	5	4
Parsnips, ⅔ cup	15	7	5	4
FRUIT DISHES				
Grapefruit half	10	3½	3	2½
¼ of a large cantaloupe	10	3½	3	2½
Small glass of fruit juice, ½ cup	10	3½	3	2½
(except grape or prune juice, ¼ cup)	10	3½	3	2½
Bulky fruit (melon, berries), 1 cup	10	3½	3	2½
Average fruit (apples, apricots, grapefruit, oranges, peaches, pears, plums), ½ cup	10	3½	3	2½
Sweet fruit (bananas, cherries, dried fruits, grapes), ¼ cup	10	3½	3	2½

Food and Amount	Grams of carbohydrate	Ounces of milk or juice to replace carbohydrate*		
		Milk	Orange	Apple
DESSERTS				
Fruit, 1 serving	10	3½	3	2½
Dietetic gelatin	0	0	0	0
FATS				
Diluted fats (French or Italian salad dressing†), 1 tablespoon	0	0	0	0
Concentrated fats (oil†, mayonnaise†, margarine), 1 teaspoon	0	0	0	0
Nuts (6 peanuts, 5 olives or 4 walnut halves)	0	0	0	0

Table IV.   Measurement Equivalents

Tablespoons	Teaspoons	Ounces	Grams	Cups	
1/3 tablespoon	1 teaspoon	1/6 ounce	5 grams	—	
1 tablespoon	3 teaspoons	1/2 ounce	15 grams	—	
2 tablespoons	6 teaspoons	1 ounce	30 grams	1/8 cup	
4 tablespoons	12 teaspoons	2 ounces	60 grams	1/4 cup	
6-2/3 tablespoons	20 teaspoons	3-1/3 ounces	100 grams	scant 1/2 cup	
8 tablespoons	24 teaspoons	4 ounces	120 grams	1/2 cup	
16 tablespoons	48 teaspoons	8 ounces	240 grams	1 cup	

Bibliography

Analytical data. Crescent Manufacturing Company, Seattle, Wash., 1974.

Analytical data. Prepared by Washington State Heart Association and Northwest Lipid Research Center, Seattle, Wash., 1974.

Analytical data. Shasta Beverages, Seattle, Wash., 1974.

Average Weight of a Measured Cup of Various Foods. Agricultural Research Service 61-6, U.S. Department of Agriculture. U.S. Government Printing Office, Washington, D.C., 1969.

Code of Federal Regulations: #21 Food and Drugs, Parts 1 to 119. Office of the Federal Register, National Archives and Records Service, General Services Administration. U.S. Government Printing Office, Washington, D.C., 1972.

Conversion Factors and Weights and Measures for Agricultural Commodities and Their Products. Statistical Bulletin #362, Economic Research Service, U.S. Department of Agriculture. U.S. Government Printing Office, Washington, D.C., 1965.

Feeley, R. M., Criner, P. E., and Watt, B. K., "Cholesterol Content of Foods." *Journal of the American Dietetic Association* 61:134, 1972.

Food Values of Portions Commonly Used, Bowes and Church (11th edition). Revised by C.F. Church and H. N. Church. J. P. Lippincott Co., Philadelphia, 1970.

Goddard, V. R., and Goddall, L. *Fatty Acids in Food Fats.* Home Economics Research Report #7, U.S. Department of Agriculture. U.S. Government Printing Office, Washington, D.C., 1959.

Heinz Handbook of Nutrition. McGraw-Hill Book Company, New York, 1959.

McCance, R. A., and Widdowson, E. M. *Chemical Composition of Foods.* Chemical Publishing Co., Brooklyn, 1947.

Mattice, Marjorie R. *Bridges' Food and Beverage Analyses* (3rd edition). Lea and Febiger, Philadelphia, 1950.

Product data from manufacturers as shown on product labels. Margarines—Fleischmann's, Mazola and Saffola. Sweeteners—Sprinkle Sweet, Sugar Twin, Sweet & Low and Sucaryl. Instant flour—Wondra. Liquid egg substitutes—Egg Beaters and Second Nature.

Sodium-Restricted diets: The Rationale, Complications and Practical Aspects of Their Use. Natural Resources Council, Pub. #325. National Academy of Sciences, Washington, D.C., 1954.

Stansby, M. E., "Composition of Fish." Fishery Leaflet #116, U.S. Fish & Wildlife Service. U.S. Government Printing Office, Washington, D.C., 1953.

Watt, B. K., and Merrill, A. L. *Composition of Foods—Raw, Processed, and Prepared* (revised). U.S. Department of Agriculture Handbook #8. U.S. Government Printing Office, Washington, D.C., 1963.

Index